Oh No . . . IT'S CHRIS

CW00591219

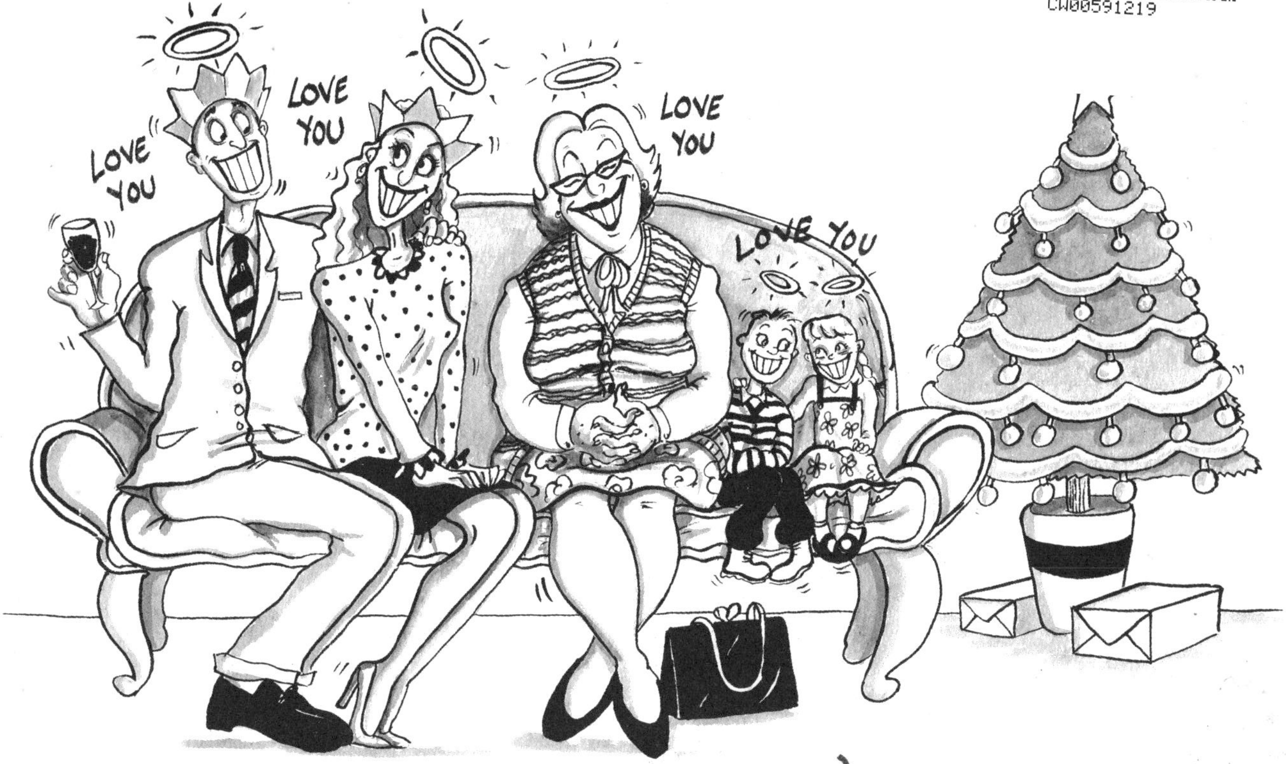
LOVE YOU
LOVE YOU
LOVE YOU
LOVE YOU

(It's Christmas... but not as **WE** know it!...)

An OPTIMA book

First published in the United Kingdom
by Optima in 1994

Copyright © 1994 Alison Everitt

The moral right of the author has been asserted

A CIP catalogue for this book is available from
the British Library

ISBN 0 356 21070 7

Typeset by Solidus (Bristol) Limited

Printed and bound in Great Britain by
BPC Hazell Books Ltd
A member of
The British Printing Company Ltd

Optima
A Division of
Little, Brown and Company (UK) Limited
Brettenham House
Lancaster Place
London WC2E 7EN

Dedicated to anyone who has ever,
just for one Christmas, wished they
were an ORPHAN ... and to my
family ... who aren't that bad really ...

CONTENTS ...

... CONTENTS

THE AUTHOR . . .

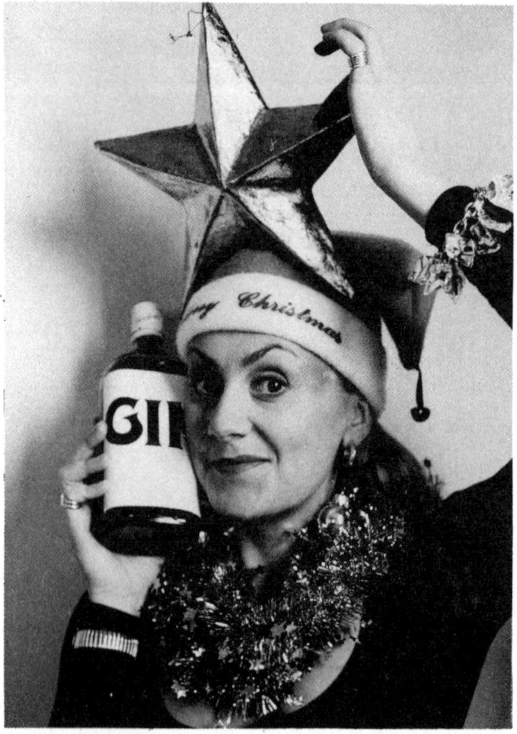
Christmas

ALISON EVERITT is a cartoonist and also writes and presents on television and radio.

Over Christmas she's guaranteed to have at least one tantrum, one hangover . . . and put on half a stone. (A day . . .)

Her ideal Christmas will be spent on a hot beach, sipping cocktails, going slowly brown, but unless this book sells really well, Christmas will be forever spent in freezing Britain, knocking back the Gin, going slowly MAD!

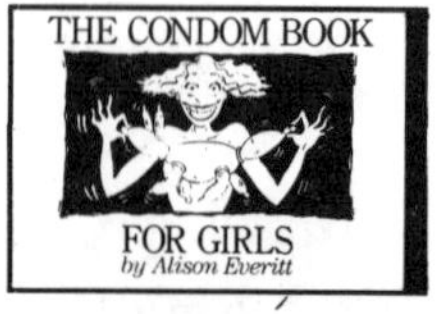
THE CONDOM BOOK
FOR GIRLS
by Alison Everitt

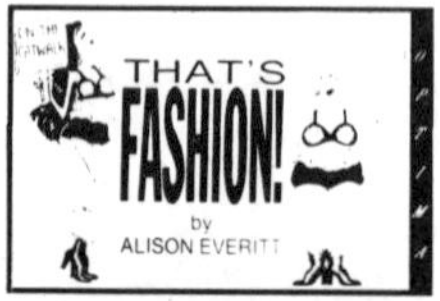
THAT'S
FASHION!
by
ALISON EVERITT

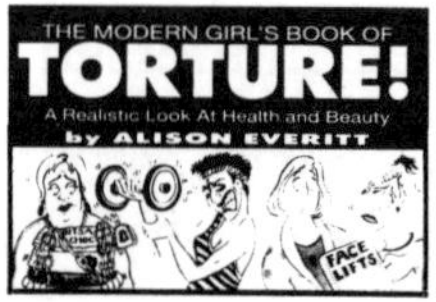
THE MODERN GIRL'S BOOK OF
TORTURE!
A Realistic Look At Health and Beauty
by ALISON EVERITT
FACE LIFTS

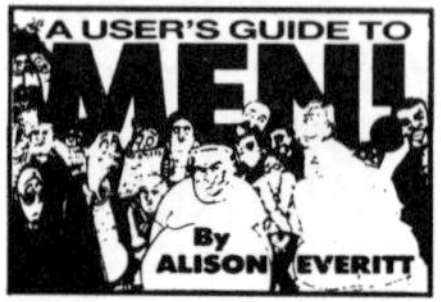
A USER'S GUIDE TO
MEN!
By
ALISON EVERITT

. . . Other books by the Author . . .
(STILL AVAILABLE!)

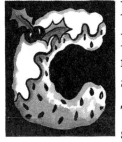 HRISTMAS!

It comes once a year, you look forward to it for months, you over-indulge for a couple of days ... and you pay for it for the rest of the year.

The traditional image of Christmas comes from snow-covered cards where everybody's smiling, old movies when everyone spends days on end with their entire family without ever contemplating murder, and adverts where the cupboards are bursting with food and drink, they can buy their families everything they want and *still* afford that February skiing holiday!

... But what happens if your life isn't like an old movie, you don't happen to live in an advert, and you spend the entire time with your hands inside an oven, immersed in soapy water or halfway up the less appealing end of a Turkey? What is Christmas like then? ... Read on ...

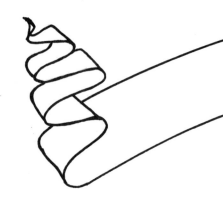

THE BUILD UP ...

Christmas seems to get earlier
and earlier. This year you spot
the first bit of tinsel in the
middle of MARCH!
(Then you realise it's that piece you
haven't taken down since 1975 ...)

… WHAT DOES CHRISTMAS MEAN TO YOU?

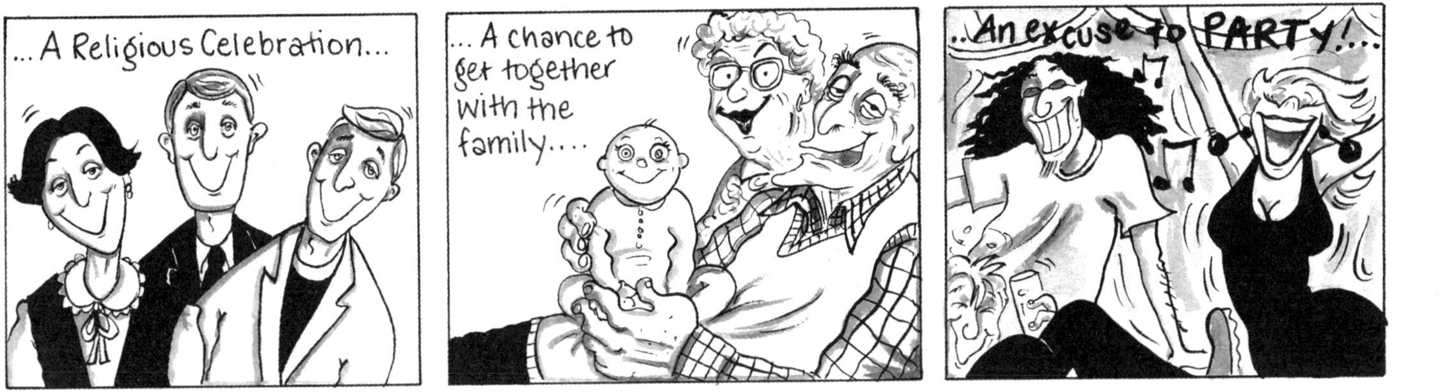
… A Religious Celebration…
… A chance to get together with the family….
..An excuse to PARTY!…

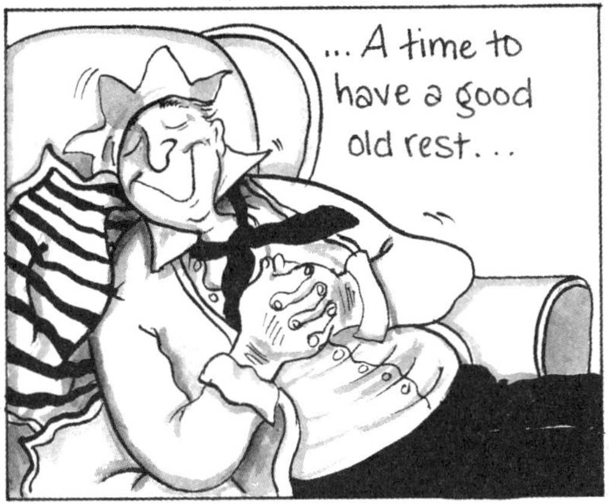
… A time to have a good old rest…

… And for WOMEN? …

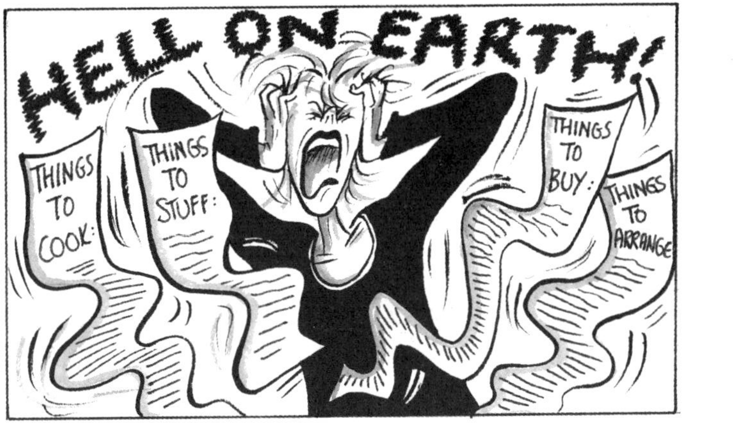
HELL ON EARTH!
THINGS TO COOK:
THINGS TO STUFF:
THINGS TO BUY:
THINGS TO ARRANGE

THE TWELVE DAYS OF CHRISTMAS

Believe it or not, they rarely have anything to do with partridges and pear trees. Normally you find that you've got too used to seeing Christmas cards in April and hearing so many Christmas adverts on the television . . .

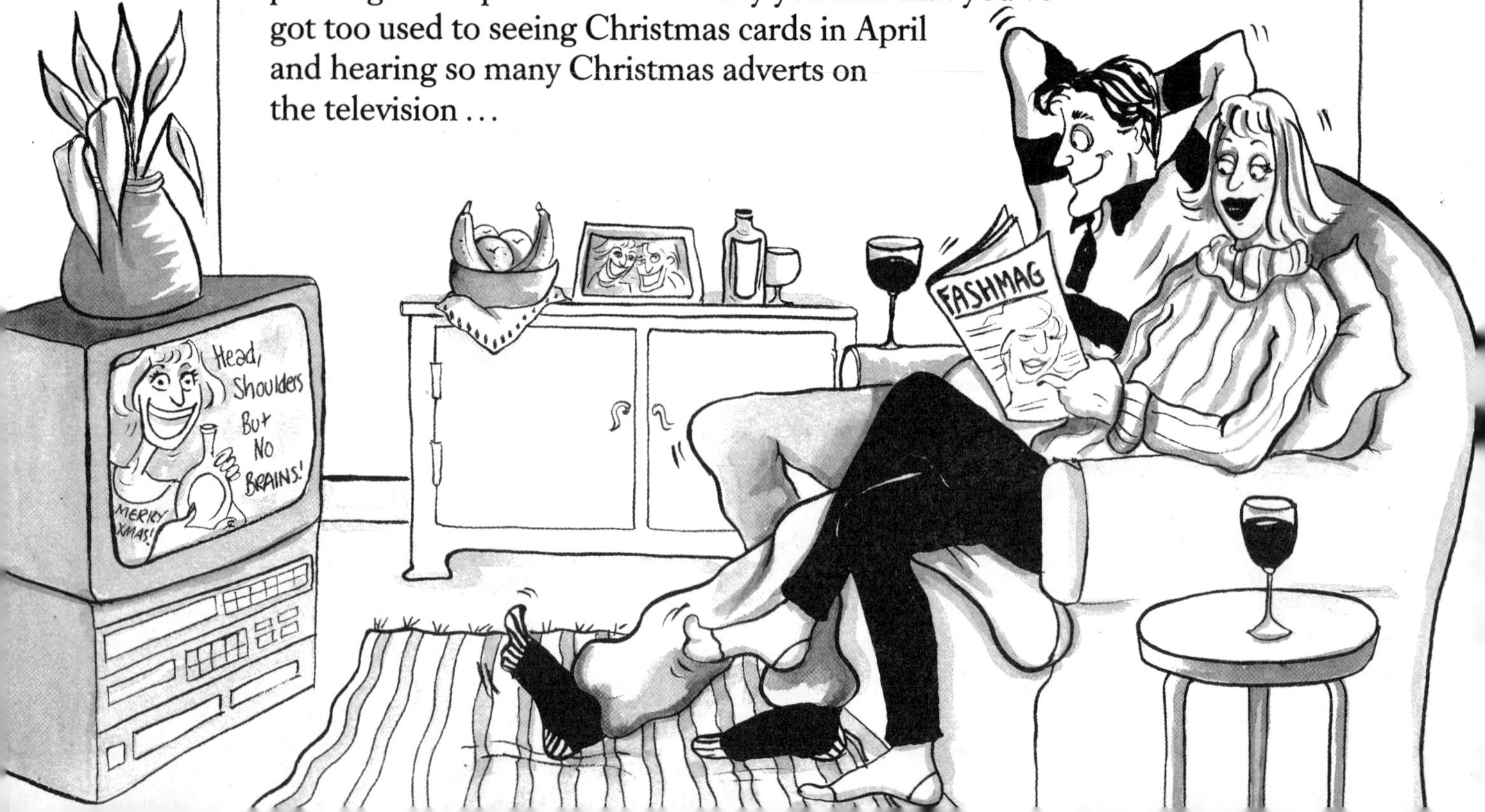
Head, Shoulders But No BRAINS!
MERRY XMAS!
FASHMAG

... and then suddenly somebody says ...

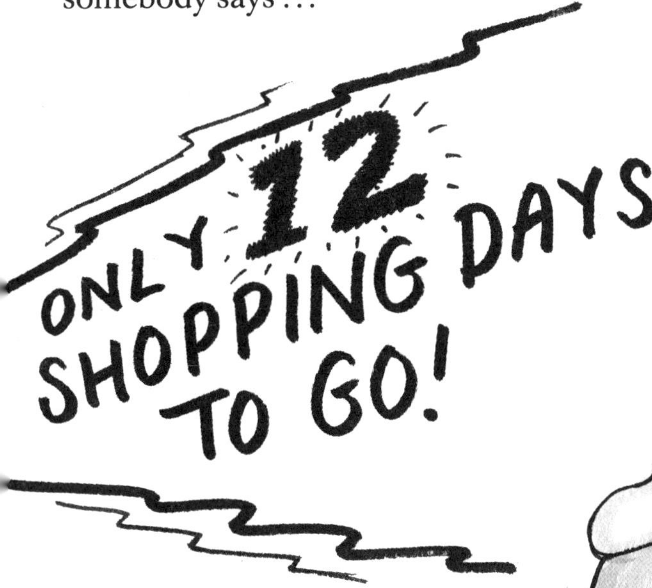
ONLY 12 SHOPPING DAYS TO GO!

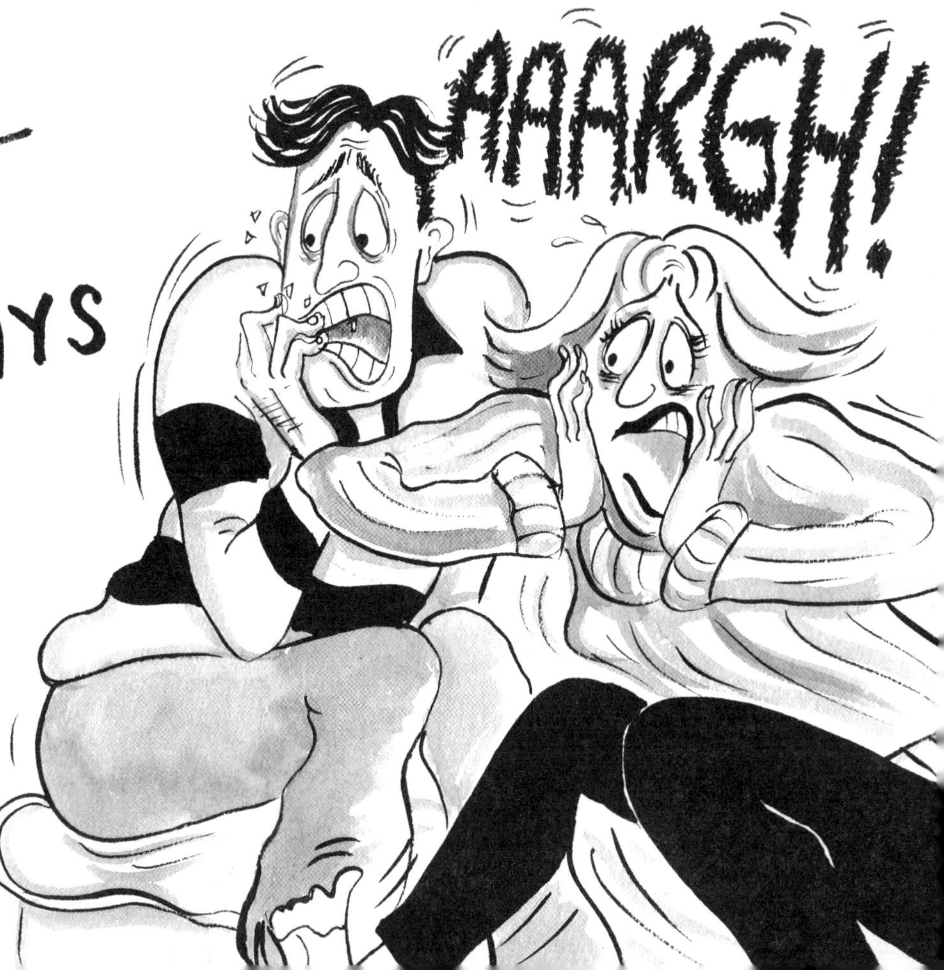
AAARGH!

... and you haven't even STARTED YET!

YOU KNOW IT'S CHRISTMAS WHEN …

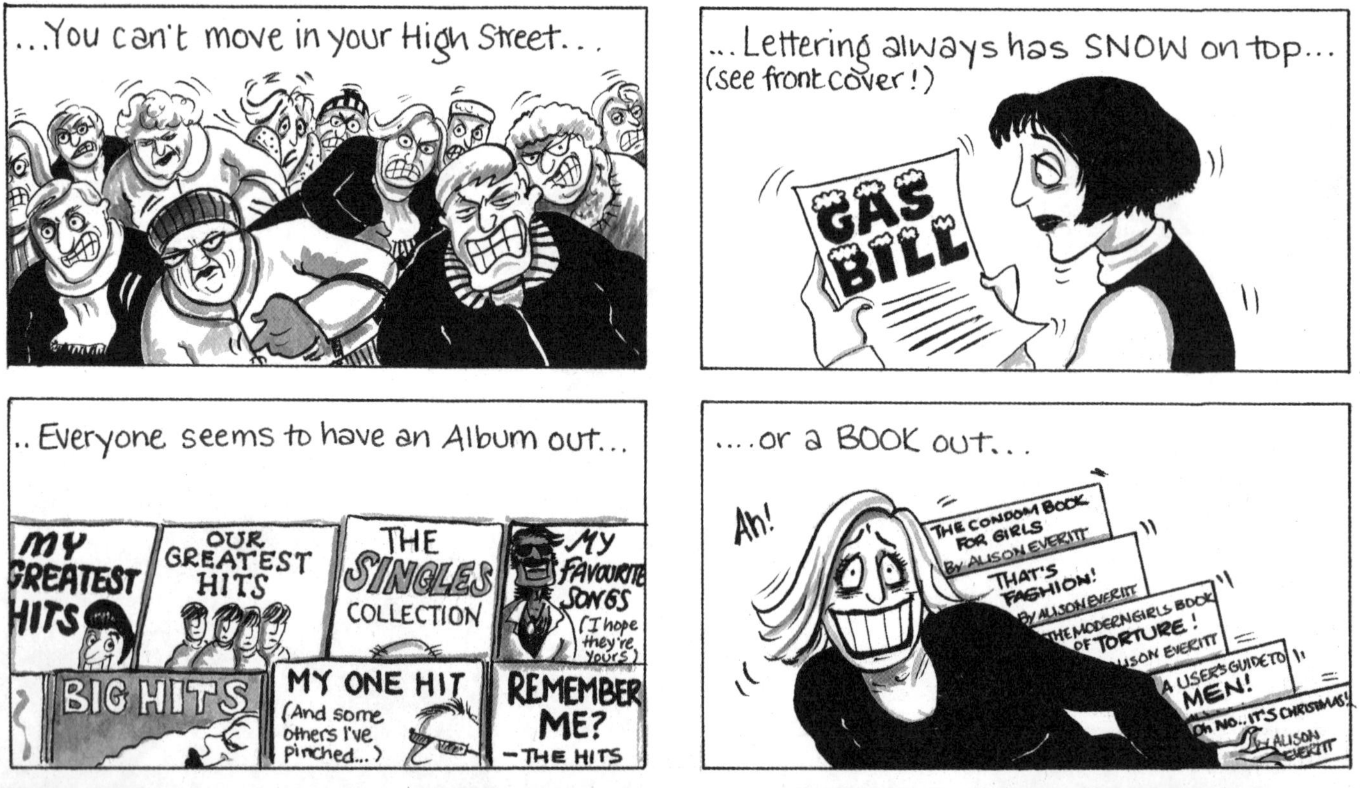

...You can't move in your High Street...
...Lettering always has SNOW on top...
(see front cover!)
GAS BILL
.. Everyone seems to have an Album out...
MY GREATEST HITS
OUR GREATEST HITS
THE SINGLES COLLECTION
MY FAVOURITE SONGS (I hope they're yours)
BIG HITS
MY ONE HIT (And some others I've pinched...)
REMEMBER ME? - THE HITS
....or a BOOK out...
Ah!
THE CONDOM BOOK FOR GIRLS By ALISON EVERITT
THAT'S FASHION! By ALISON EVERITT
THE MODERN GIRLS BOOK OF TORTURE!
A USER'S GUIDE TO MEN!
Oh NO... IT'S CHRISTMAS! By ALISON EVERITT

. . . Adverts for extortionately priced toys appear in EVERY commercial break . . .

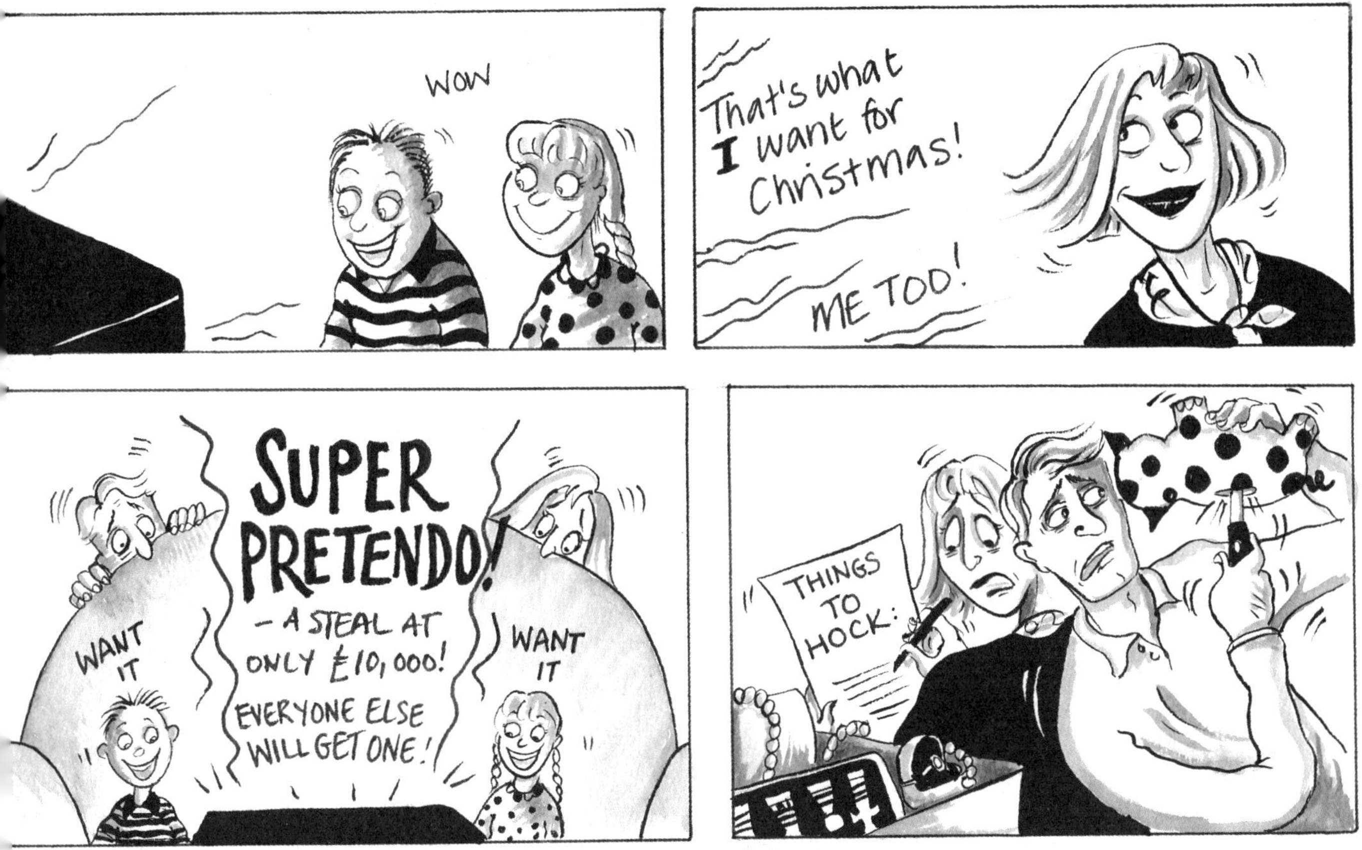
WOW
That's what I want for Christmas!
ME TOO!
SUPER PRETENDO!
– A STEAL AT ONLY £10,000!
EVERYONE ELSE WILL GET ONE!
WANT IT
WANT IT
THINGS TO HOCK:

... And everywhere you go, they're playing THAT SONG!

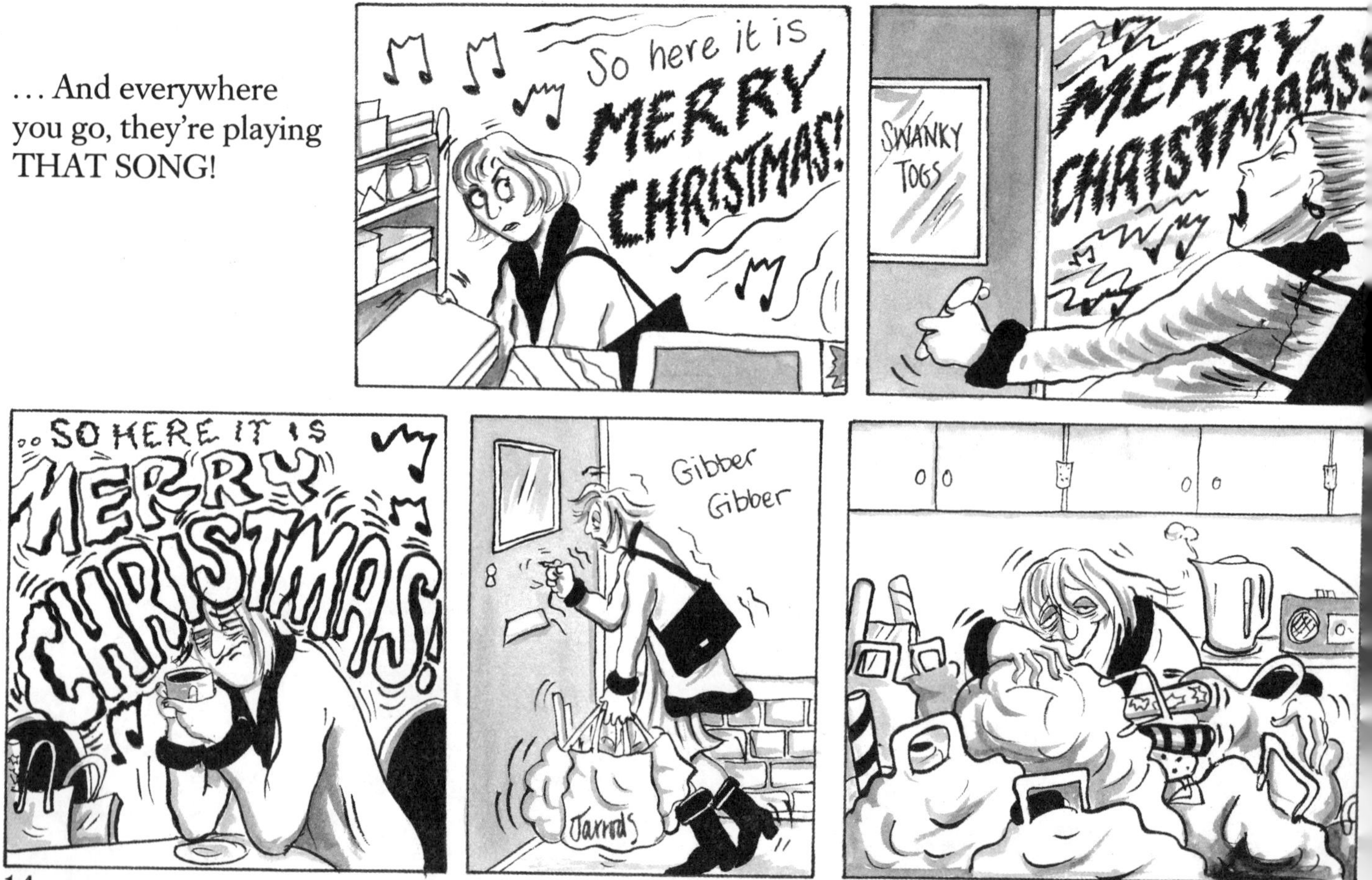

So here it is
MERRY CHRISTMAS!
SWANKY TOGS
MERRY CHRISTMAAS!
SO HERE IT IS
MERRY CHRISTMAS!
Gibber Gibber
Jarrods

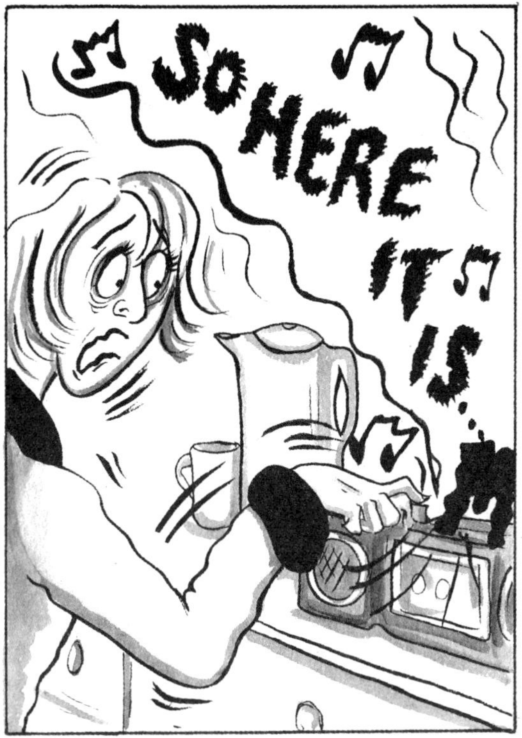
SO HERE IT IS...

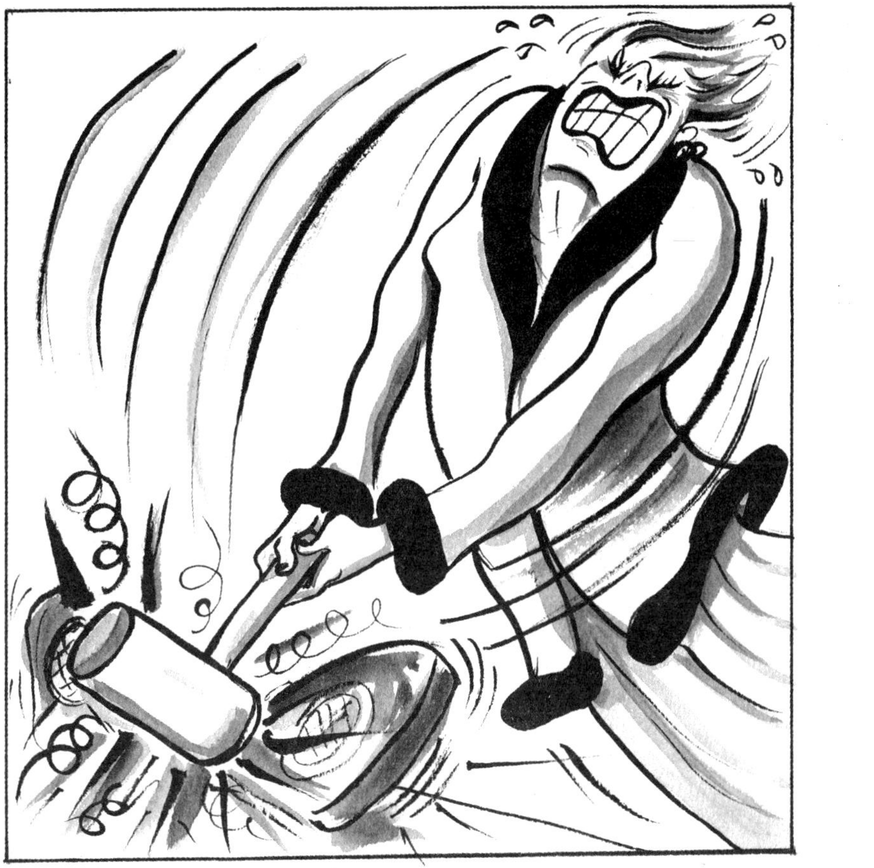

THINGS YOU HATE ABOUT CHRISTMAS

(1) Doing The Same Thing Every Year …

Every year you have to listen to other people making exotic or unusual plans for Christmas whilst you are facing the same old routine …

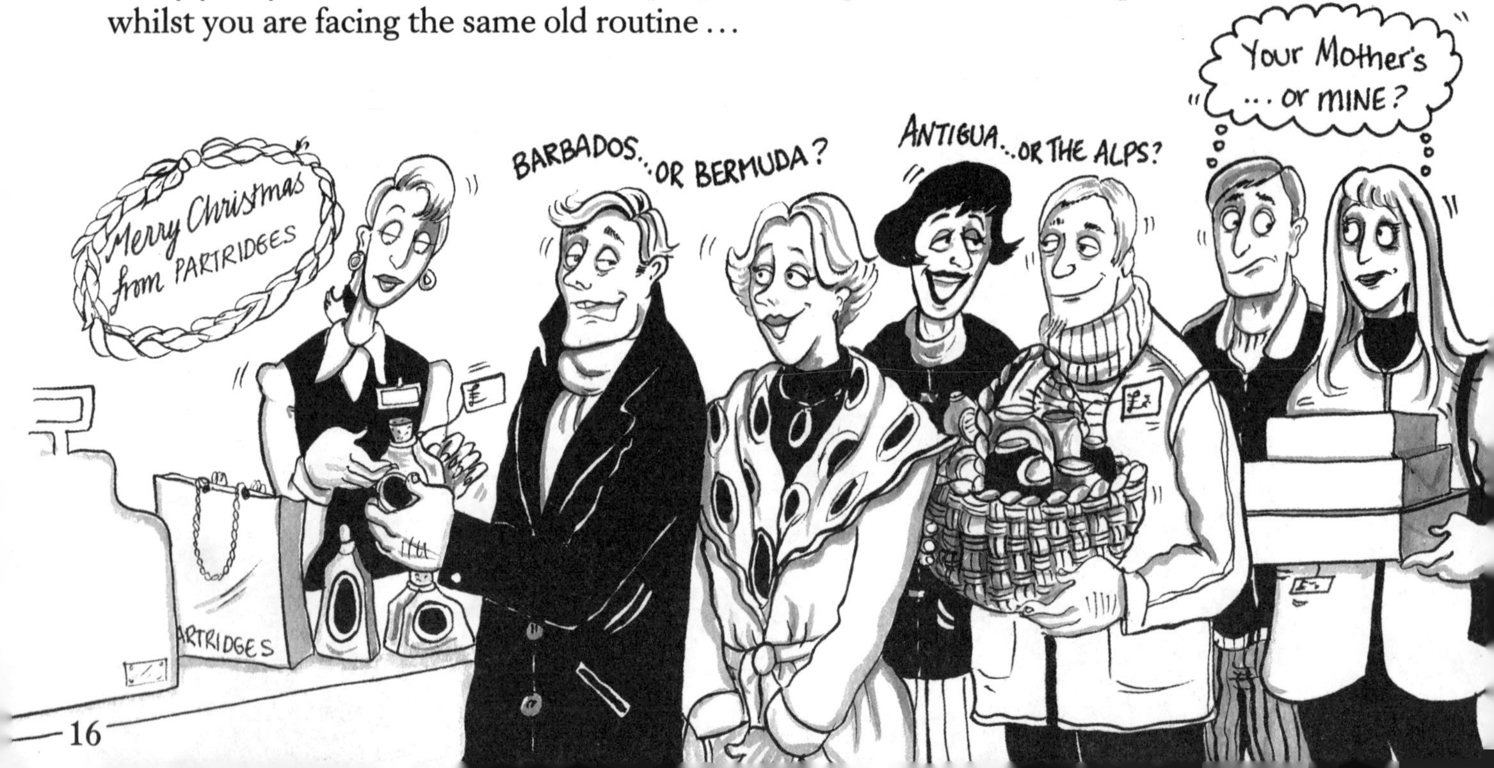

Merry Christmas from PARTRIDGES
BARBADOS… OR BERMUDA?
ANTIGUA… OR THE ALPS?
Your Mother's … or MINE?
ARTRIDGES

So you decide that this year you'll do something different. You get brochures, you buy swimsuits …

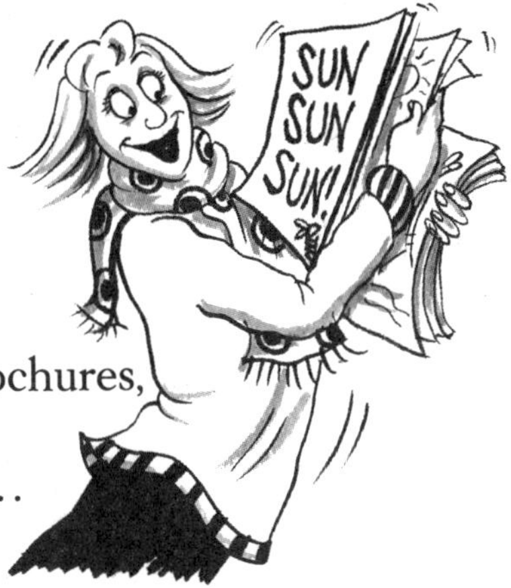
SUN SUN SUN!

… and wait for the right time to break the news to your family.

Your parents are speechless …

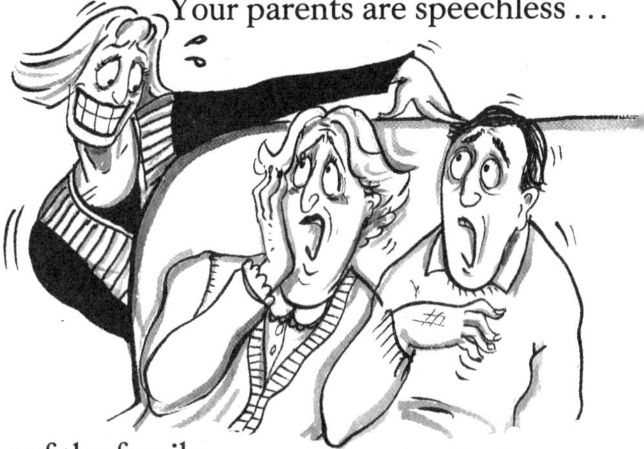

… your grandparents give you their best *"This Year Might Be Our Last"* look …

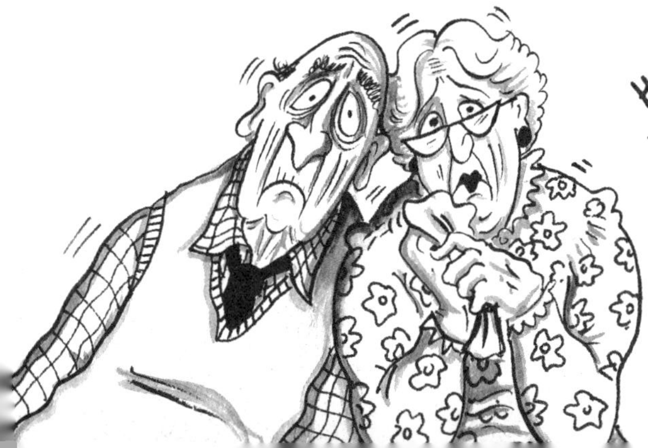

… and the rest of the family gang up on you …

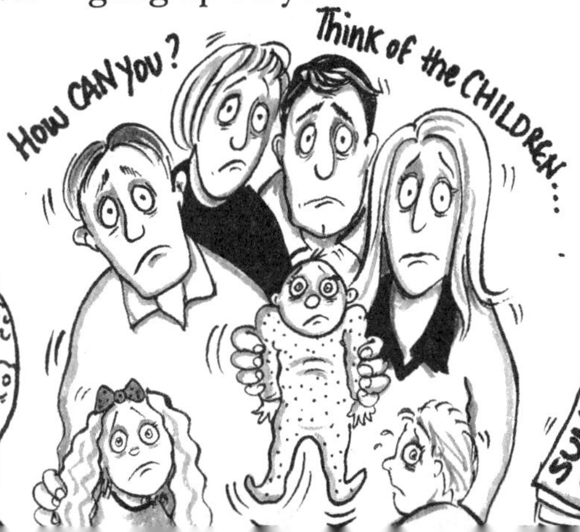
HOW CAN YOU?
Think of the CHILDREN…

So you decide that rather than spend all of next year grovelling, to GIVE IN!

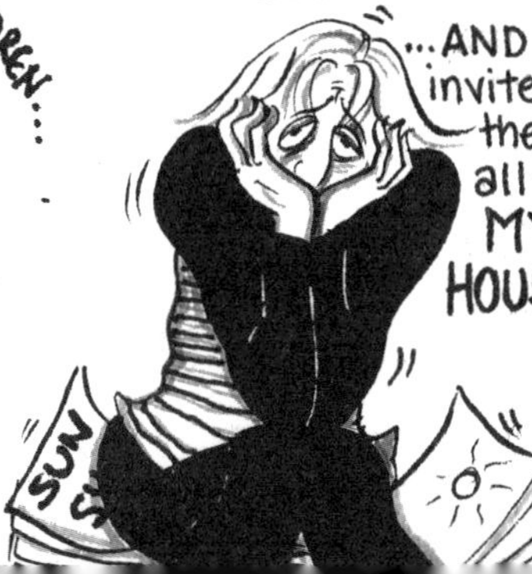
…AND I invited them all to MY HOUSE!

DECORATIONS:

Which way do YOU do it?

TRADITIONALS:

- Don't live in a mansion but wished they did.
- Keep their tree strictly traditional.
- Pretend their family has done it this way for generations.
- They really copied it from a copy of *Majesty* magazine.

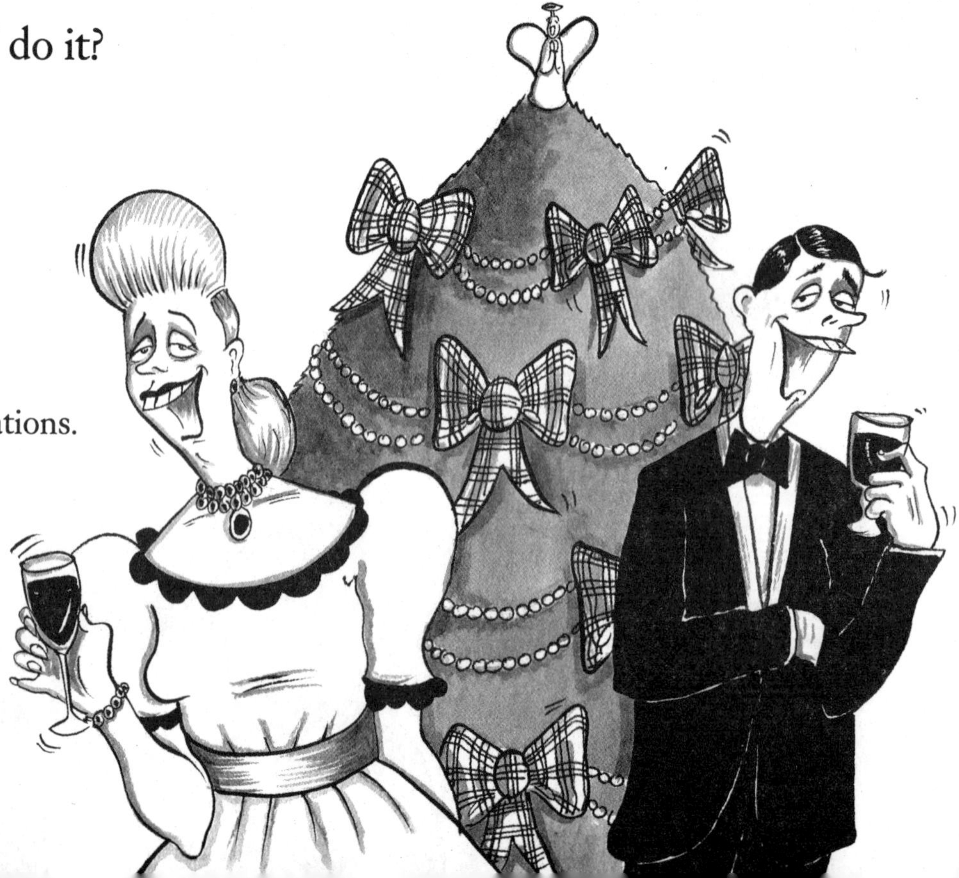

'HE MINIMALIST:

Not the person you want
) spend the festive season with.)

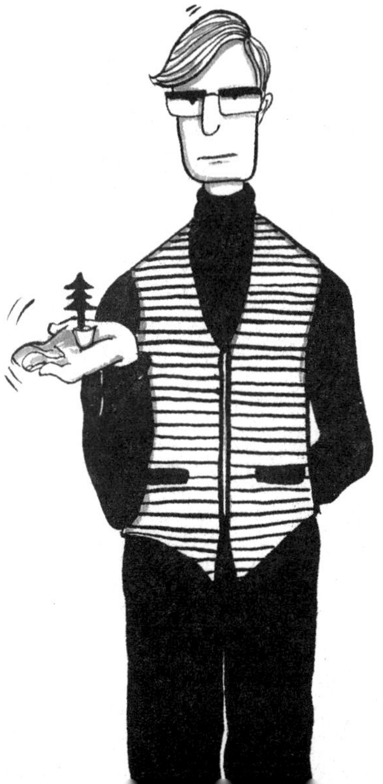

TINSELTOWNIES!

- Their tree has never even seen a forest.
- They load it with baubles, tinsels and huge bright lights.
- It's the epitome of bad taste.
- They'd STONECLAD it if they could!

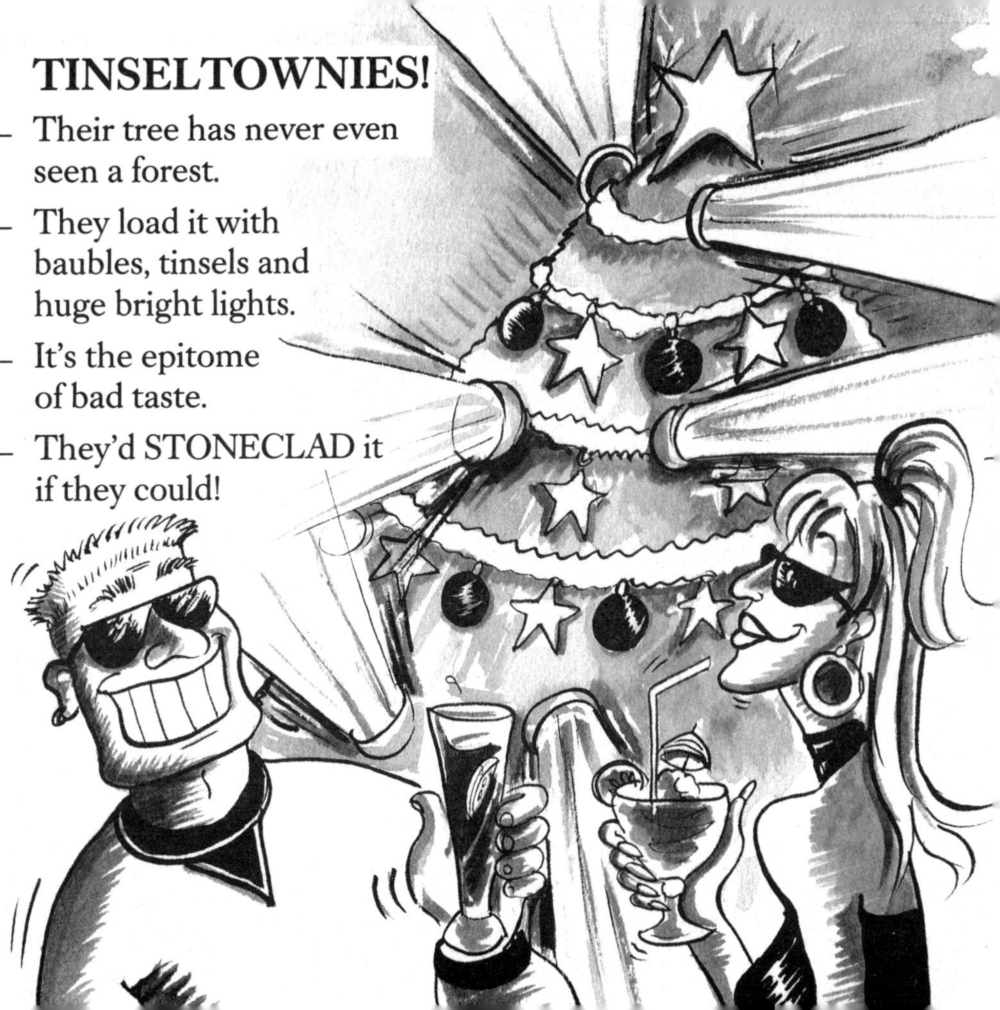

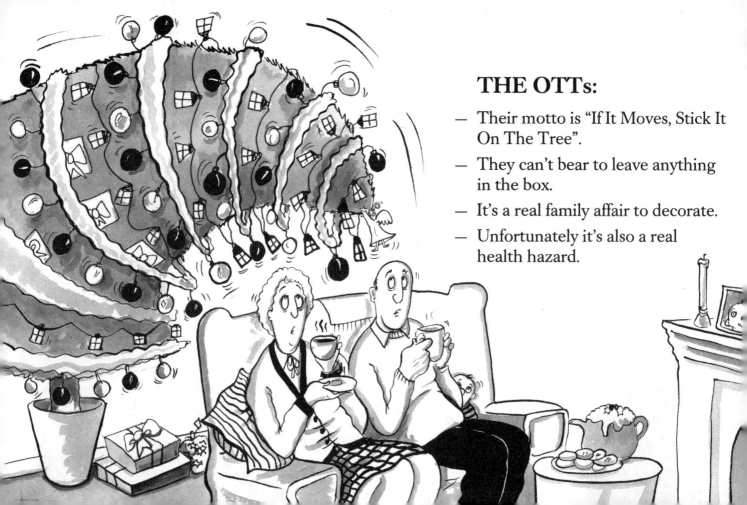

THE OTTs:

— Their motto is "If It Moves, Stick It On The Tree".

— They can't bear to leave anything in the box.

— It's a real family affair to decorate.

— Unfortunately it's also a real health hazard.

THE TRENDIES:

(Can't decorate until they know what's *'in'* this year)

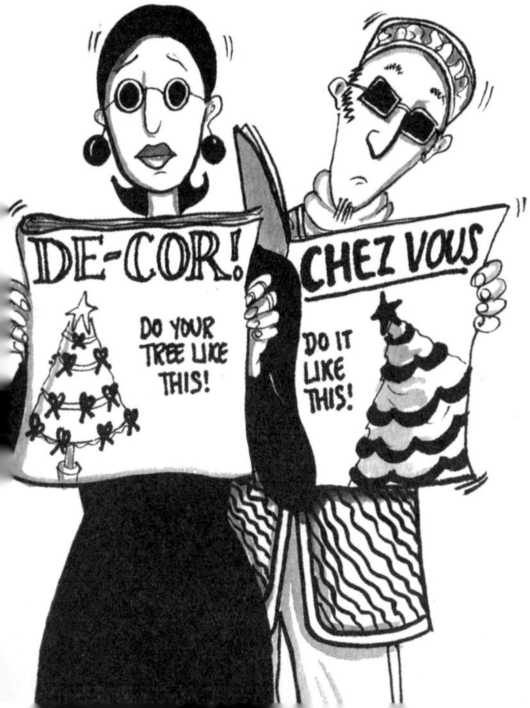
DE-COR!
DO YOUR TREE LIKE THIS!
CHEZ VOUS
DO IT LIKE THIS!

THE USUALS:

— They use the same old decorations year after year.
— Everything is held together by Sellotape and good luck.
— They can't remember a time when that fairy wasn't on the tree.
— They insist that every bauble holds a memory and every bit of tinsel tells a tale.

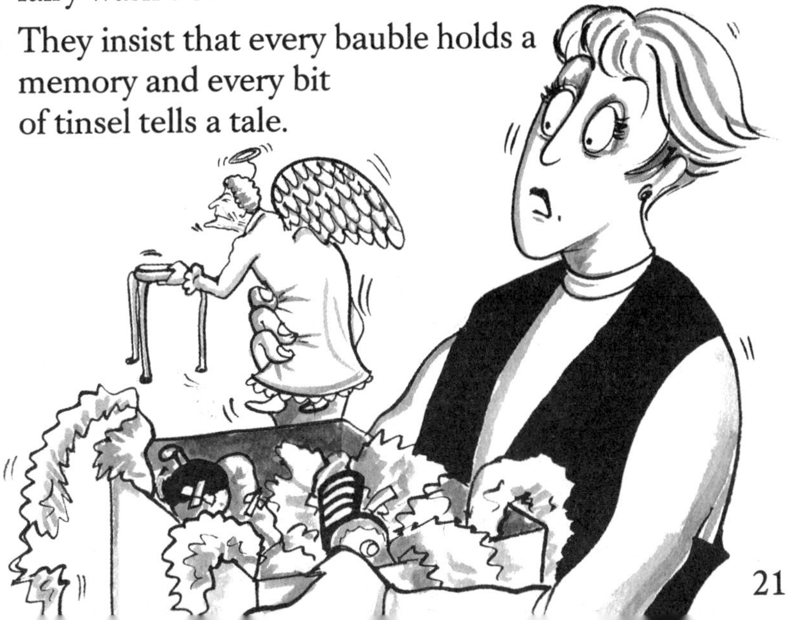

THINGS YOU HATE ABOUT CHRISTMAS

(2) Christmas People ...

All year long they're as miserable as the rest of us, but as soon as December arrives, they turn into tinsel-waving, grimace-wearing jingle-belling MANIACS!

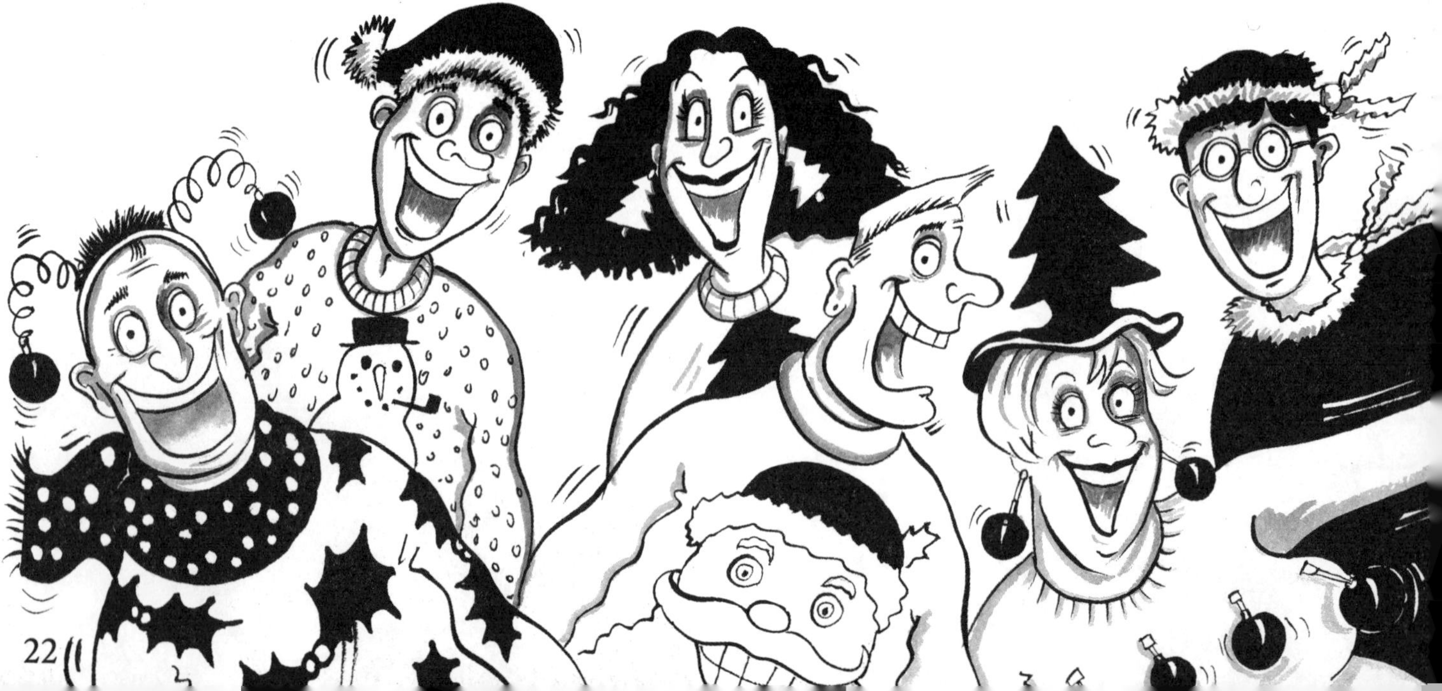

HOW TO SPOT THEM:

- They put tinsel on their car aerials.
- They wear baubles instead of earrings.
- They wear hand-knitted jumpers with seasonal slogans on, just in case you forget it's Christmas.
- They're the first people to put their tree up.
- They have huge lights outside the house, down the drive, on the gate and over any vegetation that can stand the strain.
- They say things like *"Cheer Up, It's Christmas!"* to total strangers.
- They expect you to go to pantomimes, be nice to carol singers and SMILE all the time.
- They won't leave the house unless they're in something embarrassing.

... And they're twice as bad when you're MARRIED to one!

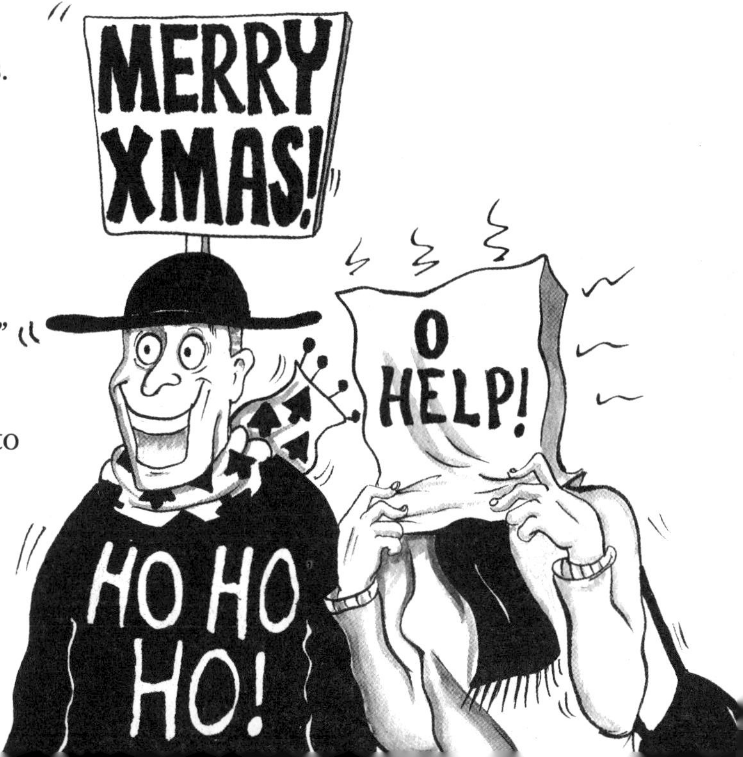
MERRY XMAS!
O HELP!
HO HO HO!

CHRISTMAS SHOPPING . . .

Every year you mean to start early, to spread the cost over a few months, but Christmas Shopping just isn't the same if it isn't done in one mad, frenzied last minute RUSH!

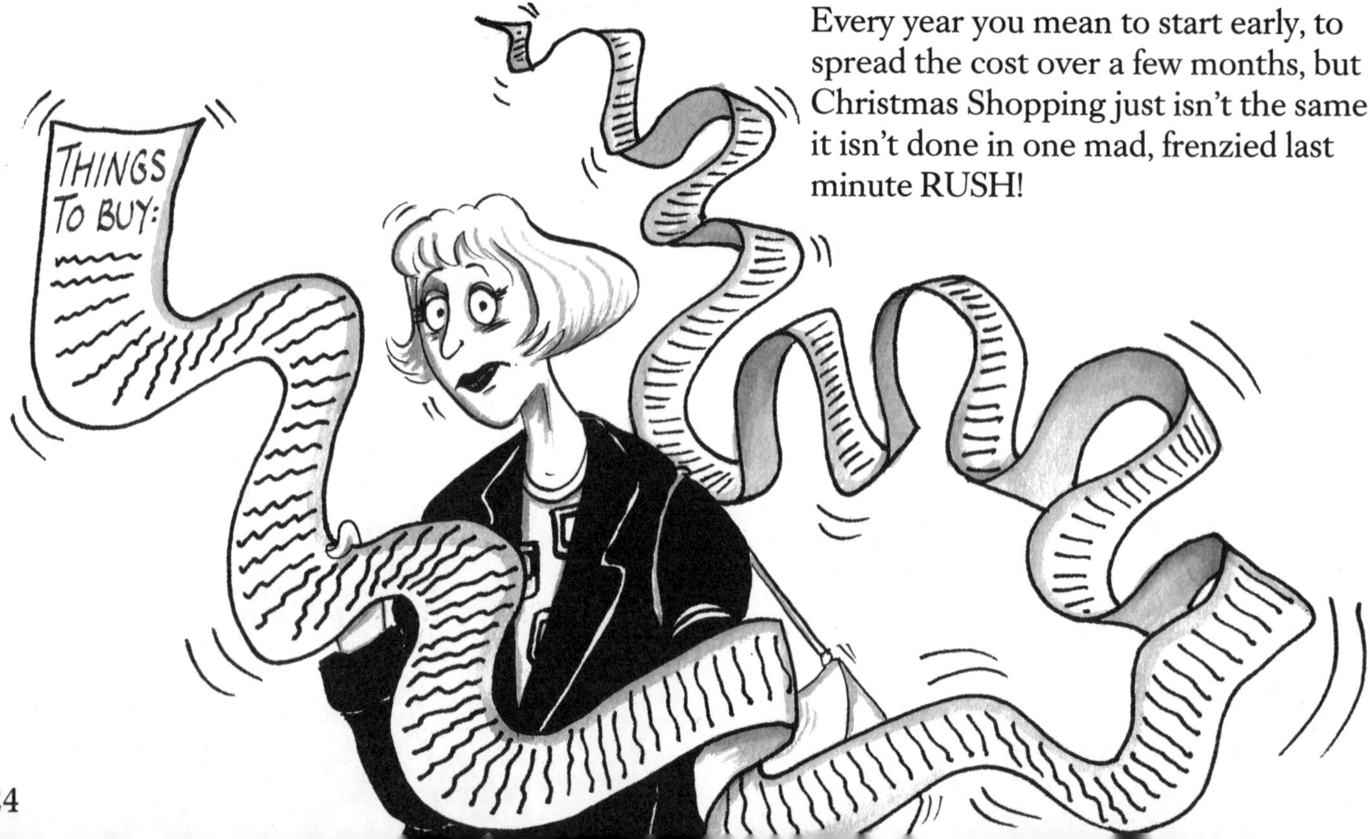
THINGS TO BUY:

THINGS YOU DON'T WANT TO HEAR …

- Sorry! Sold out of Nintendo.
- We've only got VAL DOONICAN left.
- We've got *lots* of BRUT!

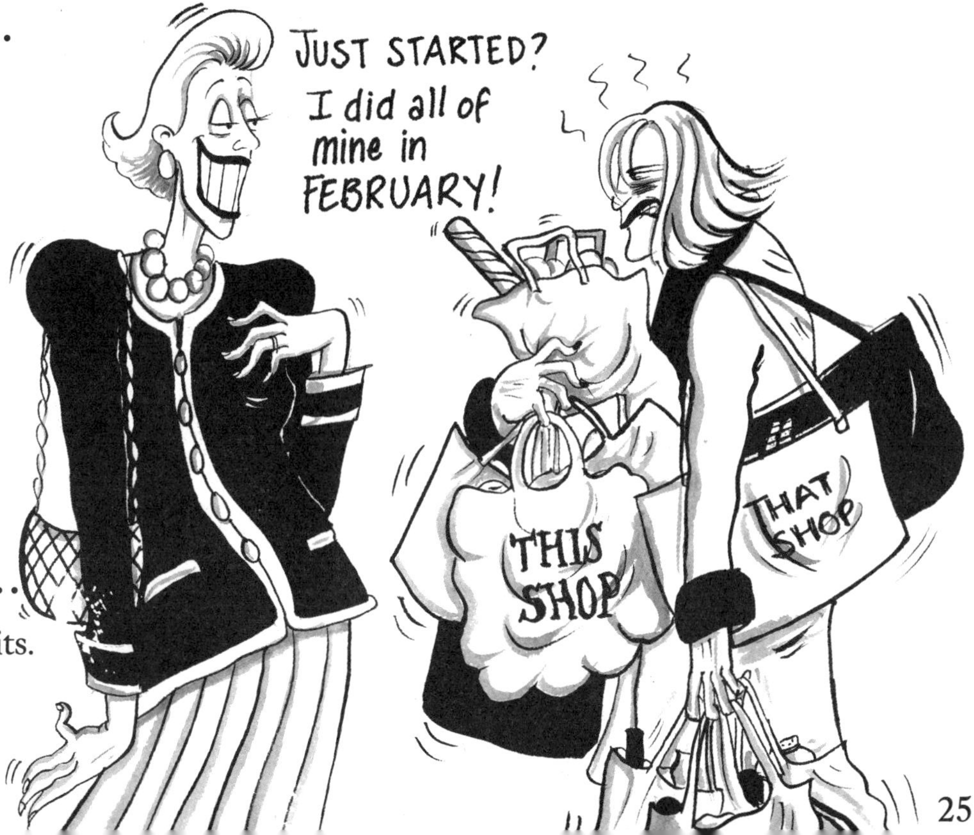
JUST STARTED?
I did all of mine in FEBRUARY!
THIS SHOP
THAT SHOP

THINGS YOU DO …

- Sorry! Sold out of Jellied Fruits.
- We've got LOTS of Alison Everitt books left.
- Christmas is nearly over!

WHAT NOT TO WEAR:

AVOID clothes that are fussy and which ride up when you walk.

ALLOW for sudden heat, sudden rain, sudden frost and sudden snow.

AVOID thick jumpers, as most shops have their heating set on 'TROPICAL', and you'll not only feel hot and sick, but HOMICIDAL too!

AVOID any colour that clashes with red ... the colour you'll be after a while.

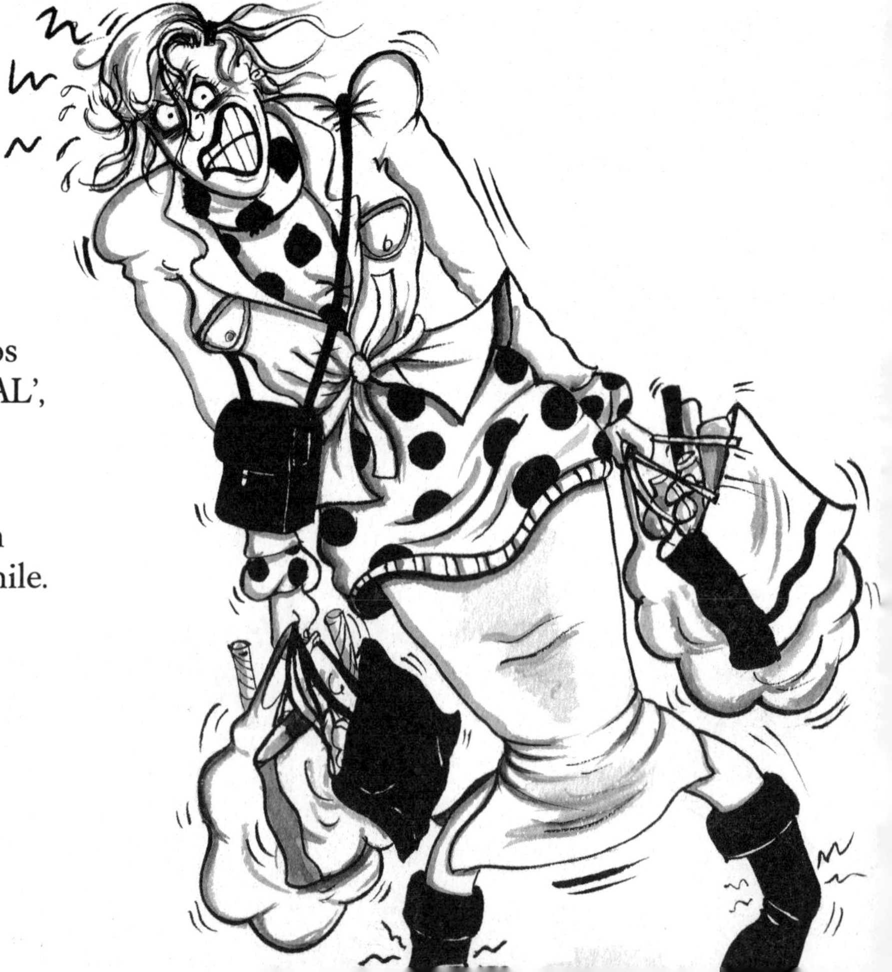

… And the **ULTIMATE SHOPPING OUTFIT** …

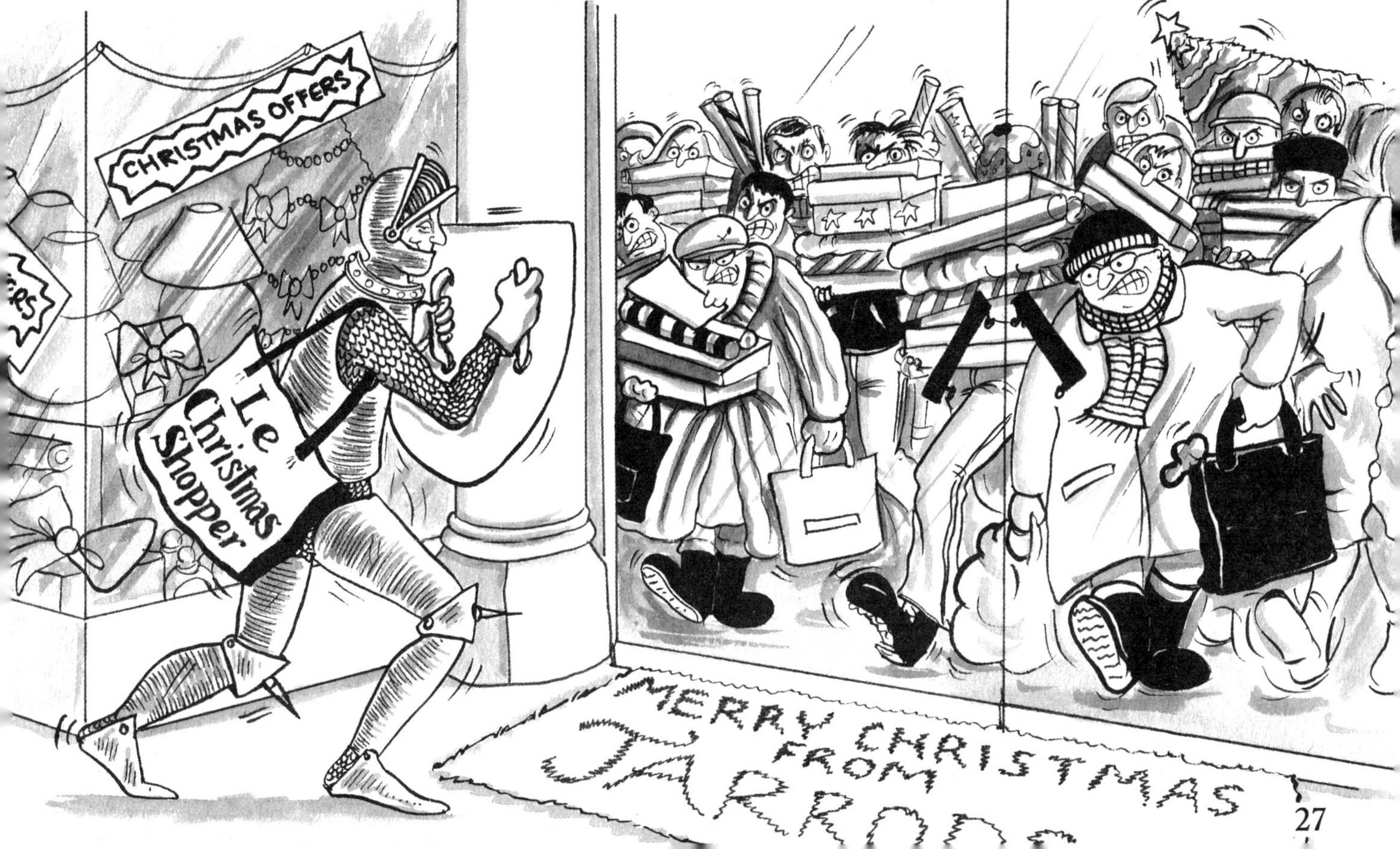
CHRISTMAS OFFERS
Le Christmas Shopper
MERRY CHRISTMAS FROM

Every year you know you buy the same old presents…

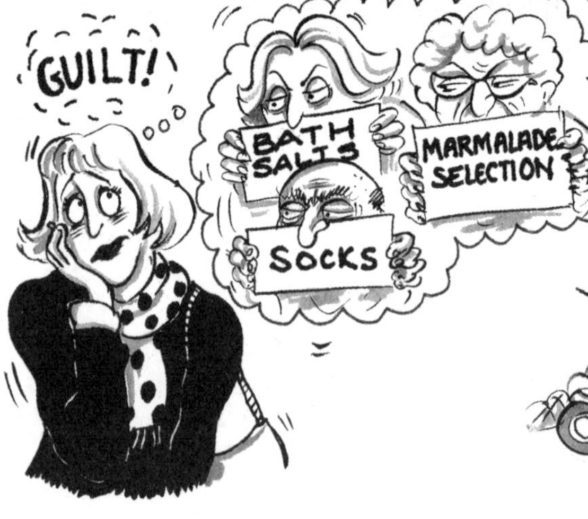
GUILT!
BATH SALTS
MARMALADE SELECTION
SOCKS

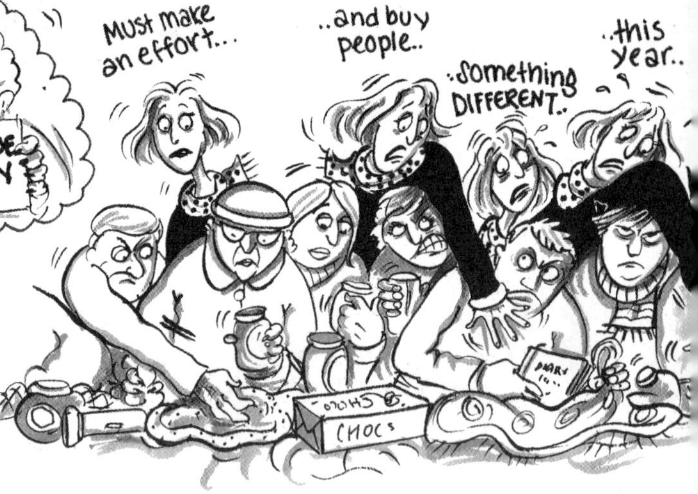
Must make an effort…
..and buy people..
..something DIFFERENT..
..this year..
CHOCS

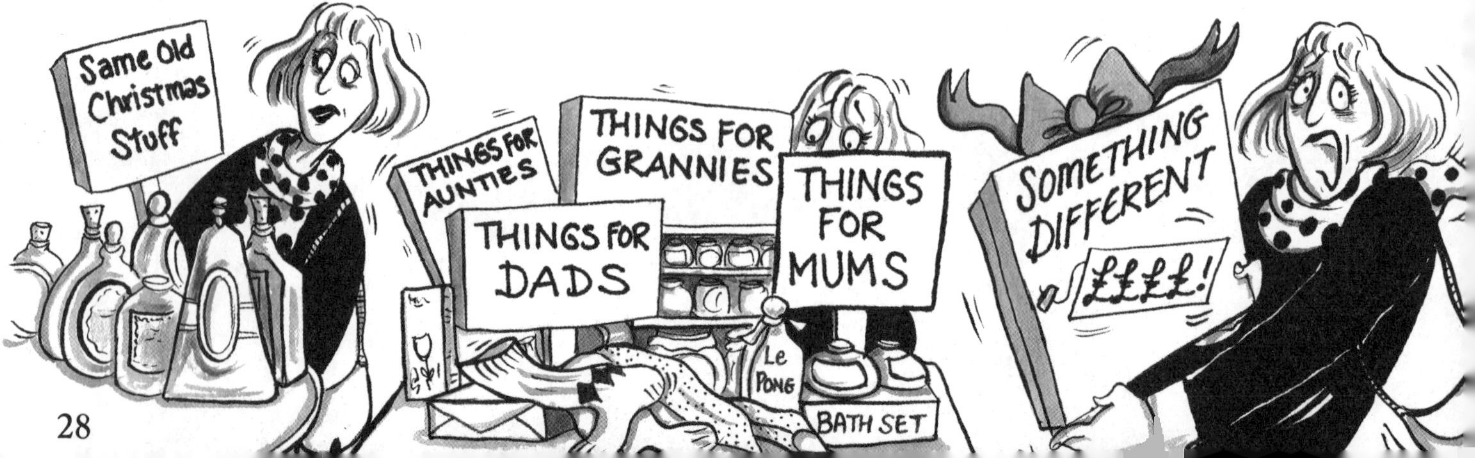
Same Old Christmas Stuff
THINGS FOR AUNTIES
THINGS FOR GRANNIES
THINGS FOR DADS
THINGS FOR MUMS
Le PONG
BATH SET
SOMETHING DIFFERENT
£££!

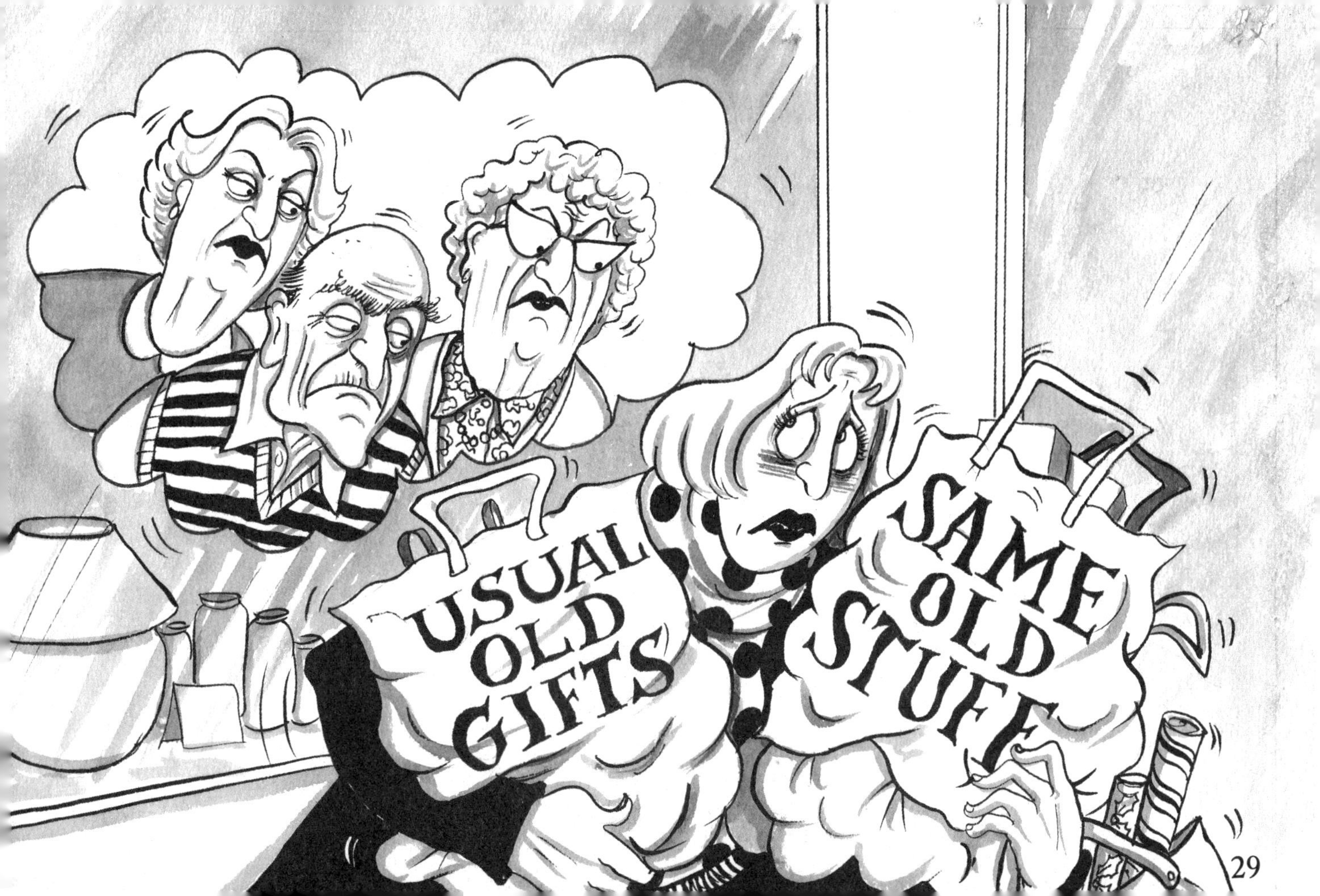
USUAL OLD GIFTS
SAME OLD STUFF

SUCCESSFUL SHOPPING:

Start buying presents early. (Like in January.)

Make a list of what you're buying for whom and the price limit, and tick them off as you go, so you don't end up totally confused.

Make another list because you're bound to leave the first one at home.

Try and get people something they'll actually like, rather than what you hope they'll give you back later.

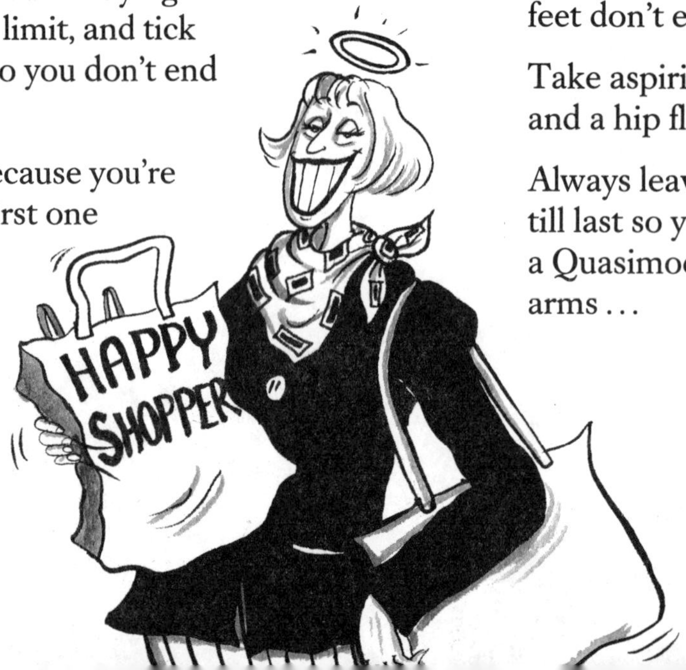
HAPPY SHOPPER

Get organised and work out a route for which shops you're going to, including lots of coffee stops so your feet don't explode.

Take aspirins, plasters, an umbrella and a hip flask. Just in case.

Always leave the heaviest presents till last so you don't end up with a Quasimodo back and Gorilla arms . . .

… AND WHEN YOU KNOW YOU'RE DOOMED …

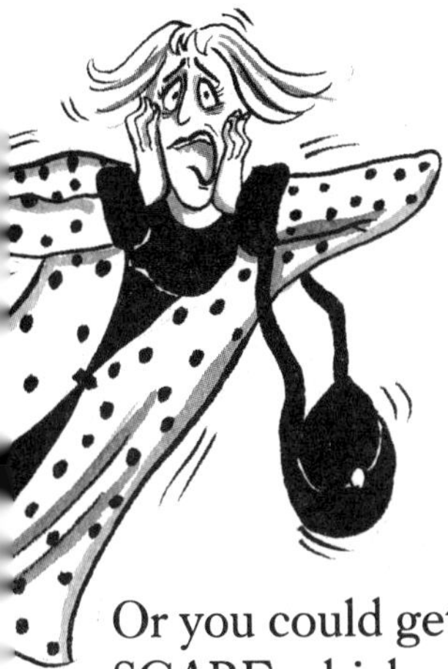

You not only forget your lists, but you also forget every member of your family, never mind what you were planning to get them … and by the time you get yourself together …

… all the good stuff's LONG GONE!

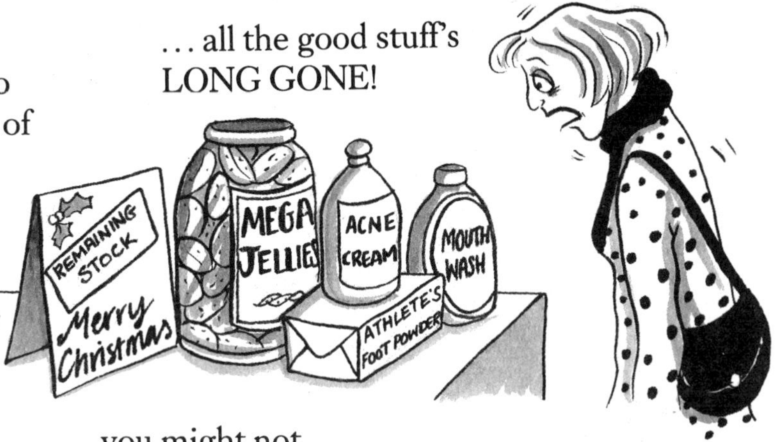
REMAINING STOCK
Merry Christmas
MEGA JELLIES
ACNE CREAM
MOUTH WASH
ATHLETE'S FOOT POWDER

Or you could get caught in a BOMB SCARE which means you have to do a day's shopping in an hour and a half because of all the delays …

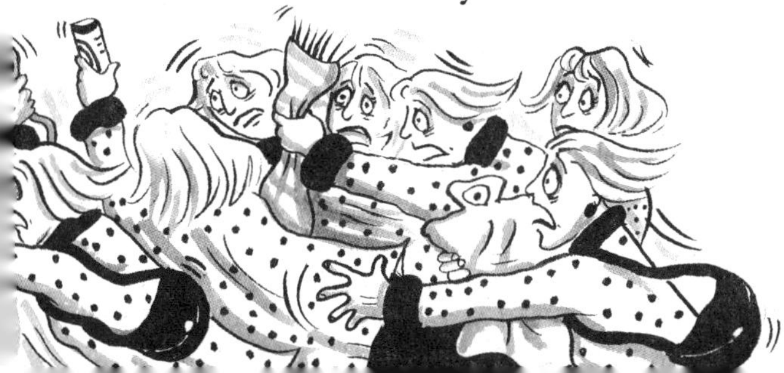

… you might not even be allowed off the train and have to buy all your presents from British Rail!

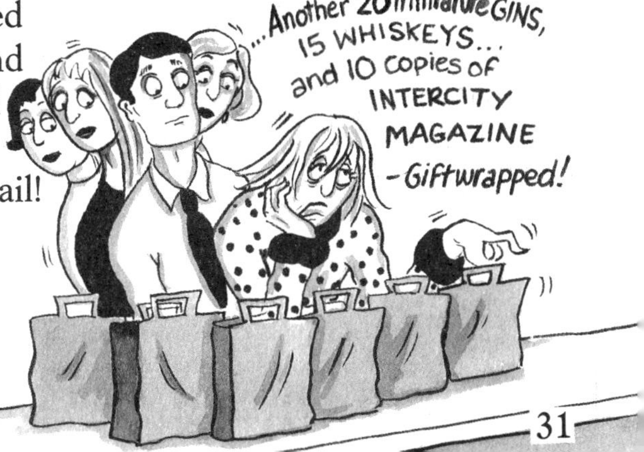
…Another 20 miniature GINS, 15 WHISKEYS… and 10 copies of INTERCITY MAGAZINE -Giftwrapped!

THINGS YOU HATE ABOUT CHRISTMAS

(3) Christmas Celebrities …

They're on Game Shows …

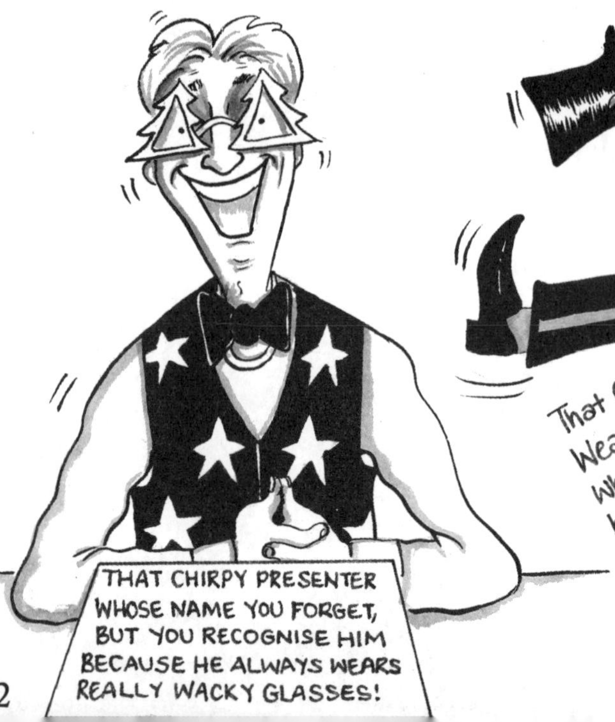
THAT CHIRPY PRESENTER
WHOSE NAME YOU FORGET,
BUT YOU RECOGNISE HIM
BECAUSE HE ALWAYS WEARS
REALLY WACKY GLASSES!

… They're in Variety Shows

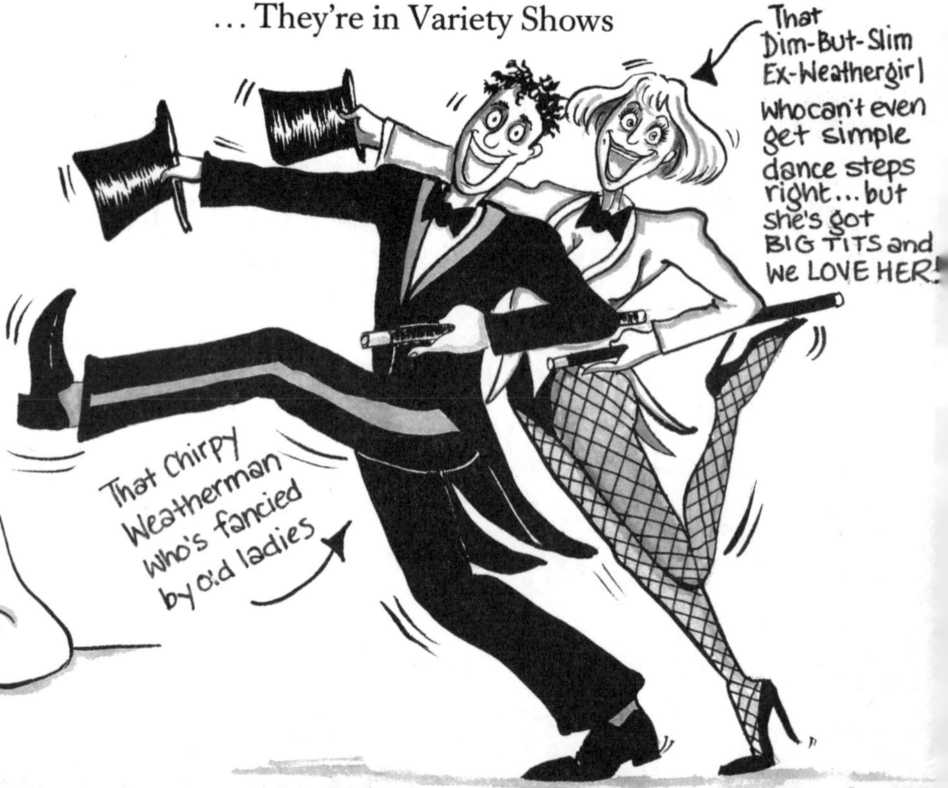
That Dim-But-Slim Ex-Weathergirl who can't even get simple dance steps right… but she's got BIG TITS and We LOVE HER!
That Chirpy Weatherman who's fancied by old ladies

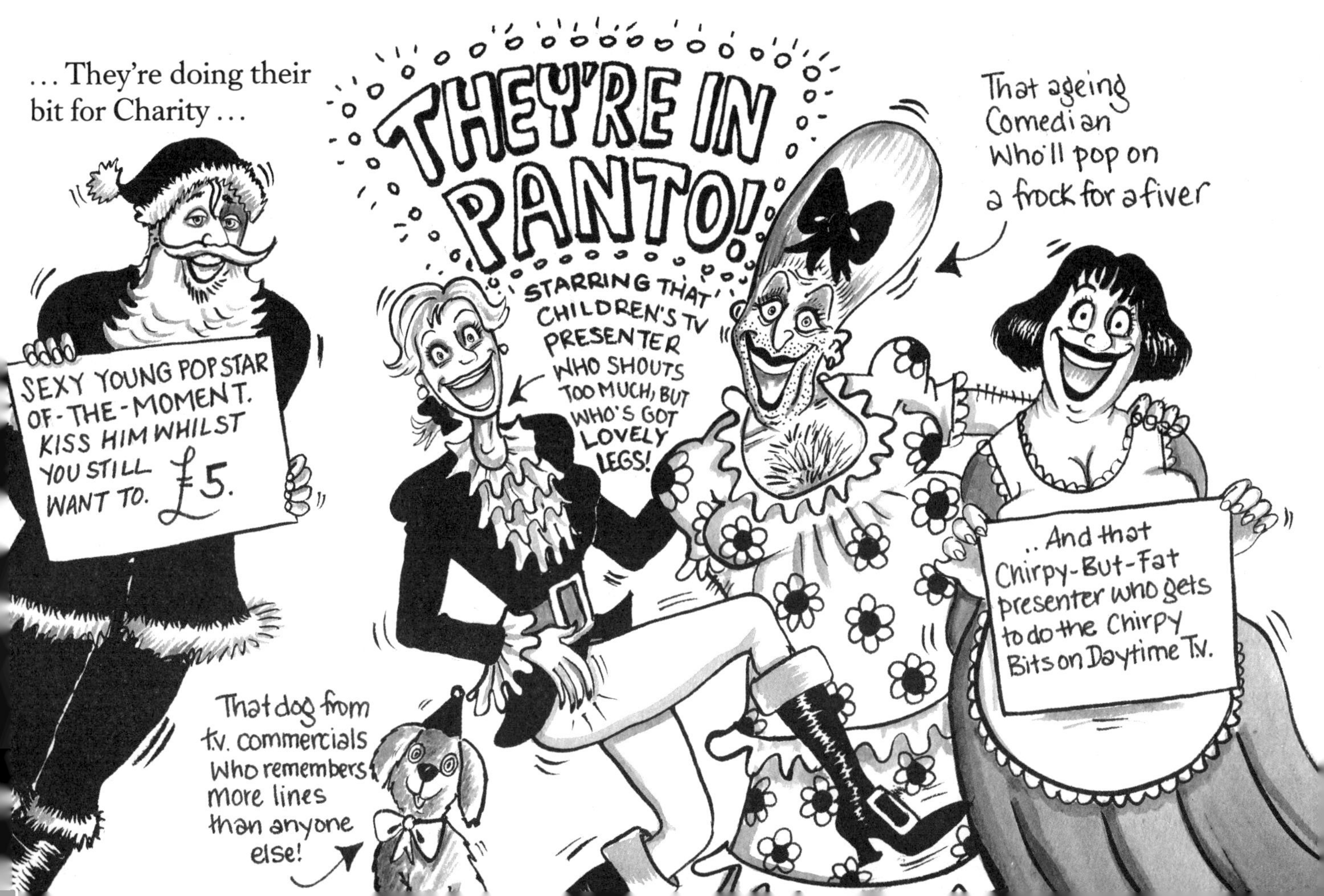

... They're doing their bit for Charity ...
THEY'RE IN PANTO!
SEXY YOUNG POP STAR OF-THE-MOMENT. KISS HIM WHILST YOU STILL WANT TO. £5.
STARRING THAT CHILDREN'S TV PRESENTER WHO SHOUTS TOO MUCH, BUT WHO'S GOT LOVELY LEGS!
That ageing Comedian Who'll pop on a frock for a fiver
.. And that Chirpy-But-Fat presenter who gets to do the Chirpy Bits on Daytime T.V.
That dog from t.v. commercials Who remembers more lines than anyone else!

CHRISTMAS SUPPLIES . . .

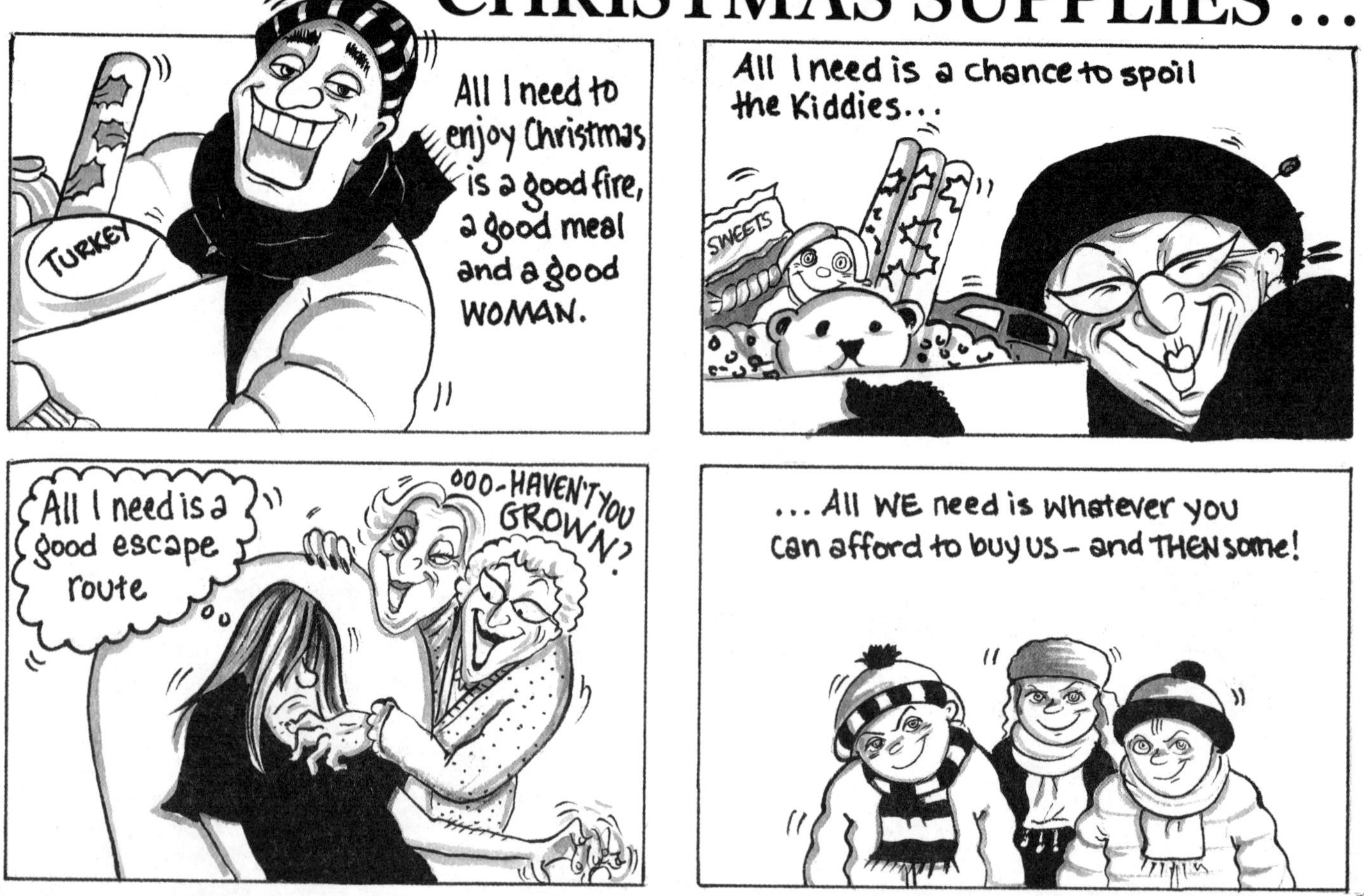
All I need to enjoy Christmas is a good fire, a good meal and a good WOMAN.
TURKEY
All I need is a chance to spoil the Kiddies...
SWEETS
All I need is a good escape route
OOO-HAVEN'T YOU GROWN?
... All WE need is whatever you can afford to buy US – and THEN some!

. . . And what does MUM need to see her through Christmas?

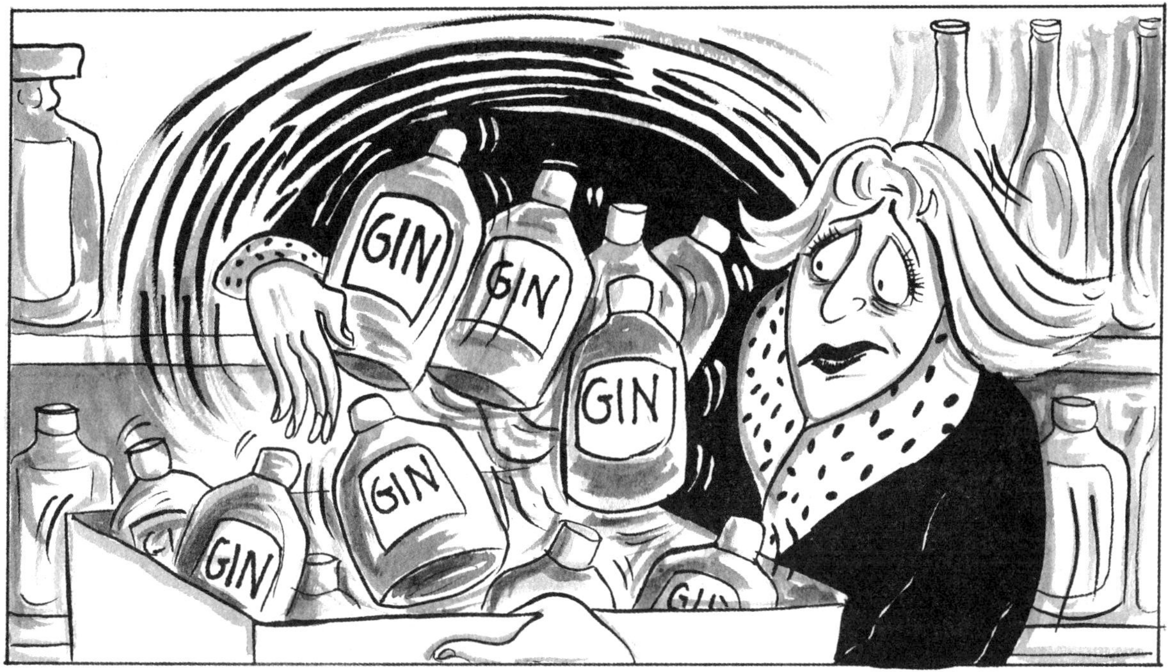
GIN
GIN
GIN
GIN
GIN

THE ESSENTIAL CHRISTMAS ACCESSORY:

THE SMILE ON A STICK ...

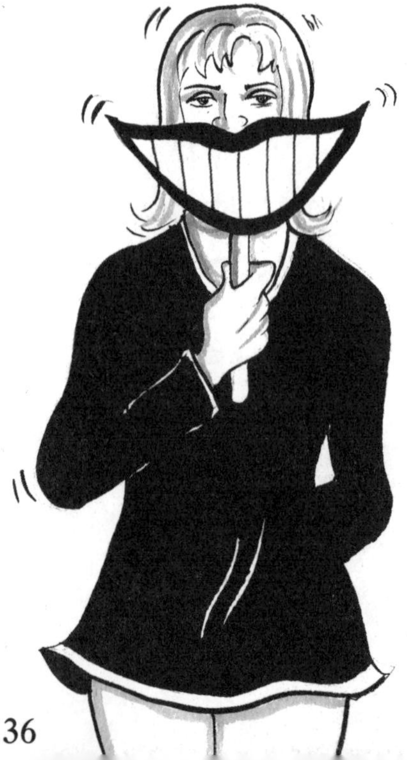

For when you're pretending to enjoy school concerts ...

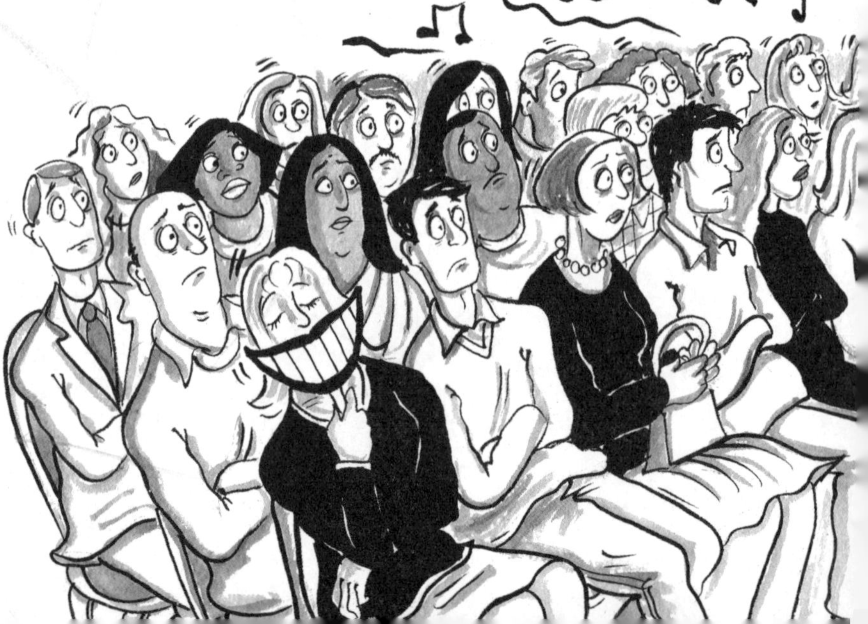

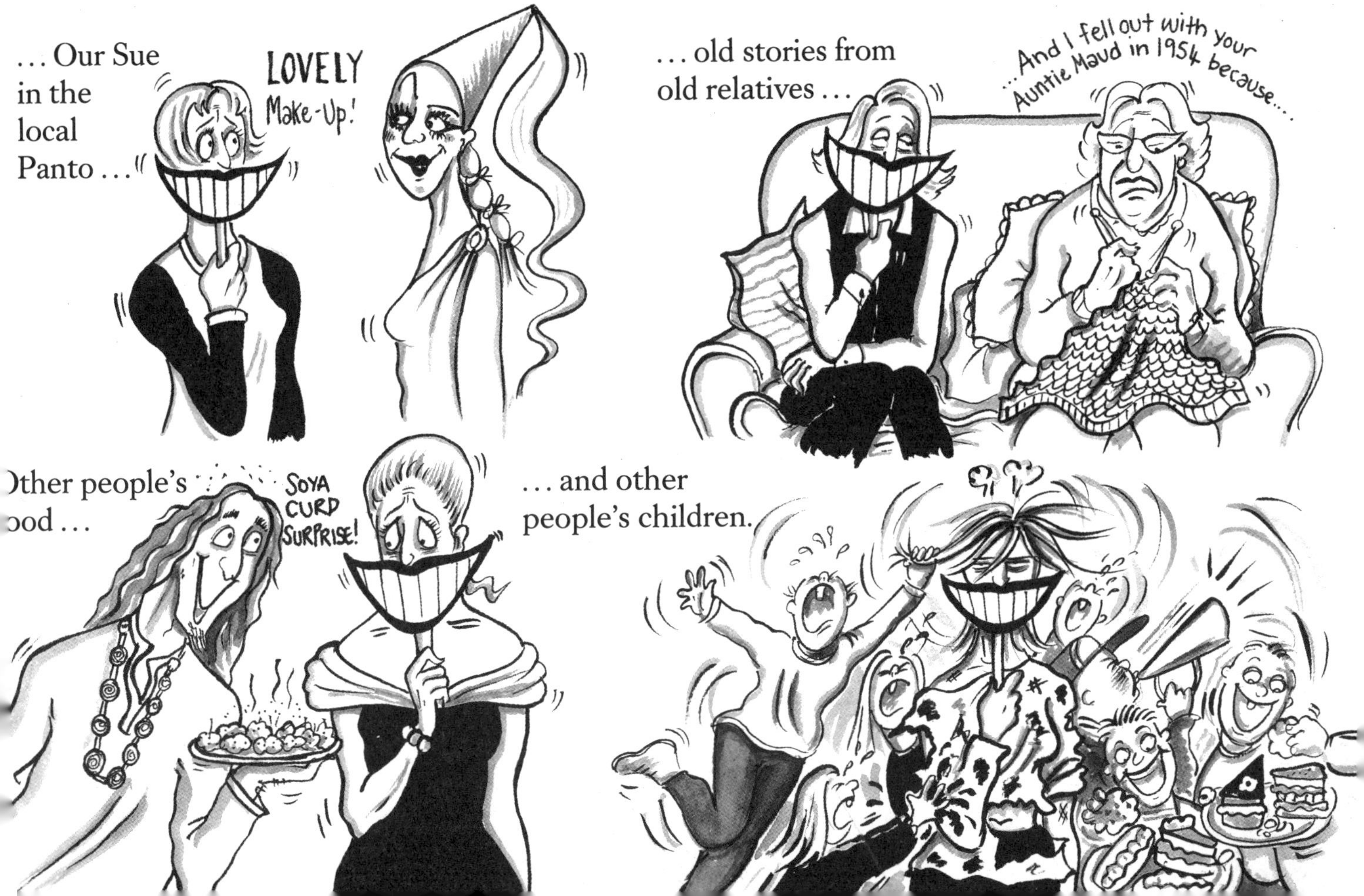

… Our Sue in the local Panto …
LOVELY Make-Up!
… old stories from old relatives …
… And I fell out with your Auntie Maud in 1954 because….
ther people's ood …
SOYA CURD SURPRISE!
… and other people's children.

THINGS YOU HATE ABOUT CHRISTMAS

(4) Once-A-Year-Drinks . . .

They're clients, they're work colleagues, they're neighbours you pretend to like, or they're old school friends who you know you've grown apart from . . .

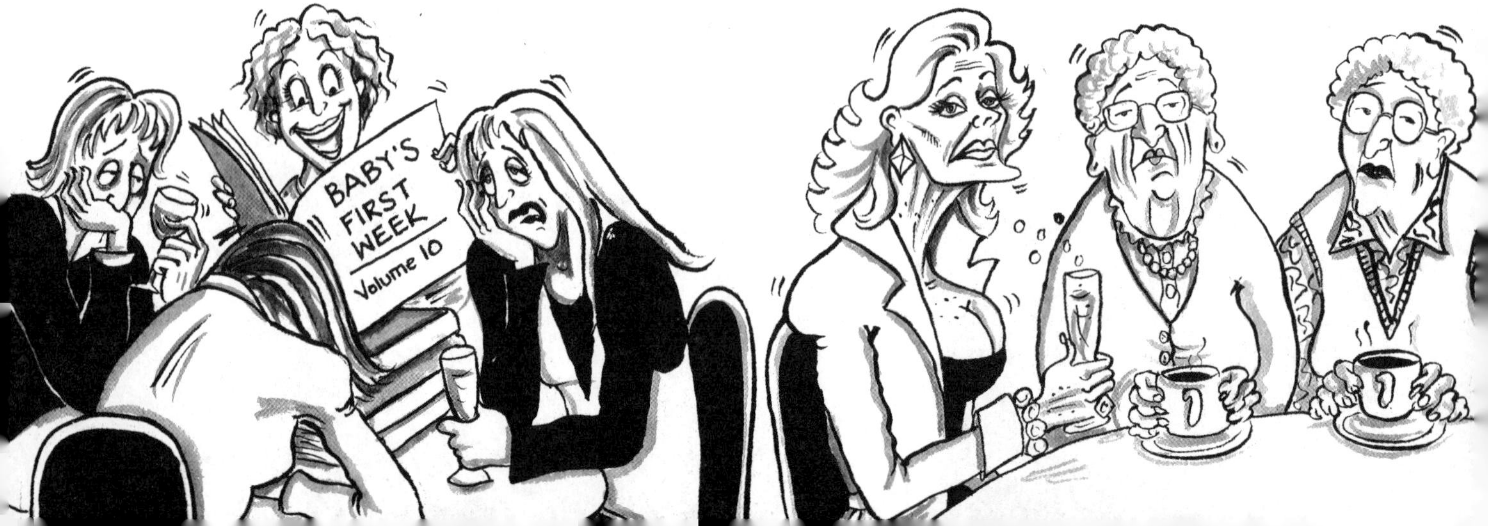
BABY'S FIRST WEEK
Volume 10

… AND AMATEUR DRINKERS …

They're either people who don't drink much and can't take it, or else they're just completely CRAP. One glass of cheap wine and they're dancing on tables, sitting naked in lifts, or wishing you a Merry Christmas and throwing up on your shoes.

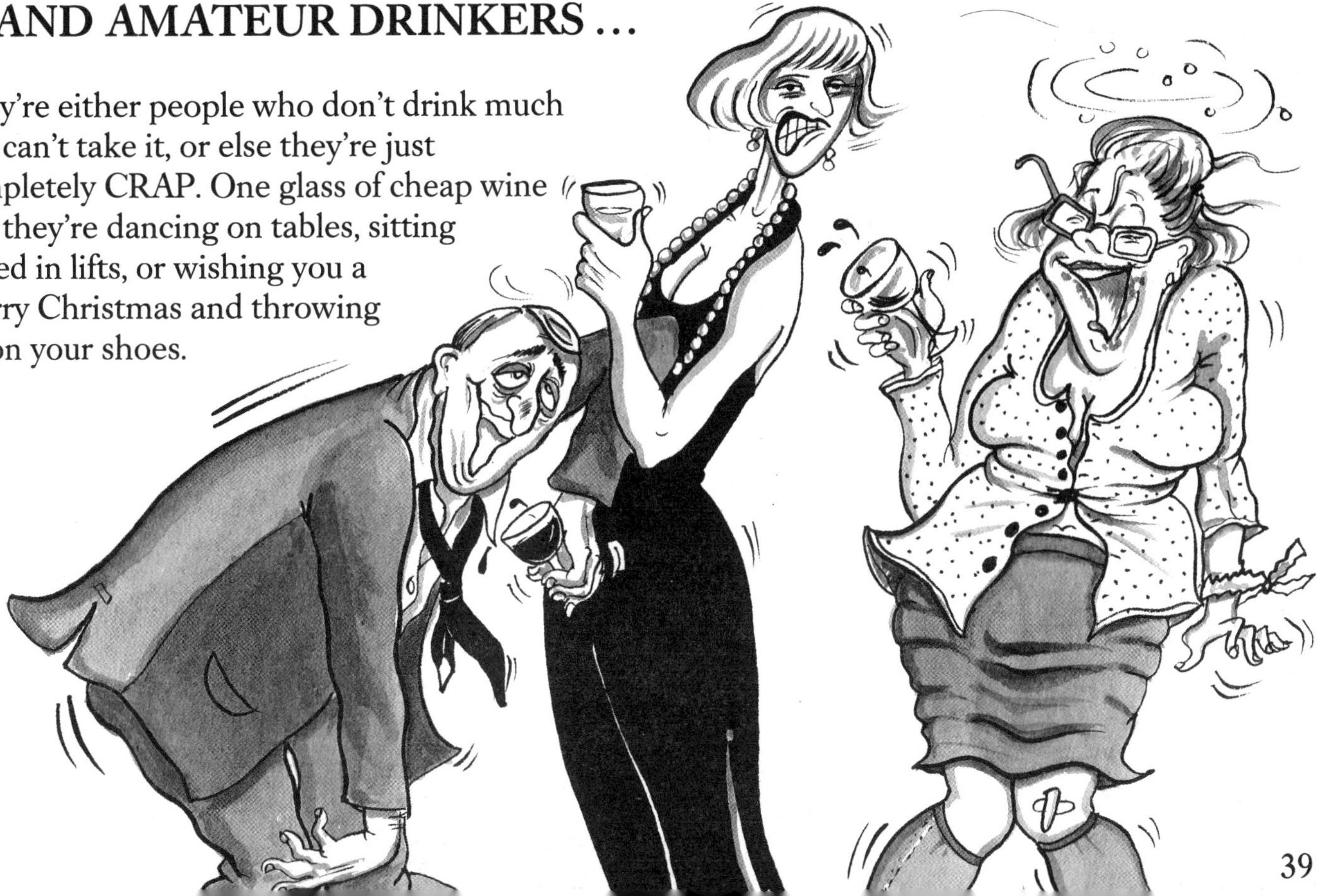

OFFICE PARTIES:

The biggest drawback about office parties is that you have to spend all night with the people you see all day.

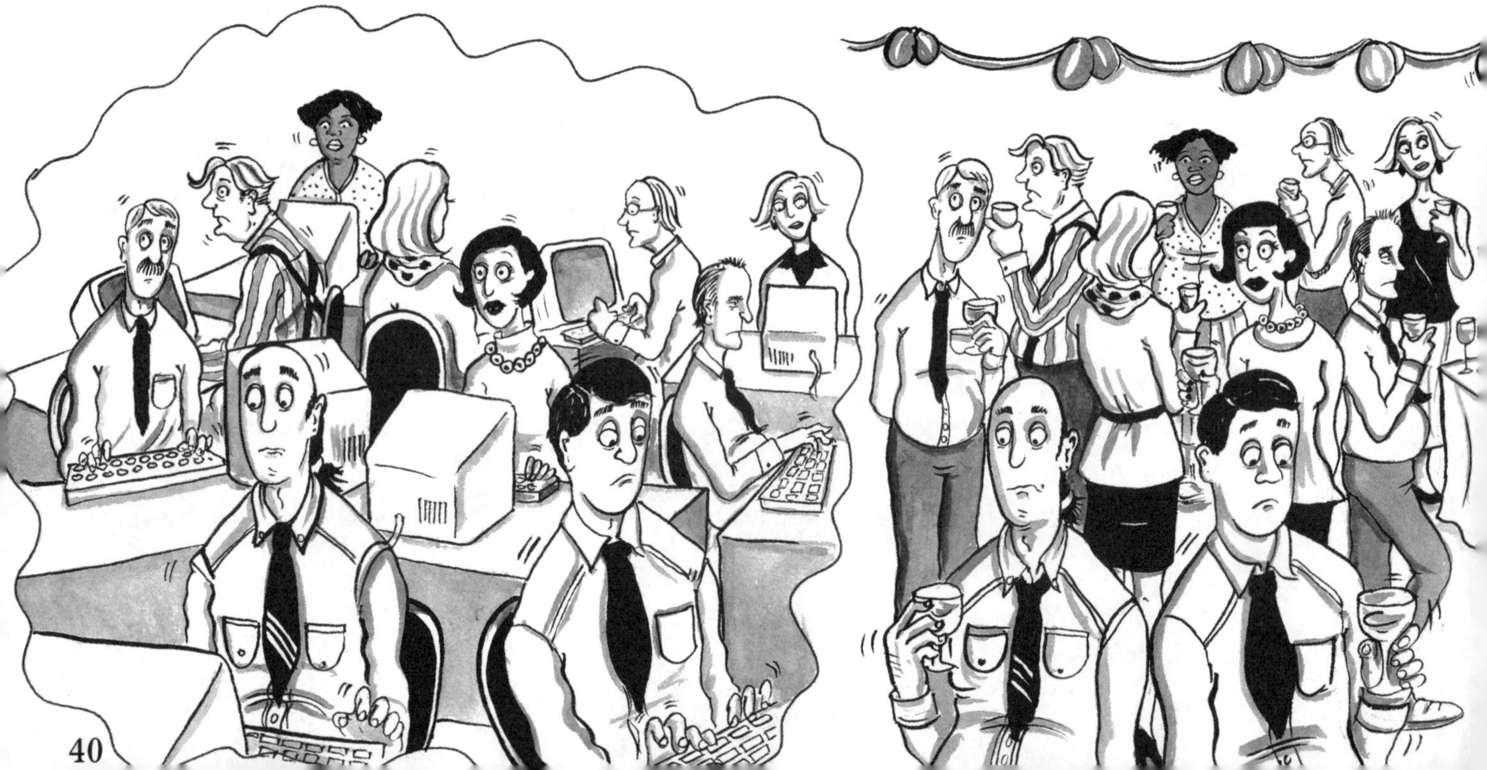

To get over this, people have to try to forget they're still at work. (Some things are harder to forget than others …)

They easily forget that they're MARRIED …

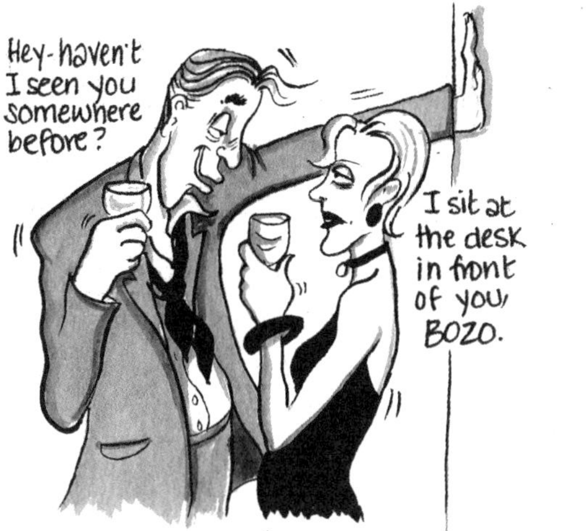
Hey-haven't I seen you somewhere before?
I sit at the desk in front of you, BOZO.

But they just can't forget that they HATE everyone else …

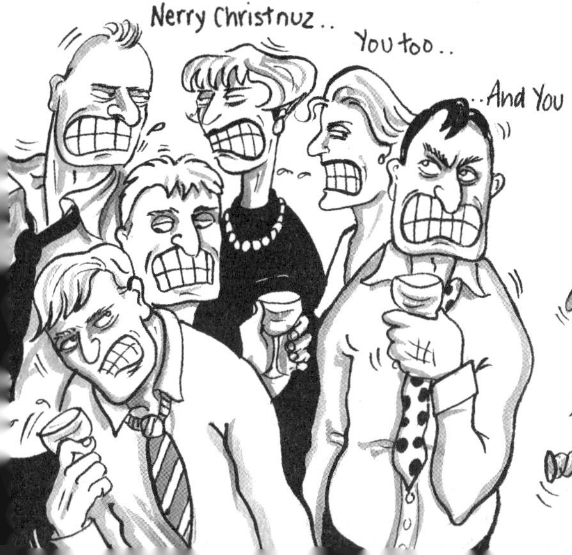
Nerry Christnuz..
You too..
..And You

… that they DIDN'T get the promotion …

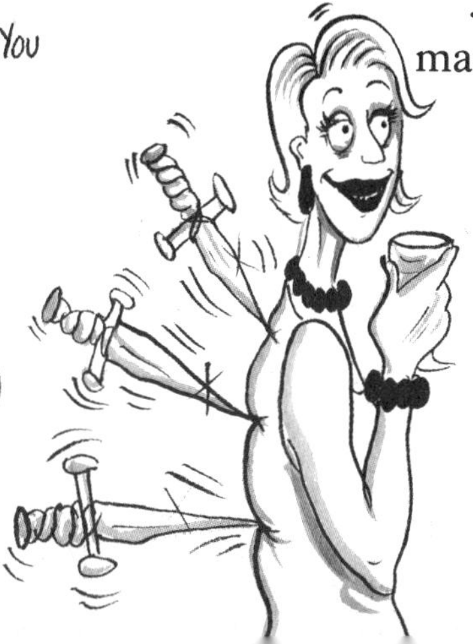

… that they've just been made REDUNDANT …

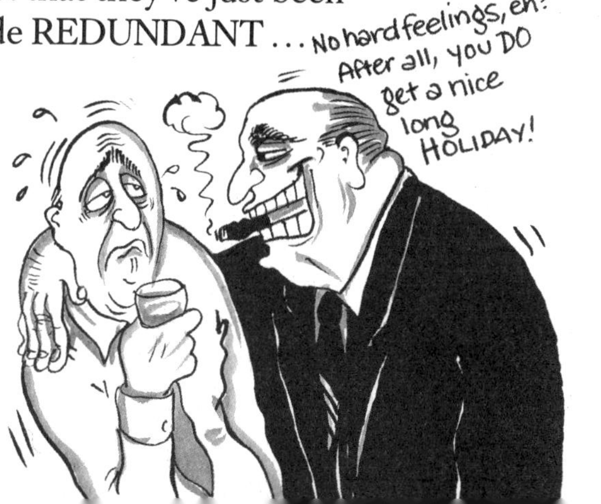
No hard feelings, eh? After all, you DO get a nice long HOLIDAY!

THINGS TO SPOT AT AN OFFICE PARTY:

When the lights are dimmed, the wine is flowing and a cheap stereo plays, you can't help your true character shining out … so watch out!

… SPOT THE: LADDER CLIMBER

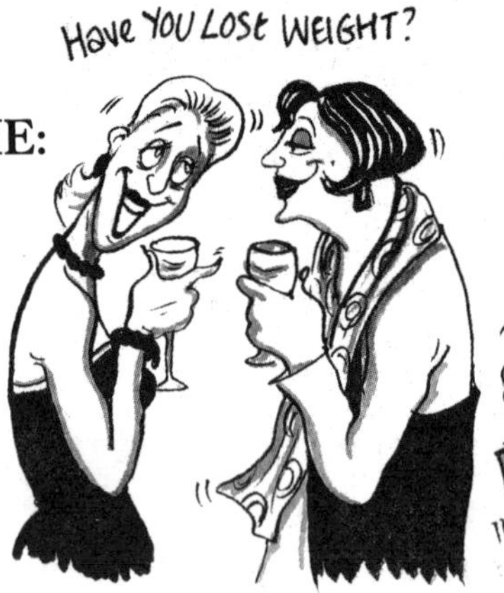
Have YOU LOST WEIGHT?

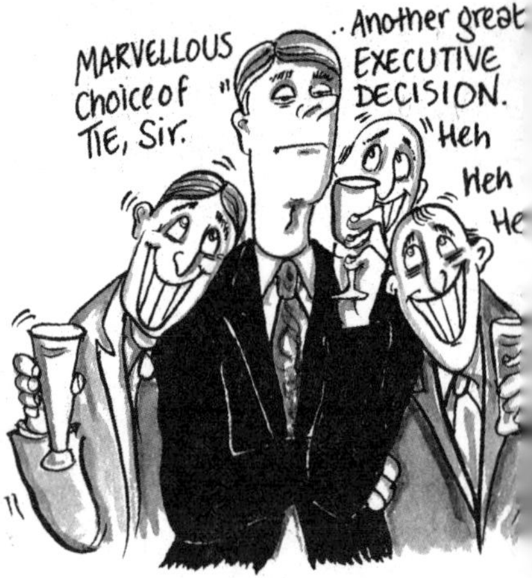
MARVELLOUS Choice of TIE, Sir.
.. Another great EXECUTIVE DECISION.
Heh Heh He

SPOT THE: ILLICIT AFFAIR

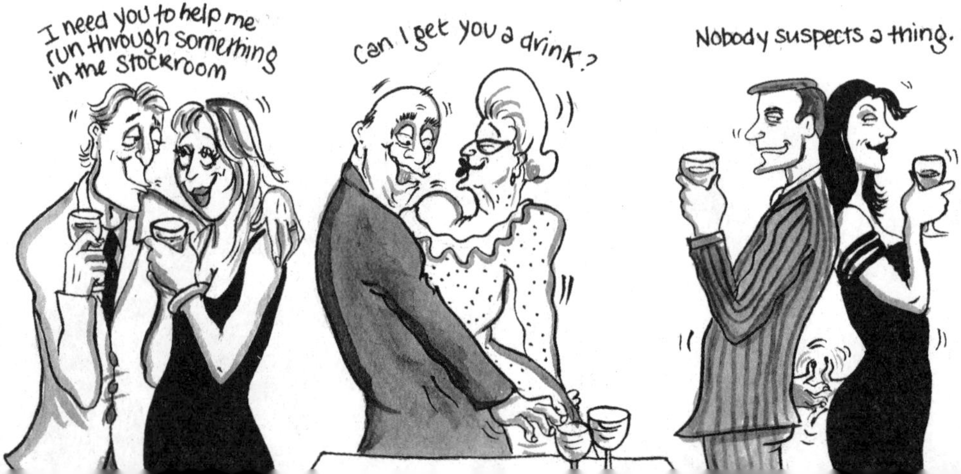
I need you to help me run through something in the stockroom
can I get you a drink?
Nobody suspects a thing.

… AND SPOT THE: MANAGING DIRECTOR (Stays for the first 10 minutes then moves on somewhere much more interesting …)

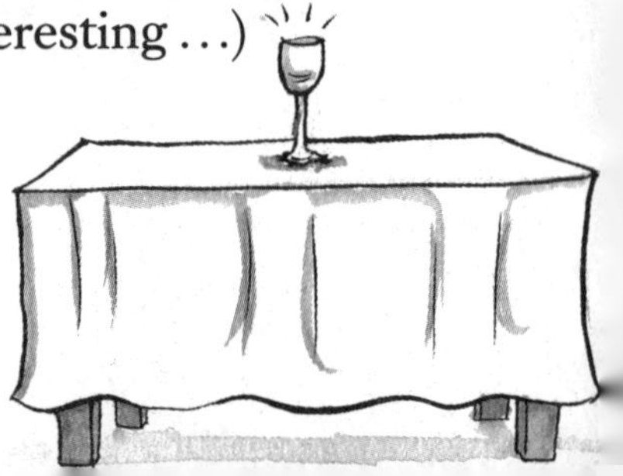

WHAT NOT TO DO AT AN OFFICE PARTY …

Drag out petty office politics …

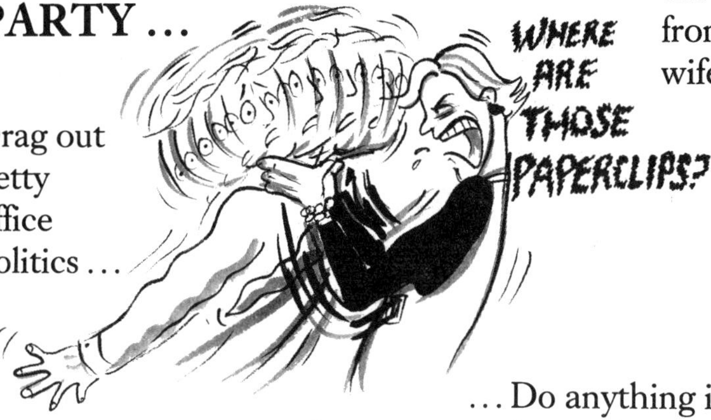
WHERE ARE THOSE PAPERCLIPS?

… Chat up the boss in front of his wife …

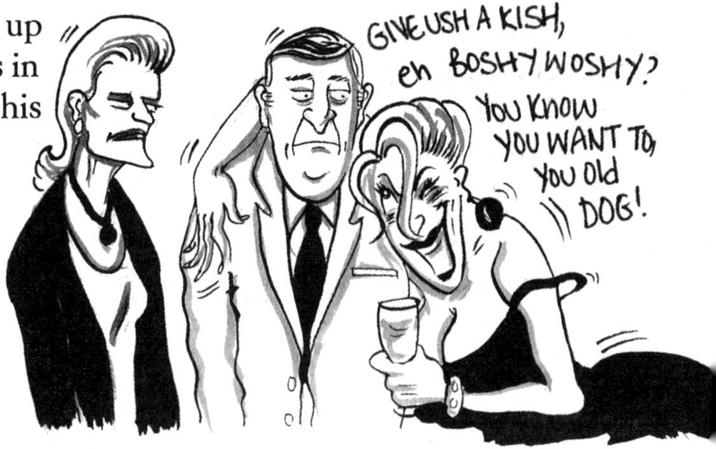
GIVE USH A KISH, eh BOSHY WOSHY?
You Know YOU WANT To, you old DOG!

… Throw up on the MD …

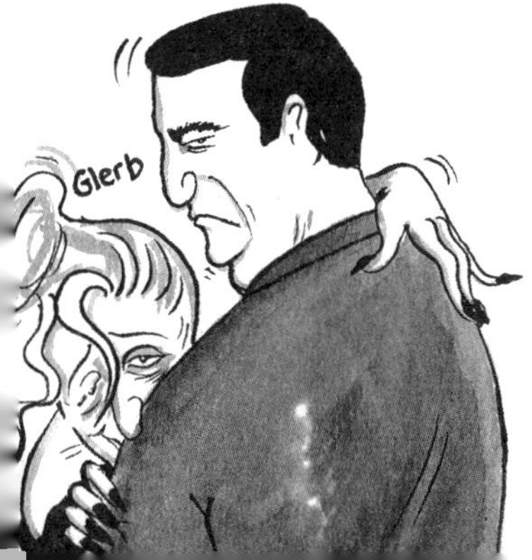
Glerb

… Do anything indiscreet in front of a camera or on a photocopier …

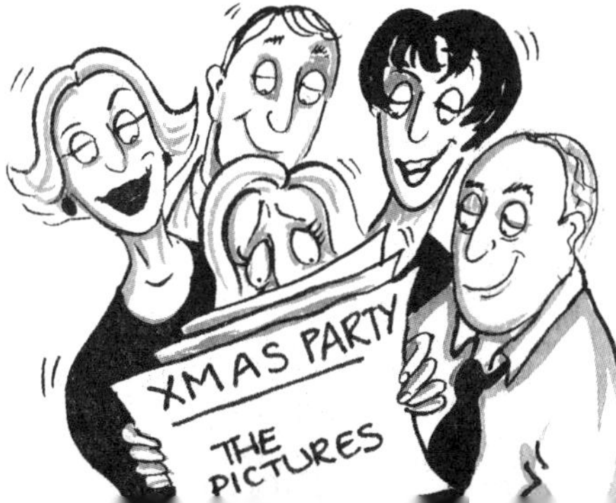
XMAS PARTY
THE PICTURES

… Declare undying love to a pot plant and show how SAD you are.

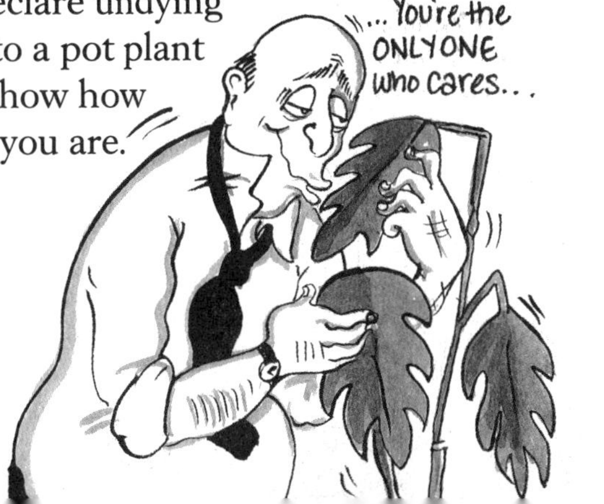
… You're the ONLY ONE who cares…

THE WORST THINGS ABOUT OFFICE PARTIES . . .

You're expected to talk about things other than work . . .

. . . You know you have to go back to work tomorrow . . .

. . . Bosses are never known for their generosity . . .

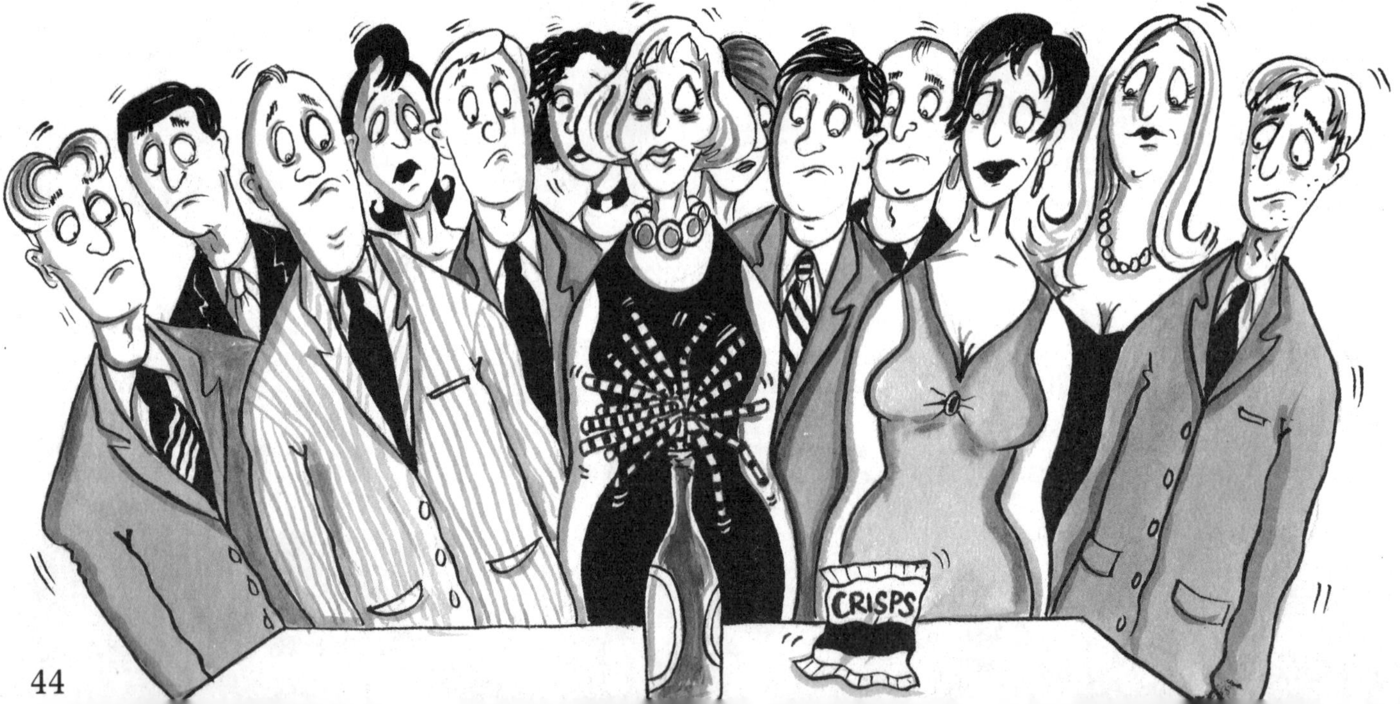
CRISPS

.. AND YOU KNOW THAT LURKING SOMEWHERE IS THE OFFICE PARTY PERVERT!

He has mistletoe superglued to his trousers.

He's covered in DIY lovebites.

He only goes to the bar when it's crowded so there are more women to rub up against.

He is DESPERATE to have his bottom photocopied.

He hangs around you just before the slow records start so he can grab you first.

He takes the blown up condoms home so his dustmen think he has a sex life.

He knows that this is the ONE TIME a year he can whip his tongue in your mouth and you'll be too drunk to throw him off.

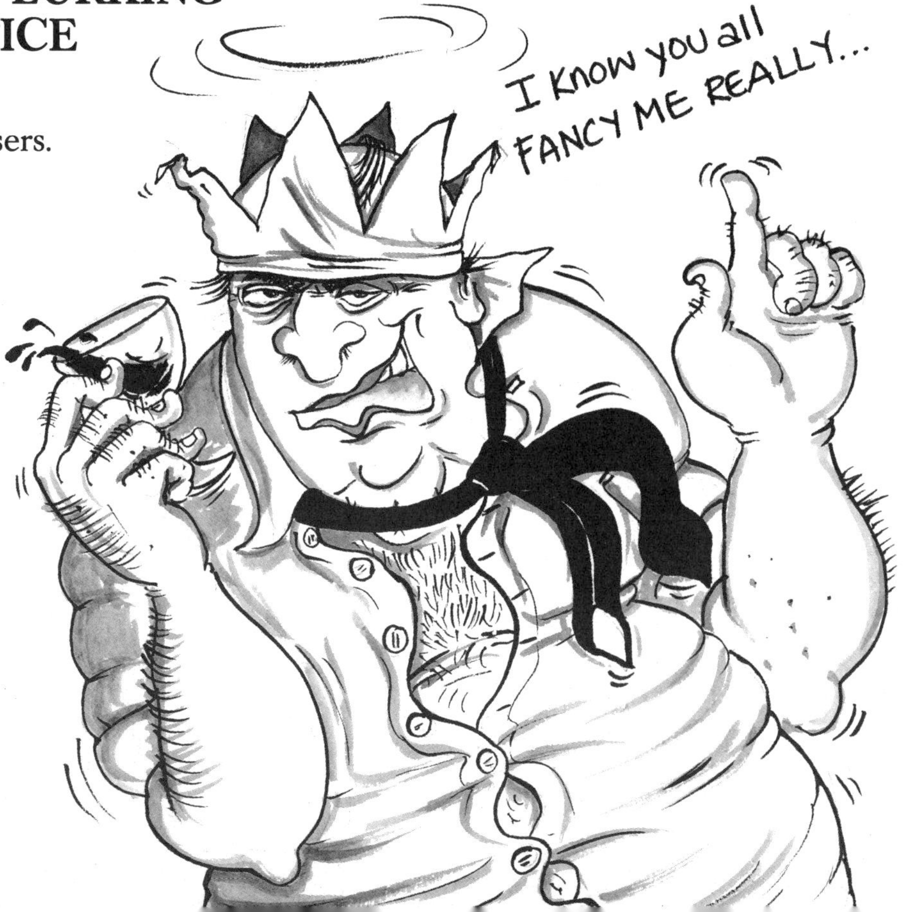
I KNOW YOU ALL FANCY ME REALLY...

THINGS YOU HATE ABOUT CHRISTMAS:

(5) Other People's Christmas Lunches …

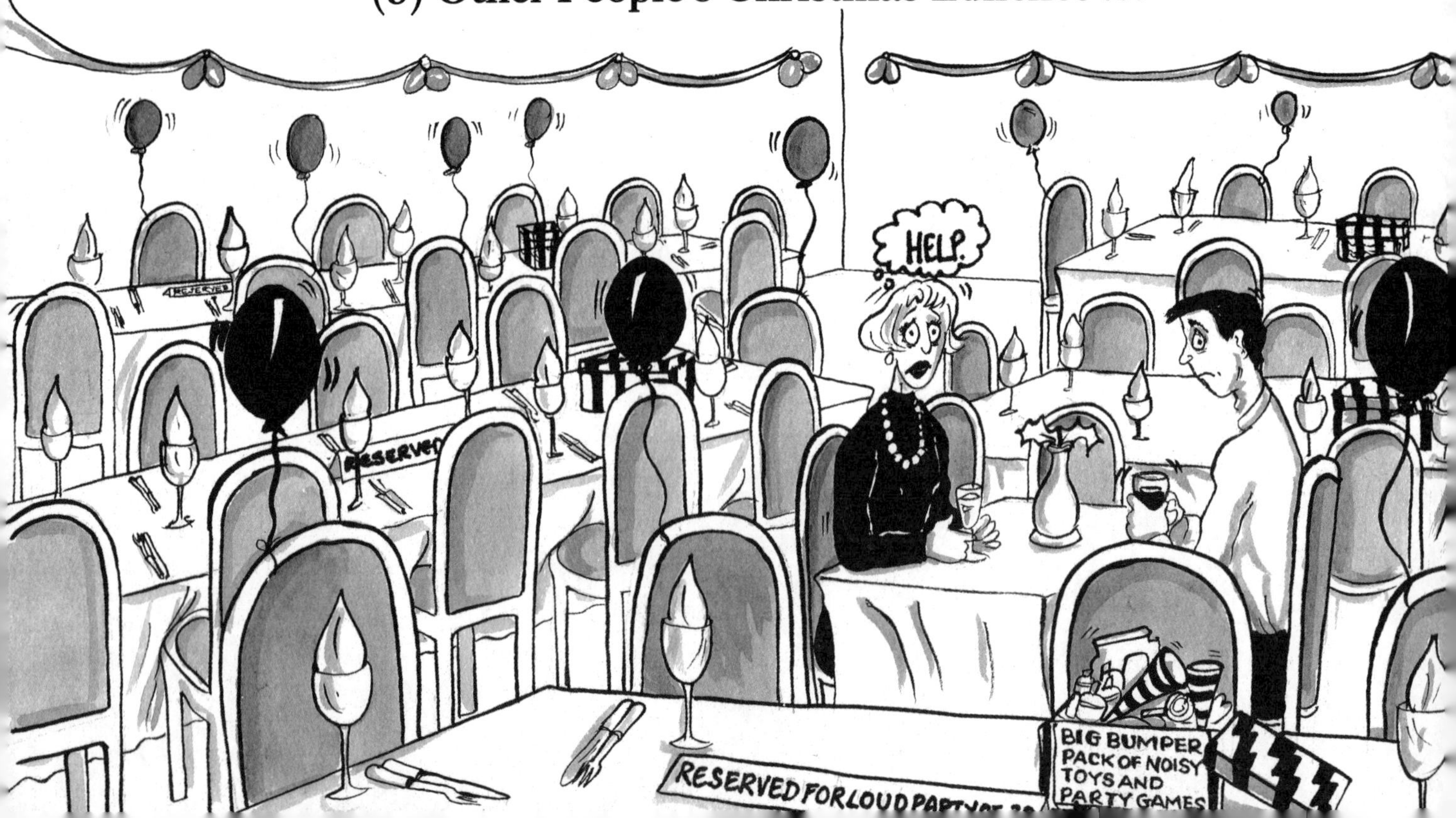
HELP.
RESERVED
RESERVED FOR LOUD
BIG BUMPER
PACK OF NOISY
TOYS AND
PARTY GAMES

Unless you're in a group of at least twenty, going for a quiet lunch at Christmas is impossible. You're surrounded by rowdy office workers, amateur drinkers and secondhand festivities, topped with the knowledge that at any moment someone will jump on a table and expect you to join in with the singing. Avoid going out until the middle of January.

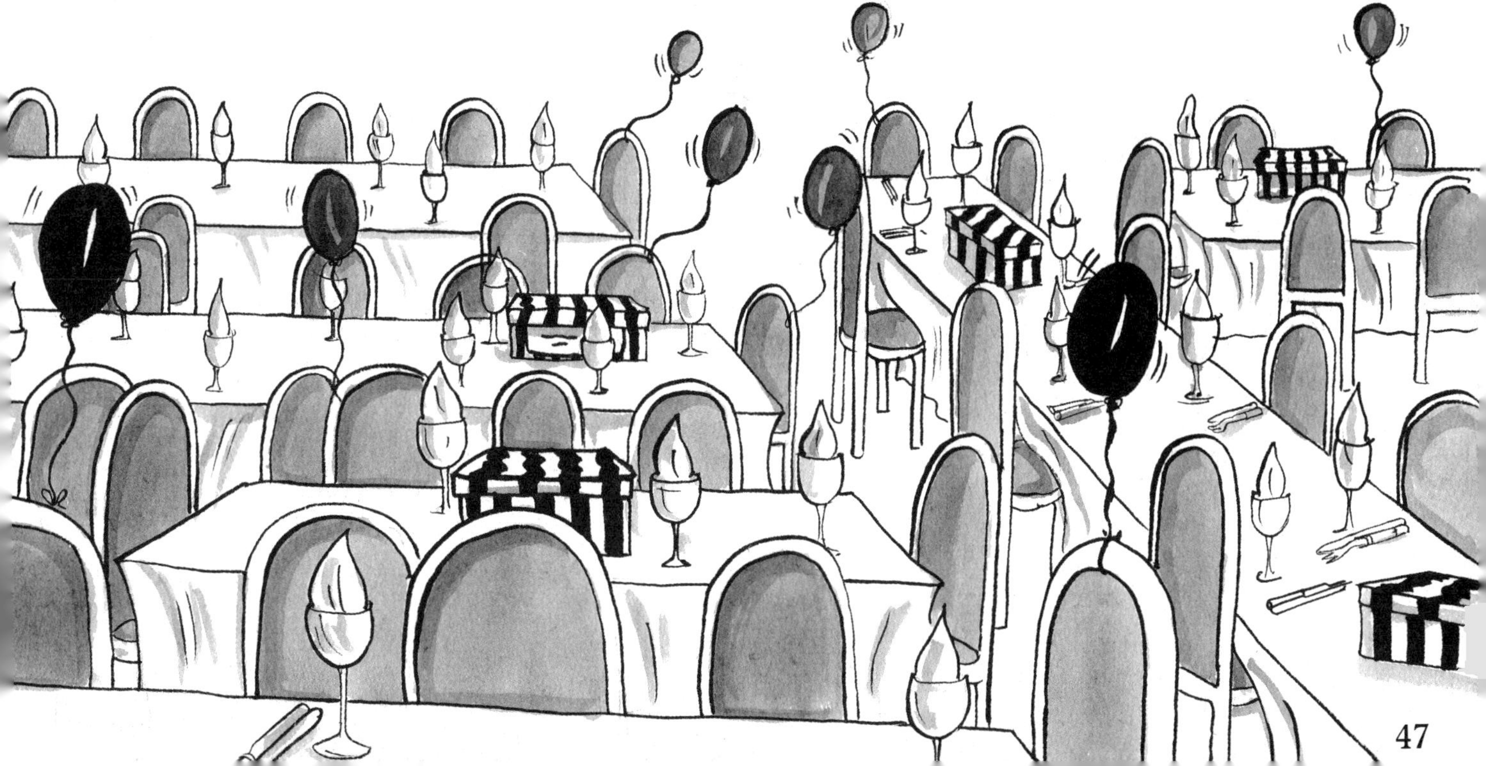

CHRISTMAS AILMENTS …

Backache …

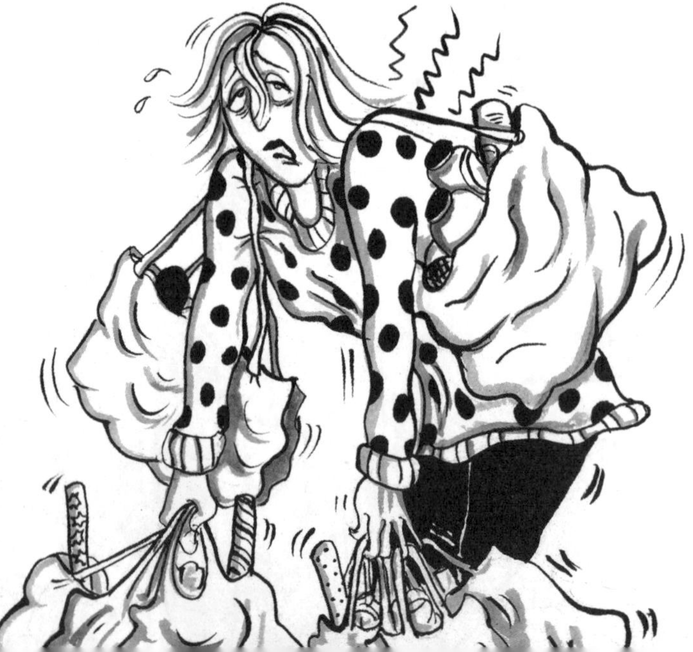

… Heatstroke …

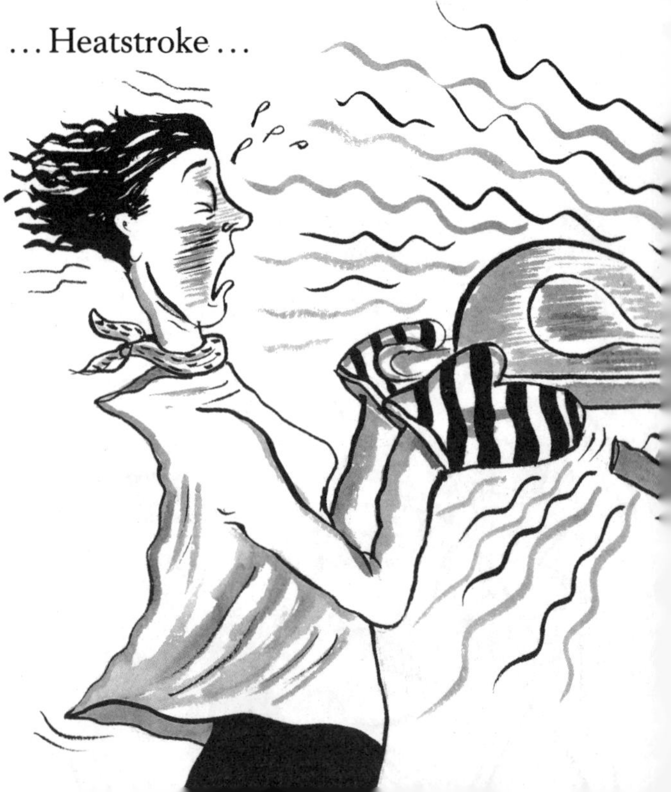

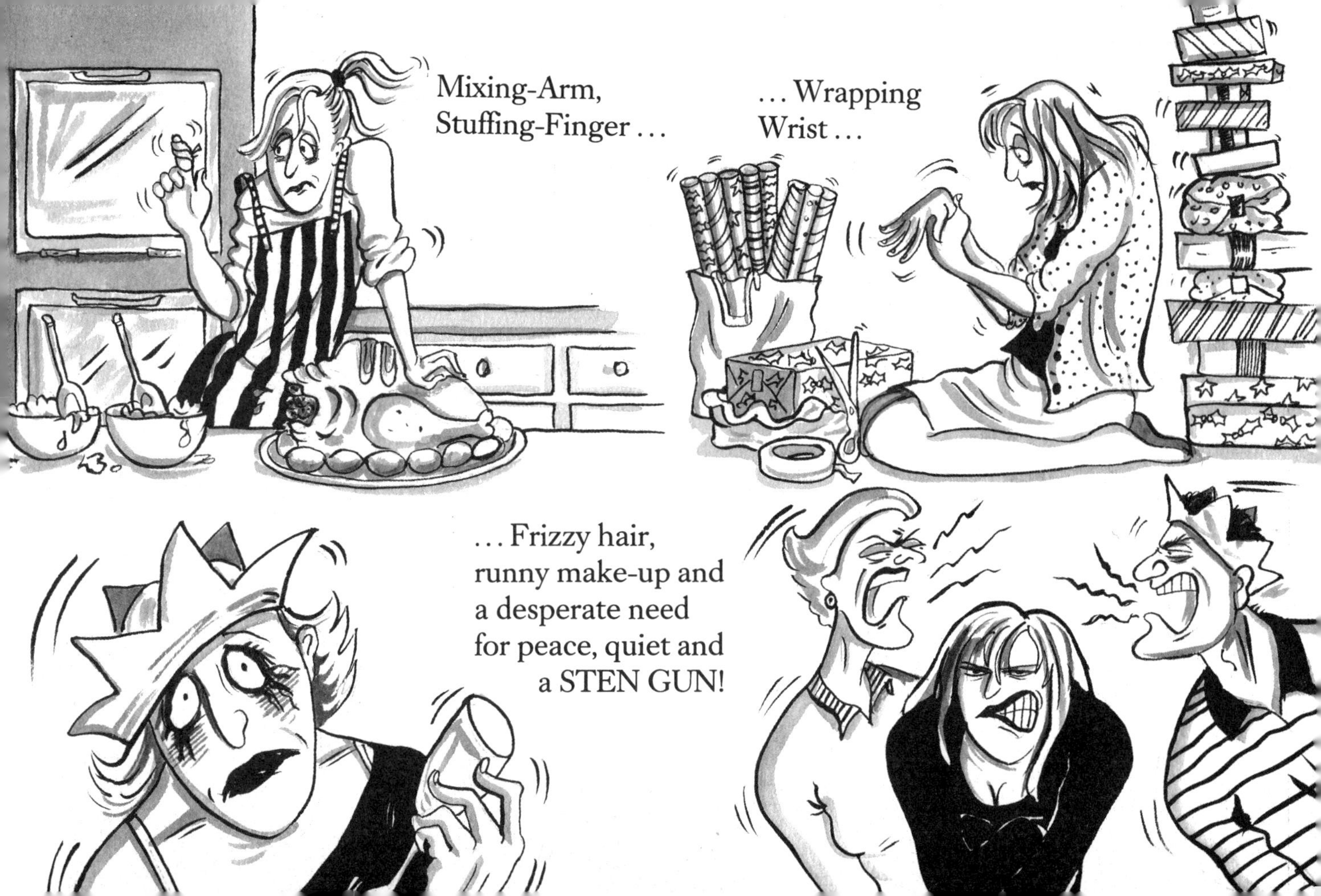
Mixing-Arm, Stuffing-Finger …
… Wrapping Wrist …
… Frizzy hair, runny make-up and a desperate need for peace, quiet and a STEN GUN!

CHRISTMAS EVE!

Not long to go now. It's your last chance to check that you haven't forgotten anyone, and to stock up on spare presents in case of any last minute present bearing visitors . . .

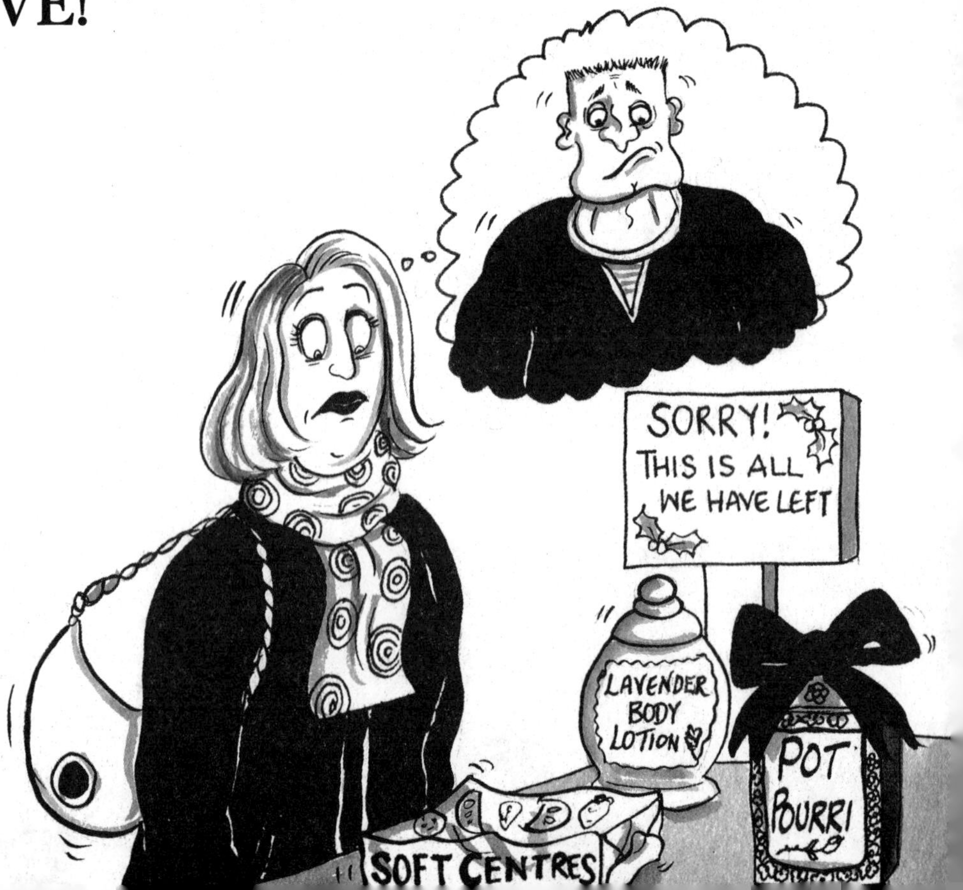
SORRY! THIS IS ALL WE HAVE LEFT
LAVENDER BODY LOTION
POT POURRI
SOFT CENTRES

... And of course, to make sure you've got enough to eat ...

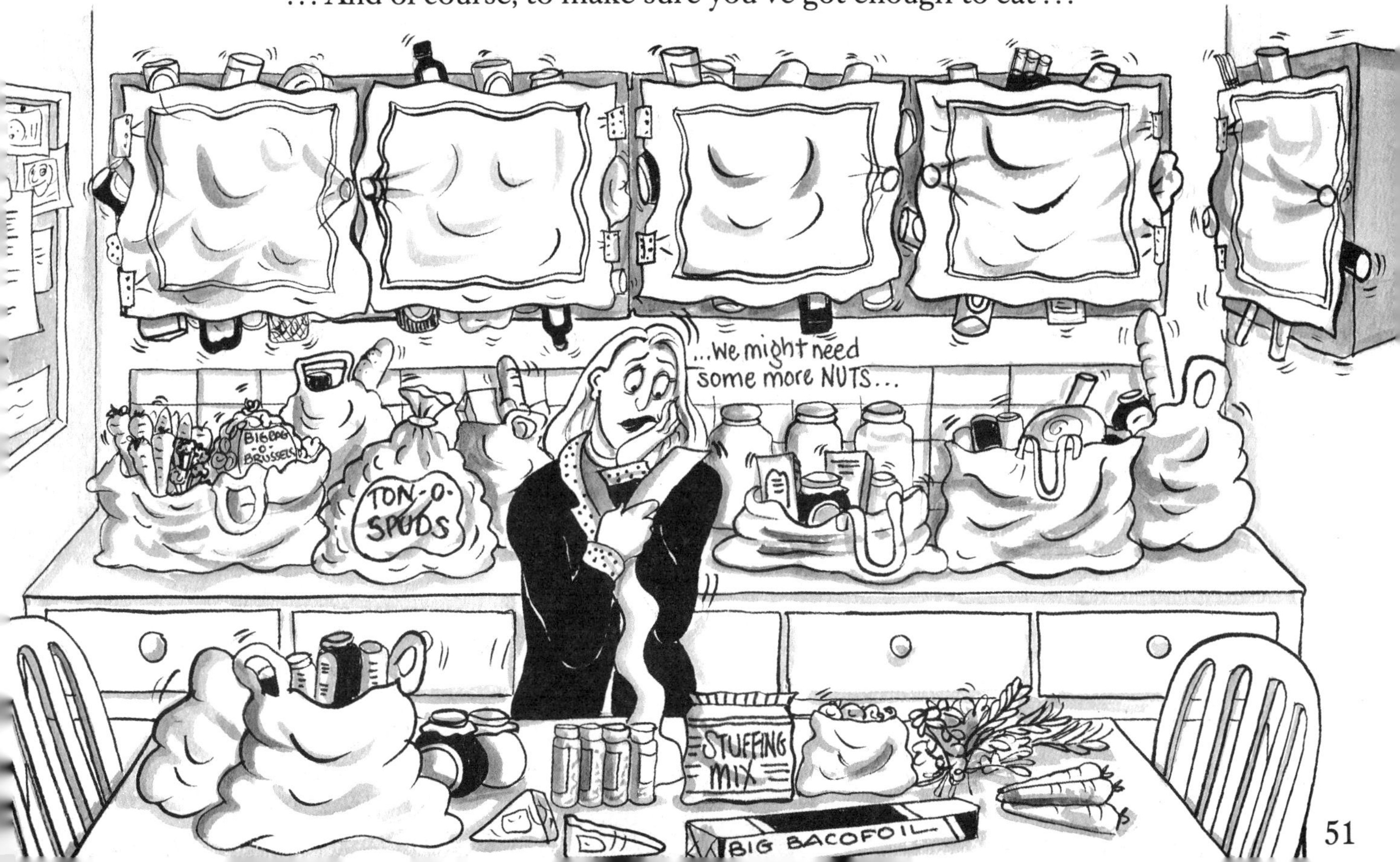
...We might need some more NUTS...
BIG BAG -O- BRUSSELS
TON-O-SPUDS
STUFFING MIX
BIG BACOFOIL

All that's left is to herd the kids off to bed with the traditional presents for Santa . . .

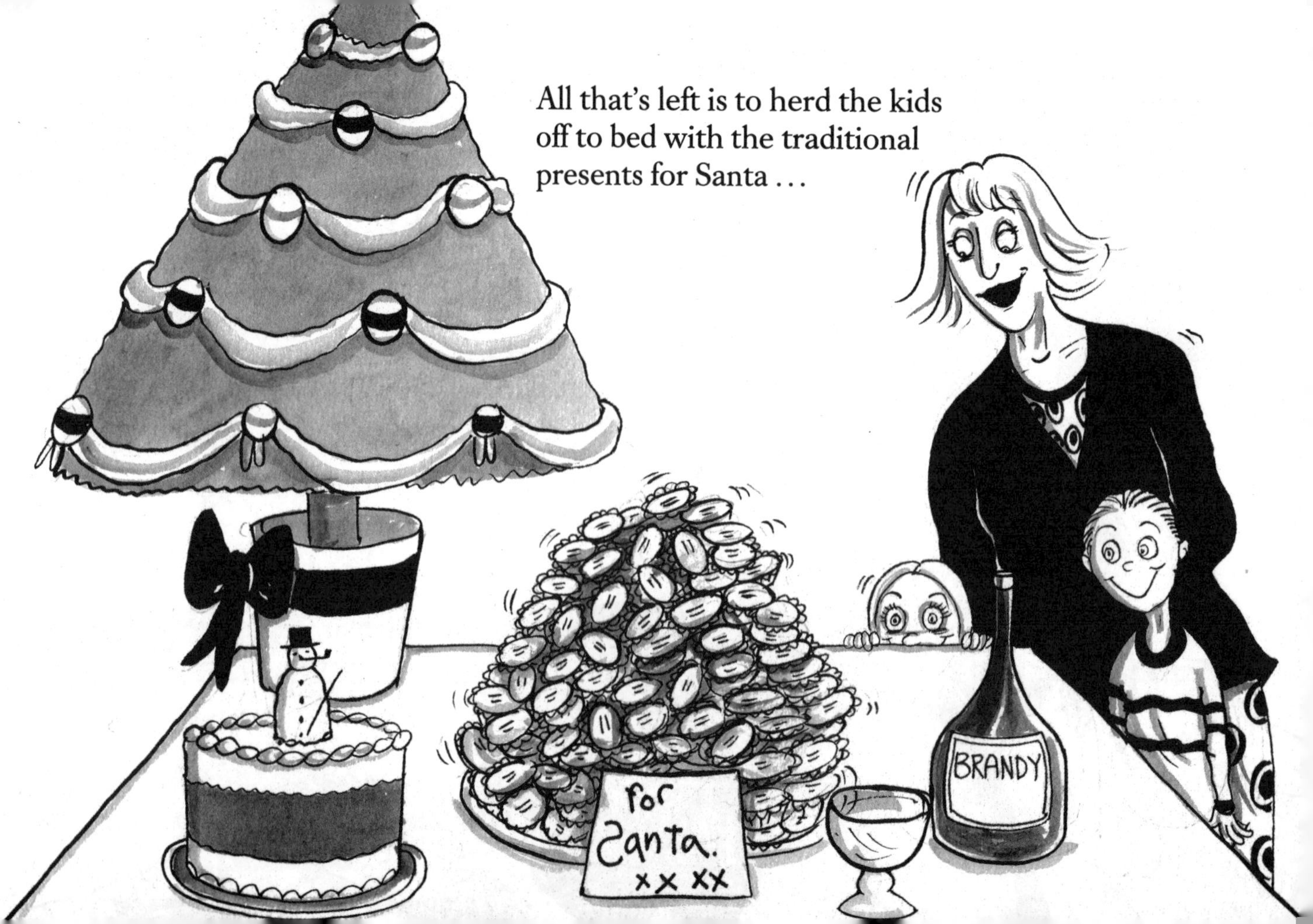
for Santa. xx xx
BRANDY

… and the traditional Bribery and Corruption …

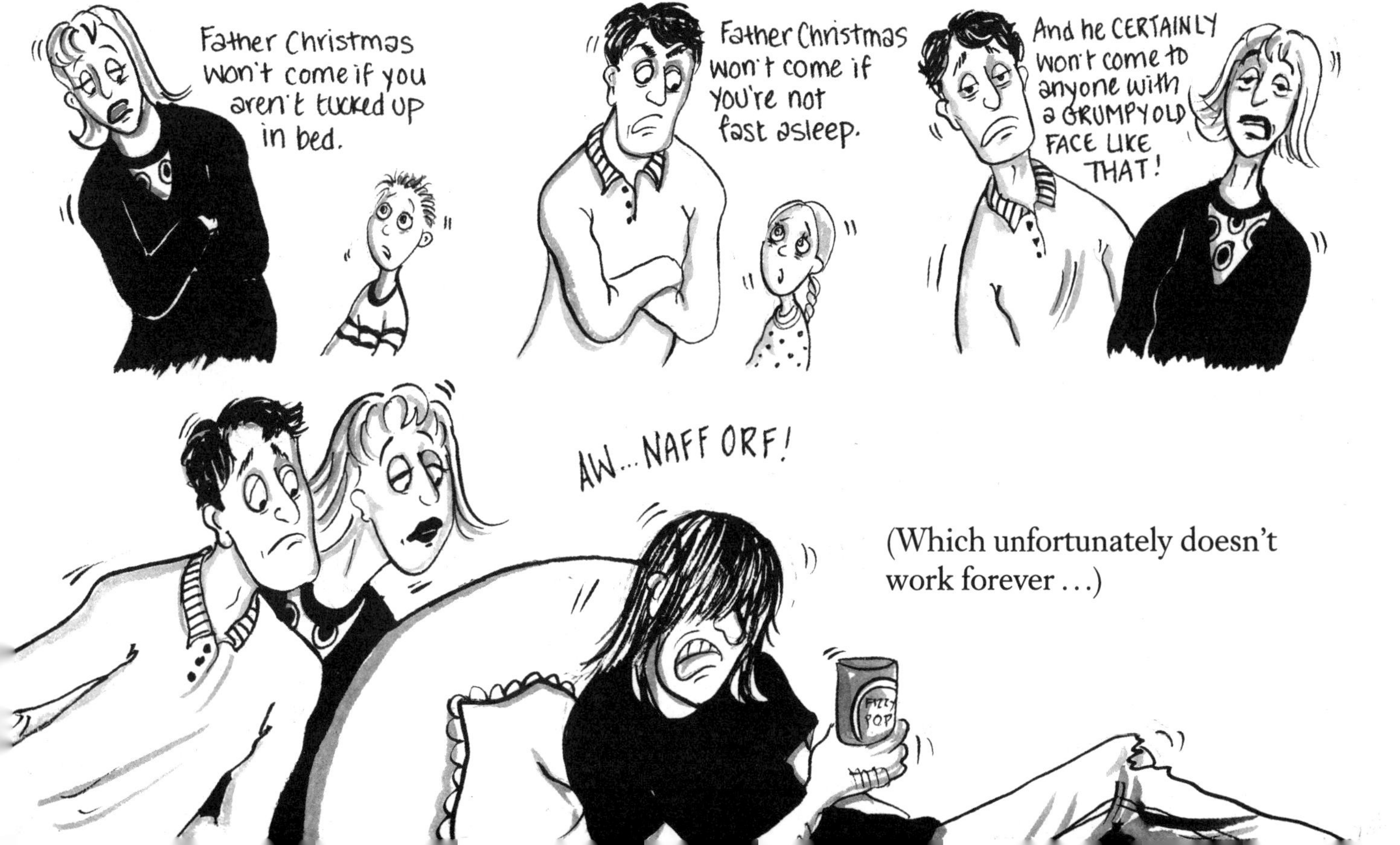
Father Christmas won't come if you aren't tucked up in bed.
Father Christmas won't come if you're not fast asleep.
And he CERTAINLY won't come to anyone with a GRUMPY OLD FACE LIKE THAT!
AW... NAFF ORF!
FIZZY POP

(Which unfortunately doesn't work forever …)

. . . And then there's just the
WRAPPING to do . . .

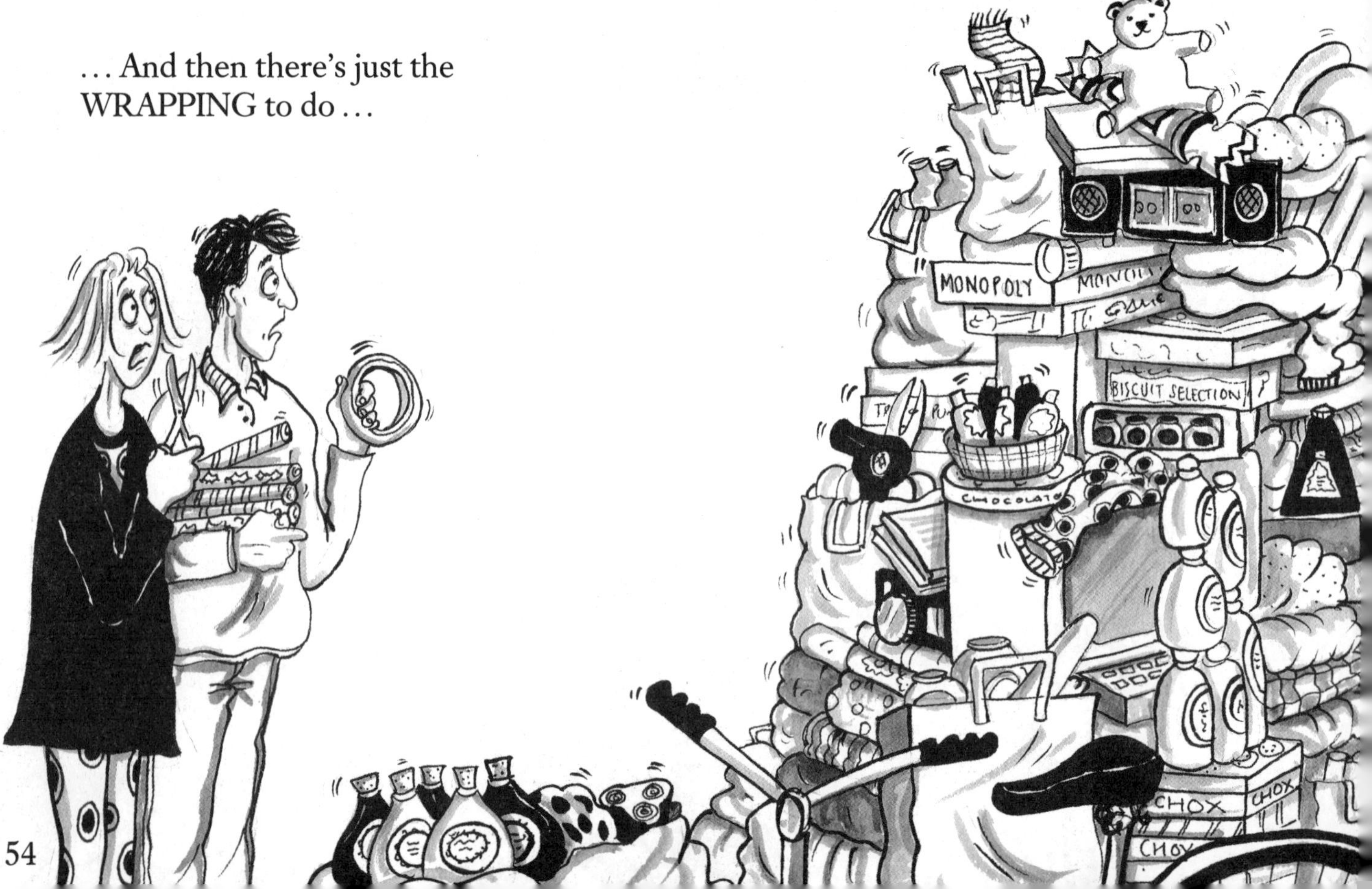
MONOPOLY
BISCUIT SELECTION
CHOCOLATE
CHOX
CHOX

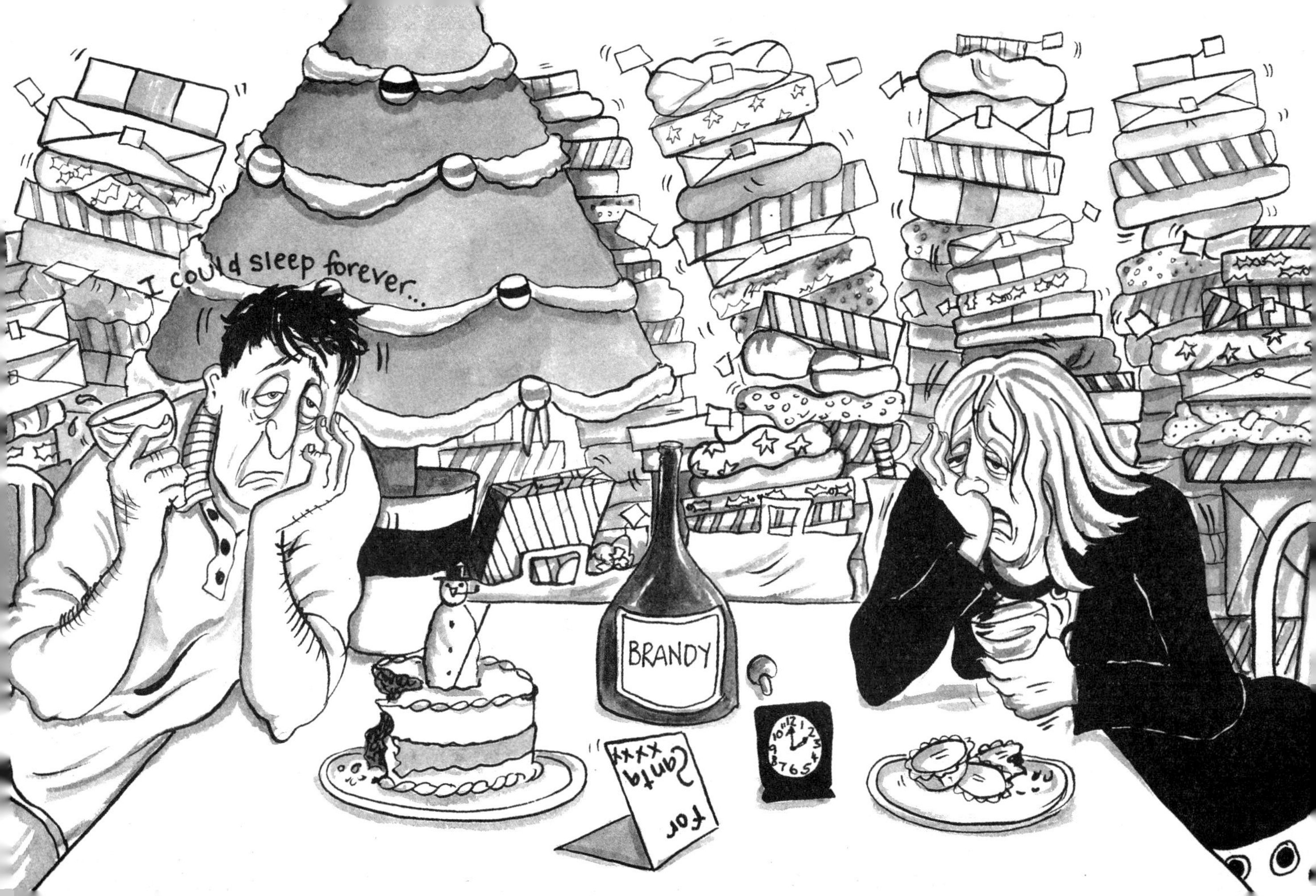
I could sleep forever...
BRANDY
For Santa xxxx

CHRISTMAS EVE THOUGHTS ...

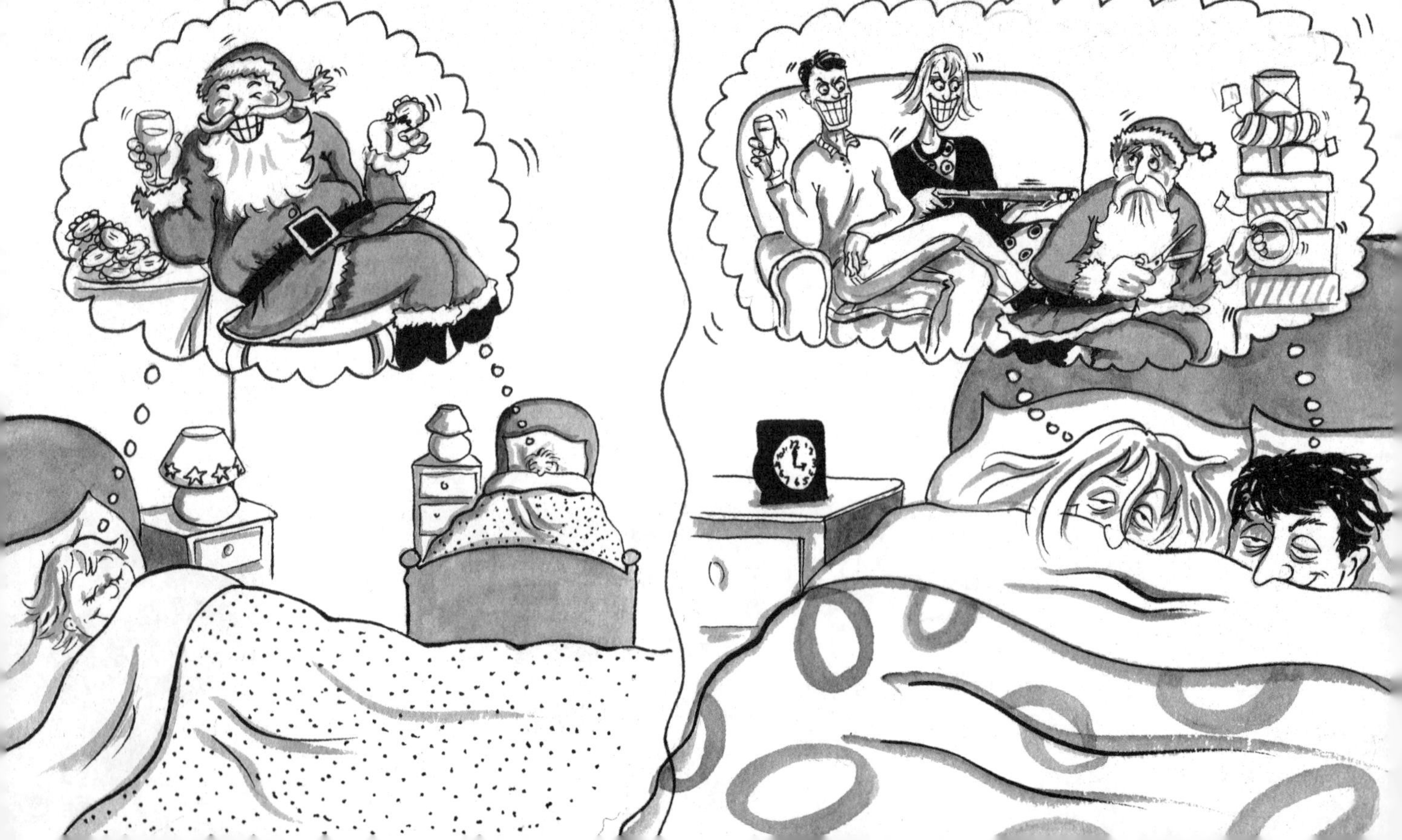

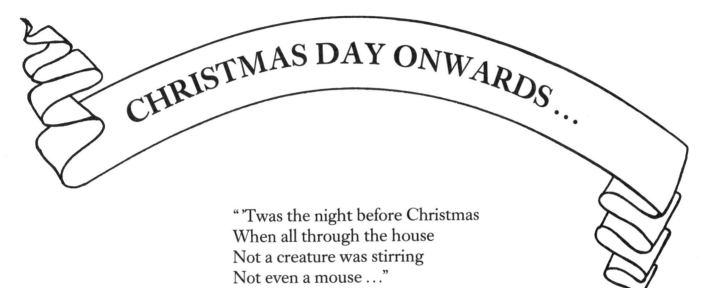

CHRISTMAS DAY ONWARDS ...

" 'Twas the night before Christmas
When all through the house
Not a creature was stirring
Not even a mouse ..."

(... AND THEN CAME 4 a.m...!)

On Christmas Day
(very early) in the morning …

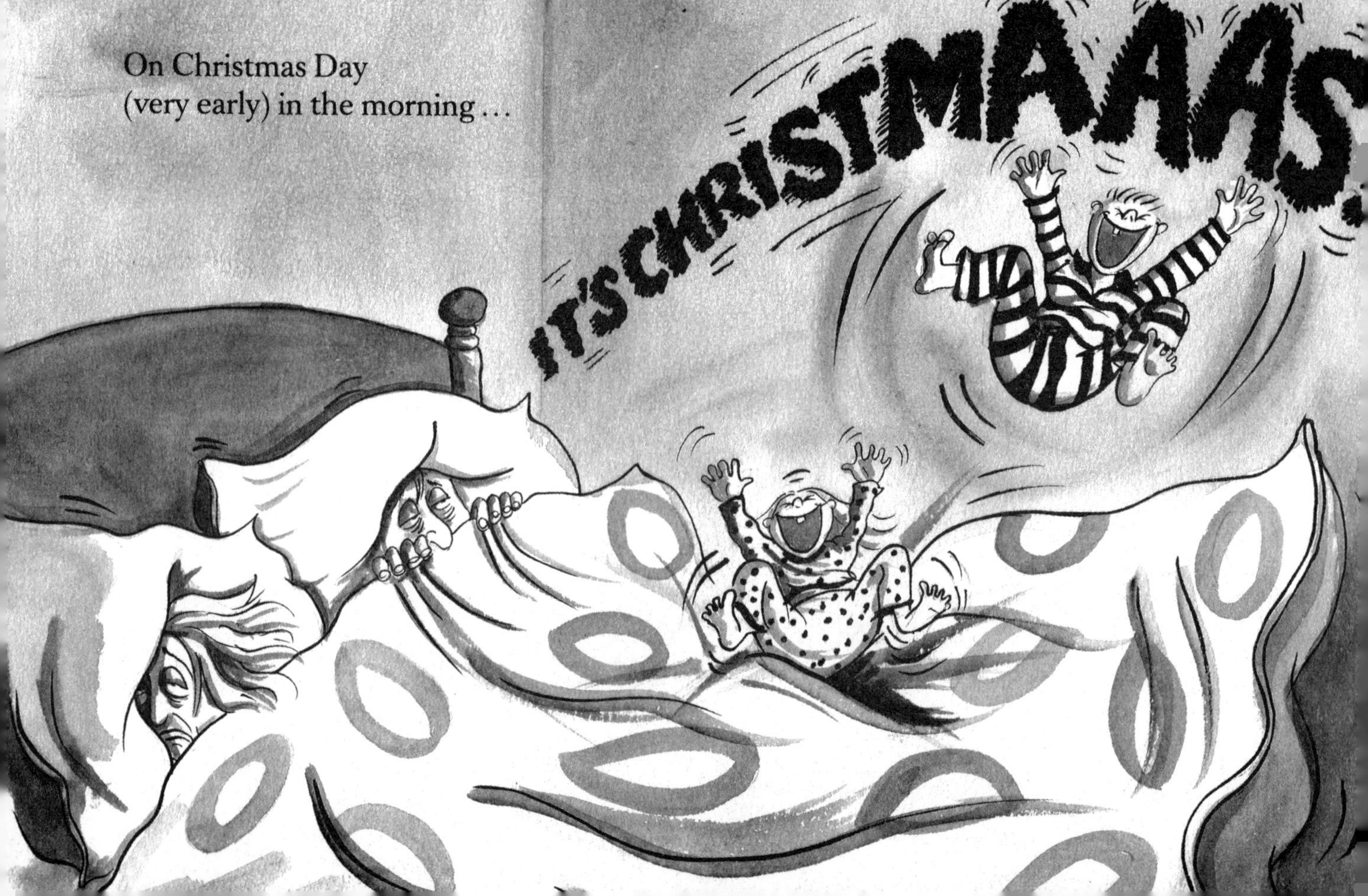
IT'S CHRISTMAAAS!

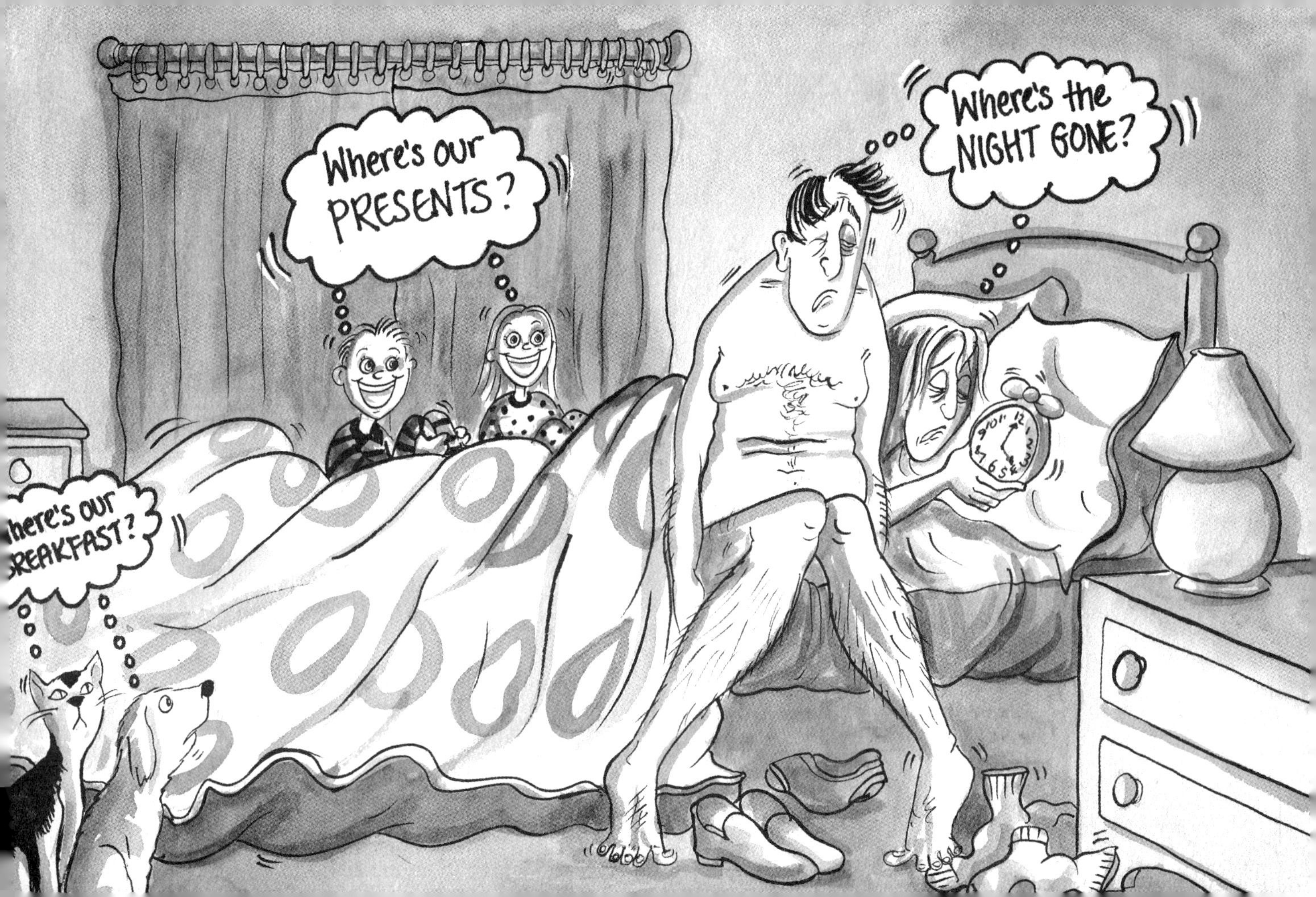
Where's our PRESENTS?
Where's the NIGHT GONE?
here's our REAKFAST?

CHRISTMAS MORNING IN THE KITCHEN ...

You have your first cup of tea and mince pie of thousands, and your first chance to look at all the work ahead. Christmas cooking needs more planning than a meeting of the United Nations and is much more likely to end in war.

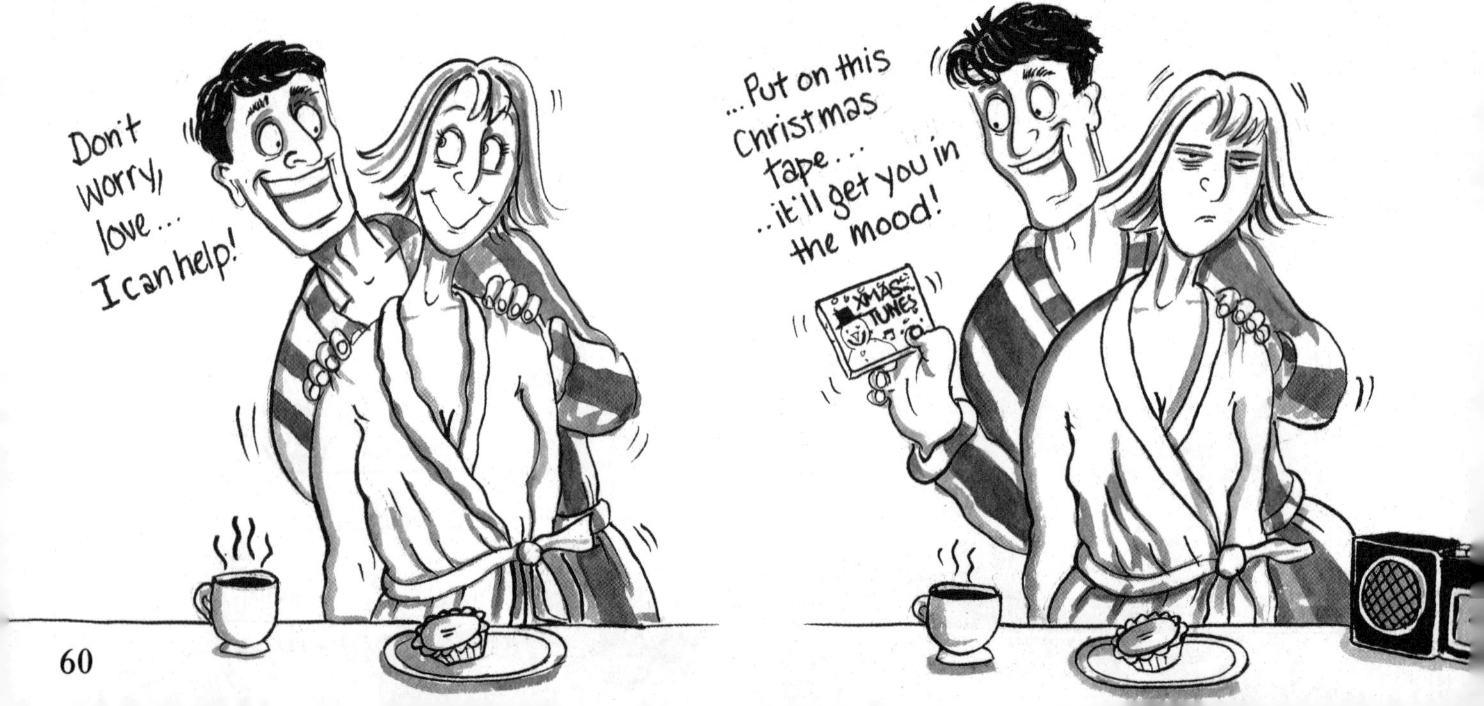
Don't worry, love... I can help!
...Put on this Christmas tape... ..it'll get you in the mood!
XMAS TUNES

THE TURKEY:

It has bigger thighs than you have and will need a nuclear explosion to cook it. All your baking trays are far too small, you need a crane to lift it into the oven, you had to start defrosting it weeks ago and you're beginning to think it won't be cooked properly until January.

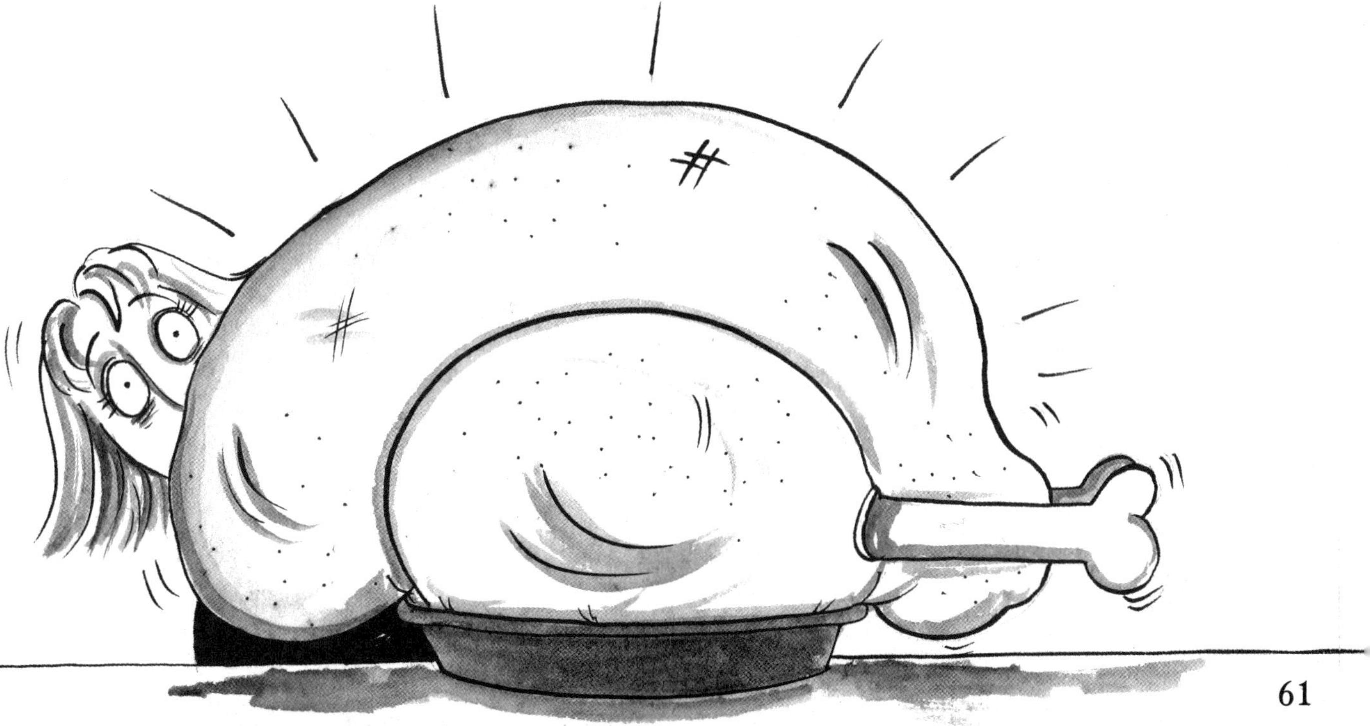

THE FANTASY CHRISTMAS ...

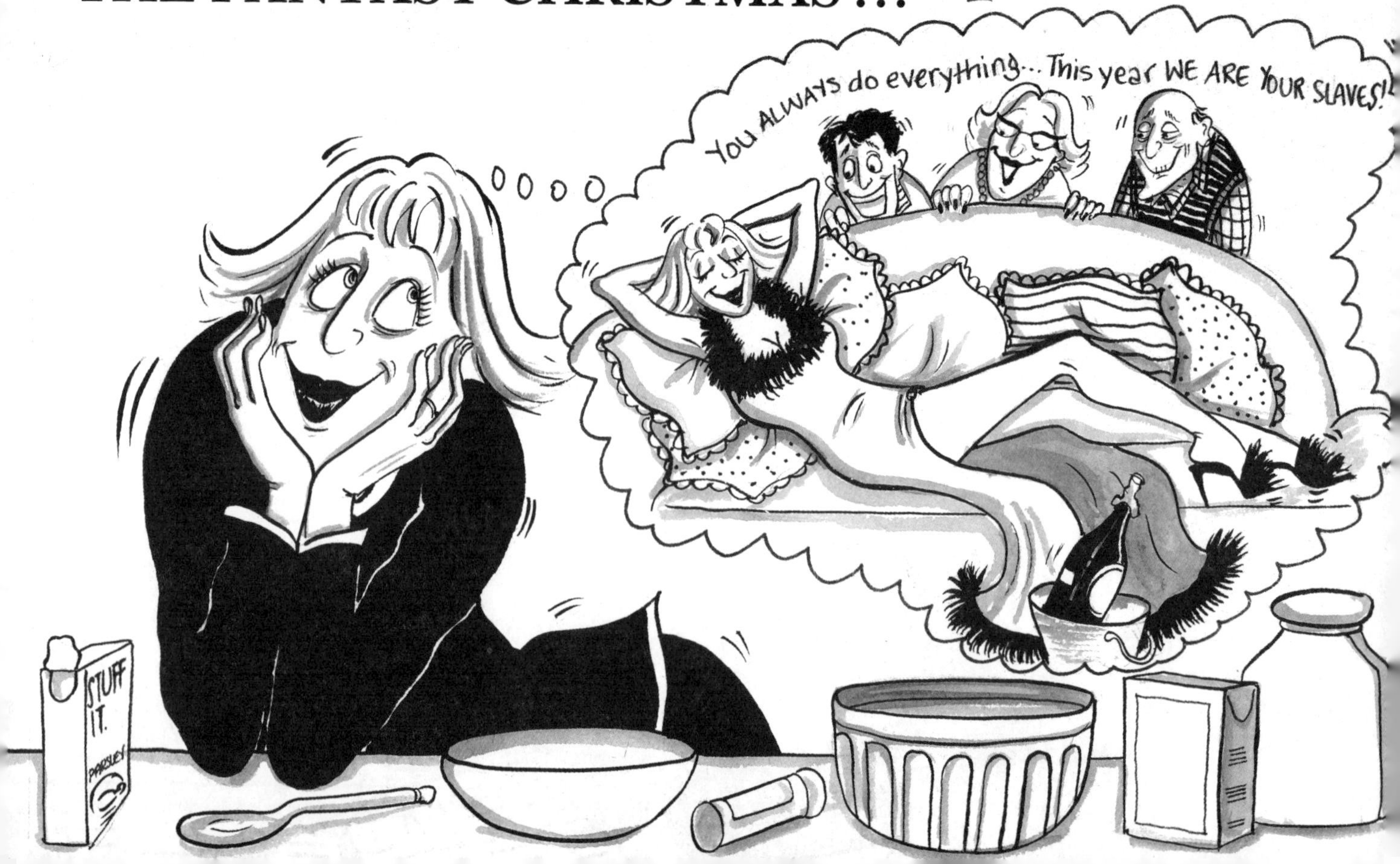

You ALWAYS do everything... This year WE ARE YOUR SLAVES!
STUFF IT.
PARSLEY

... THE REALITY ...

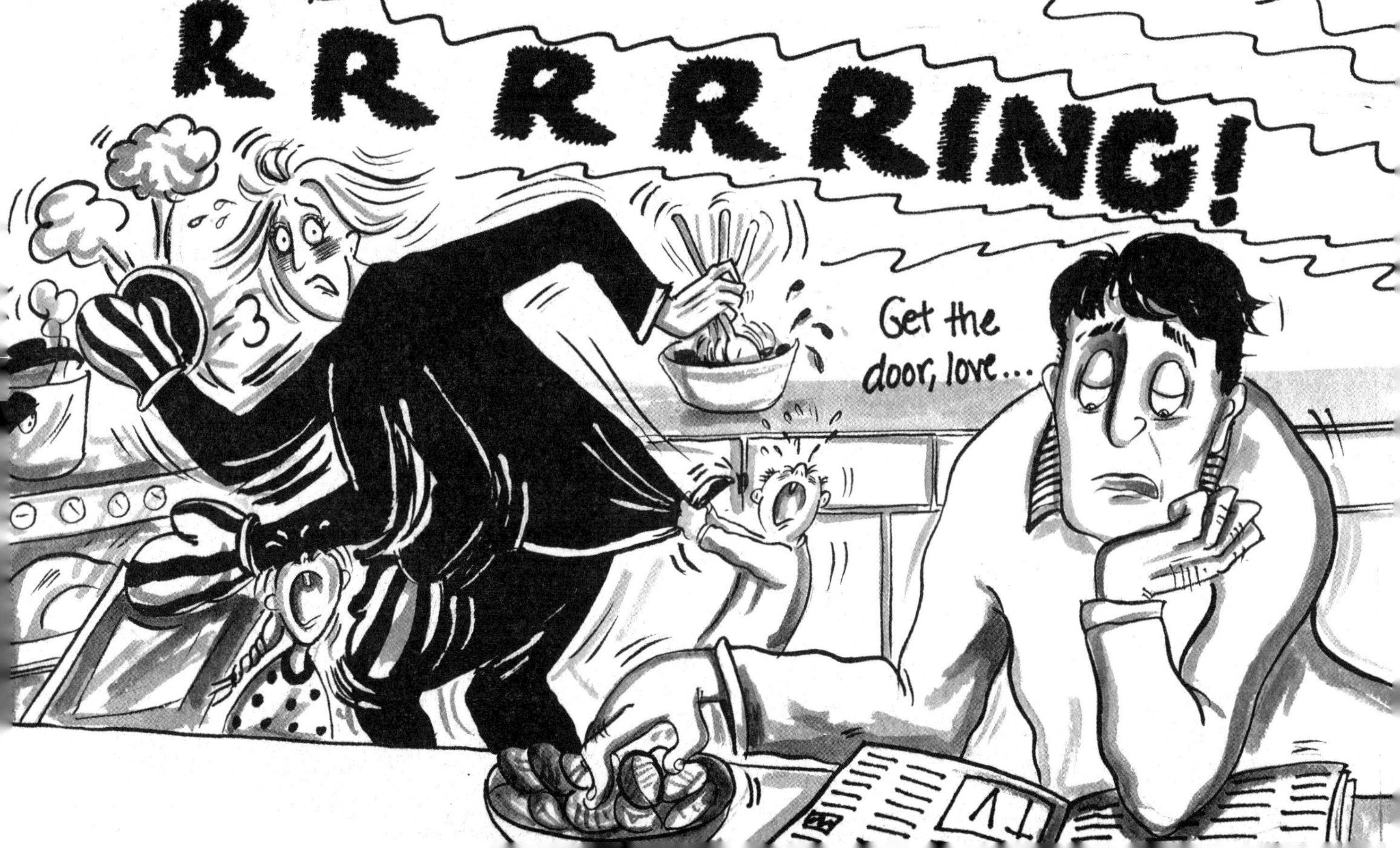
R R R R RING!
Get the door, love...

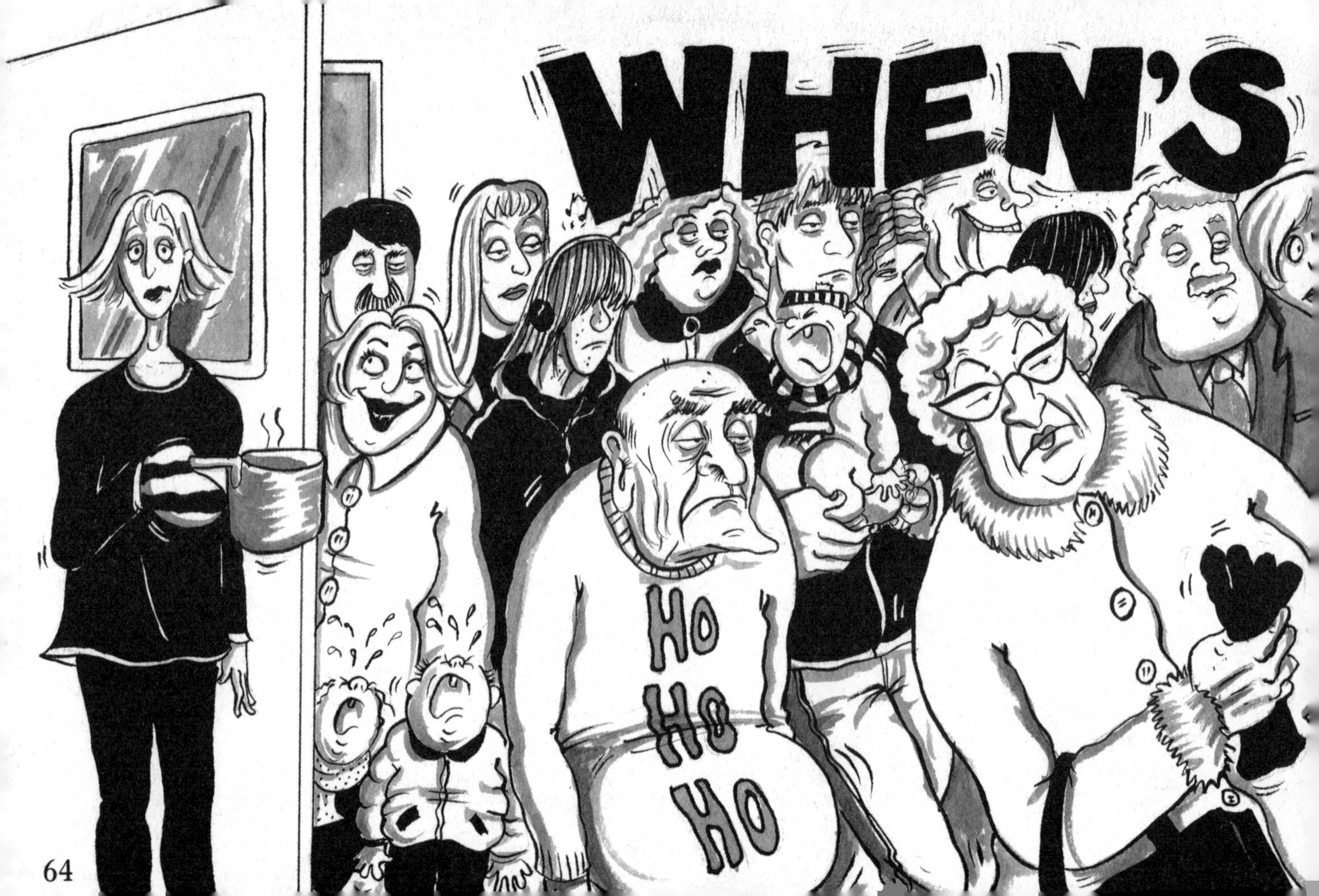
WHEN'S
HO
HO
HO
HO

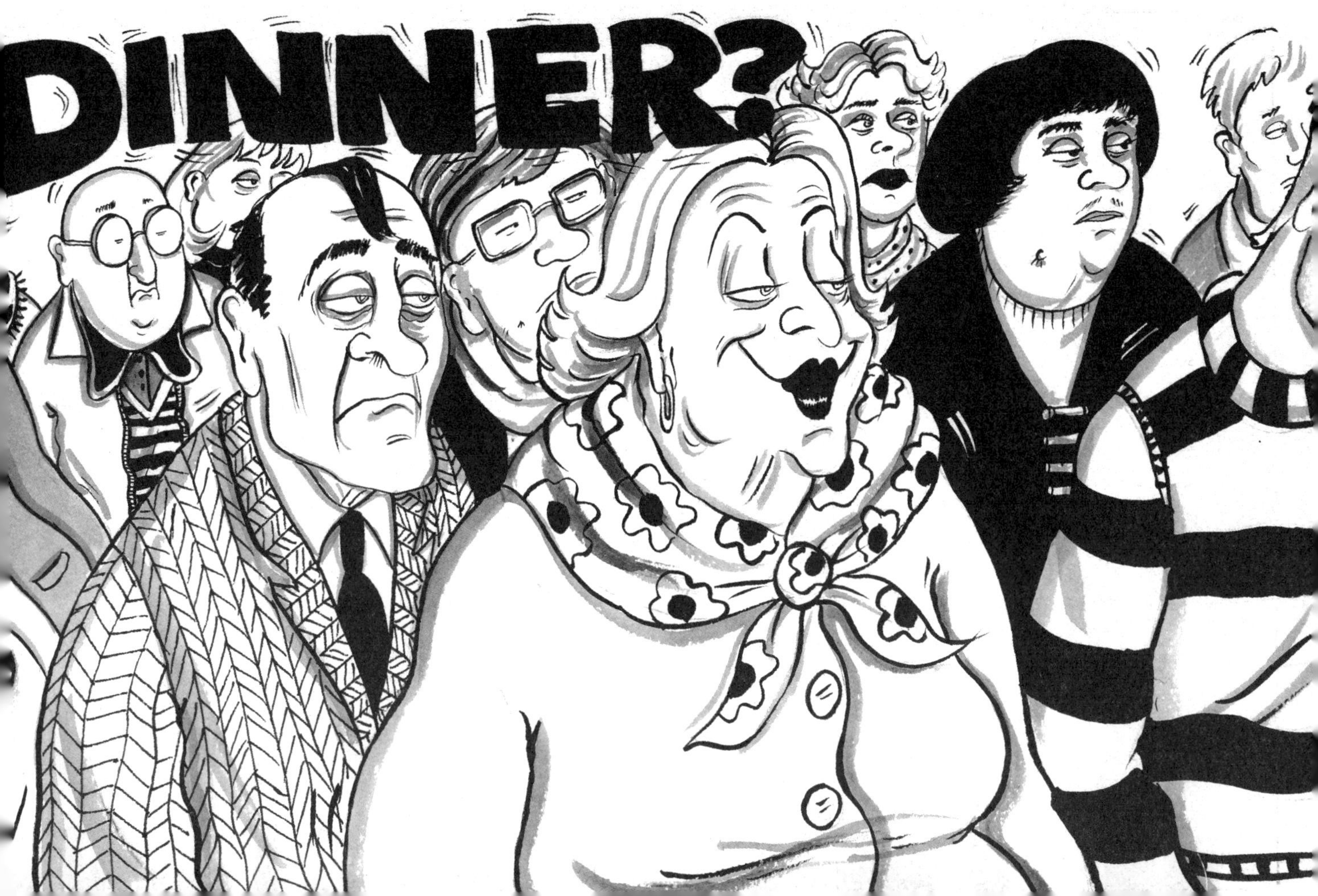
DINNER?

THINGS YOU HATE ABOUT CHRISTMAS

(6) Annual Rituals …

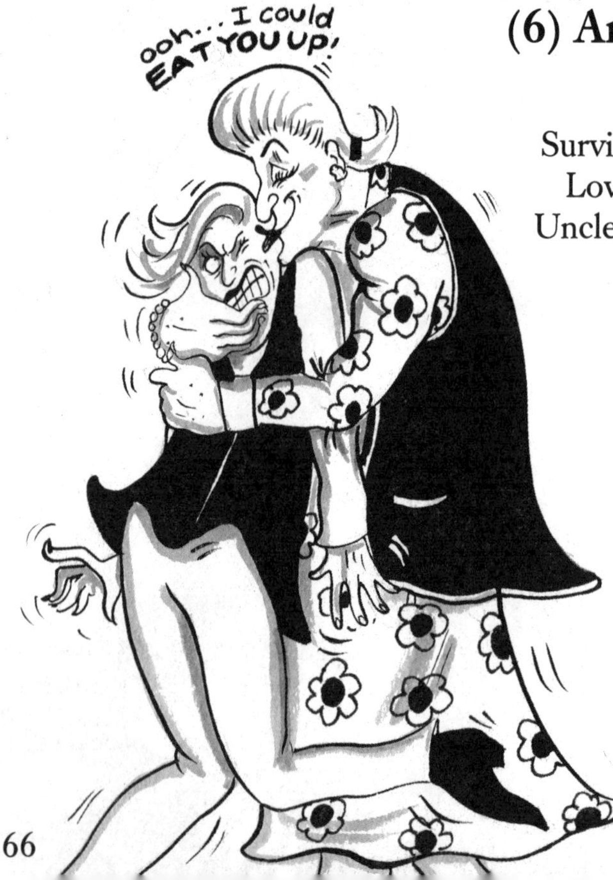
ooh… I could EAT YOU UP!

Surviving Auntie's
Love-Grip and
Uncle's Groping …

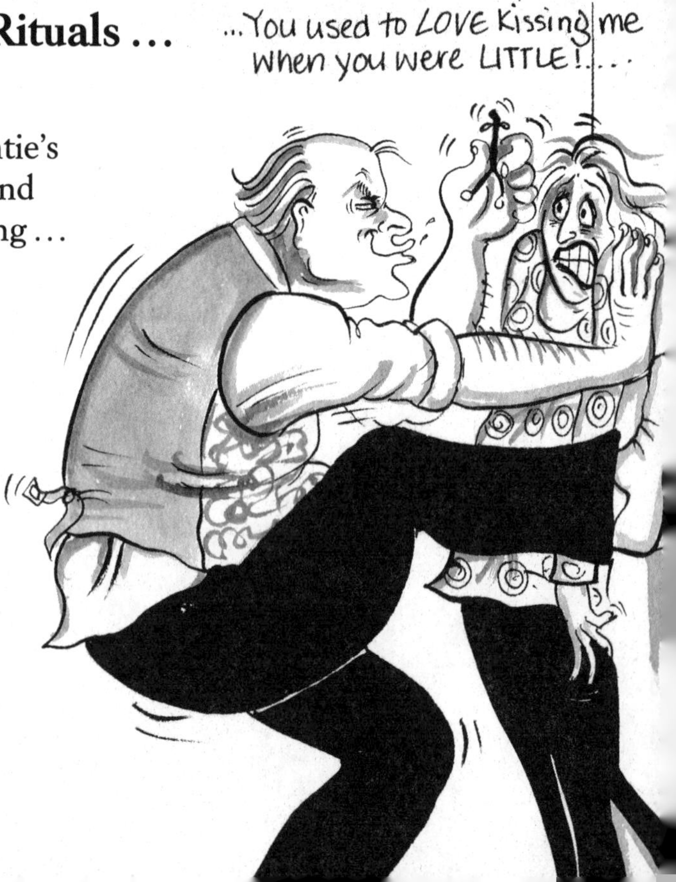
…You used to LOVE Kissing me when you were LITTLE! …

... Catching up on those operation stories ...

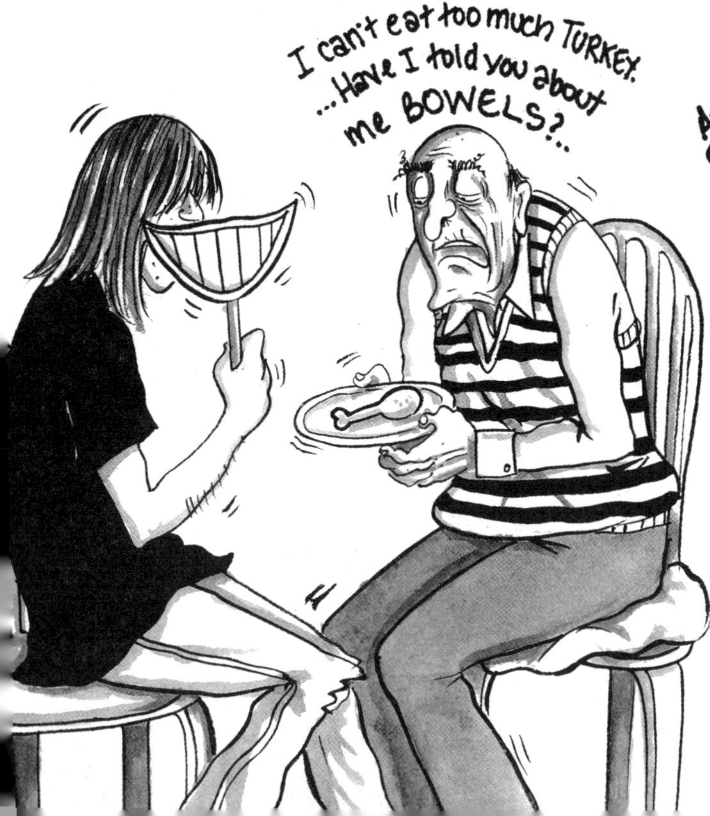
I can't eat too much TURKEY
...Have I told you about me BOWELS?...

... and going through the INQUISITION ...

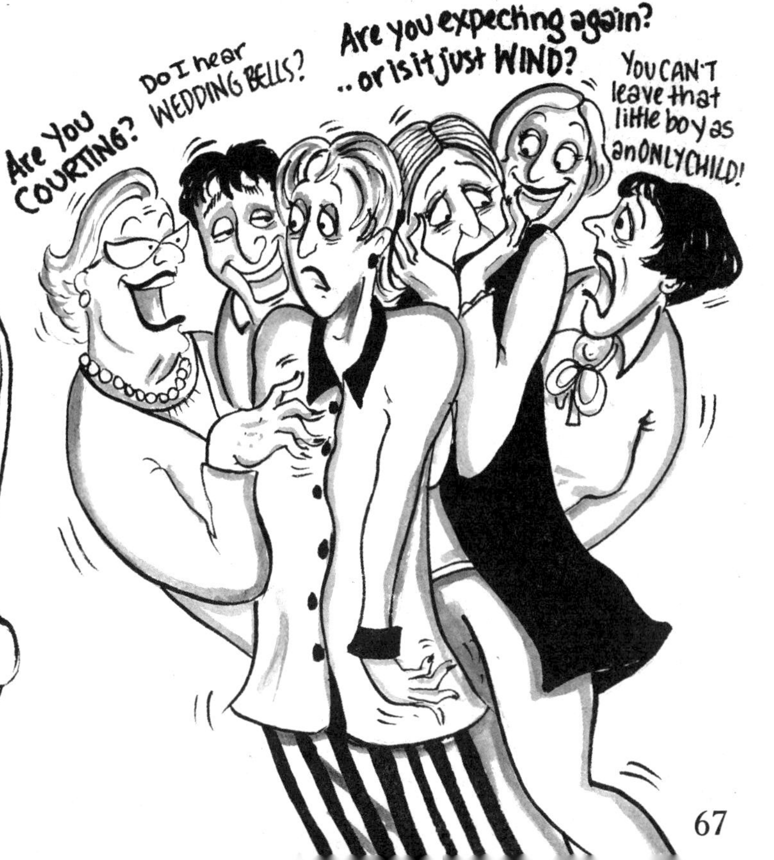
Are You COURTING?
Do I hear WEDDING BELLS?
Are you expecting again? ..or is it just WIND?
You CAN'T leave that little boy as an ONLY CHILD!

THE PRESENTS: (The older you get, the less presents you get . . .)

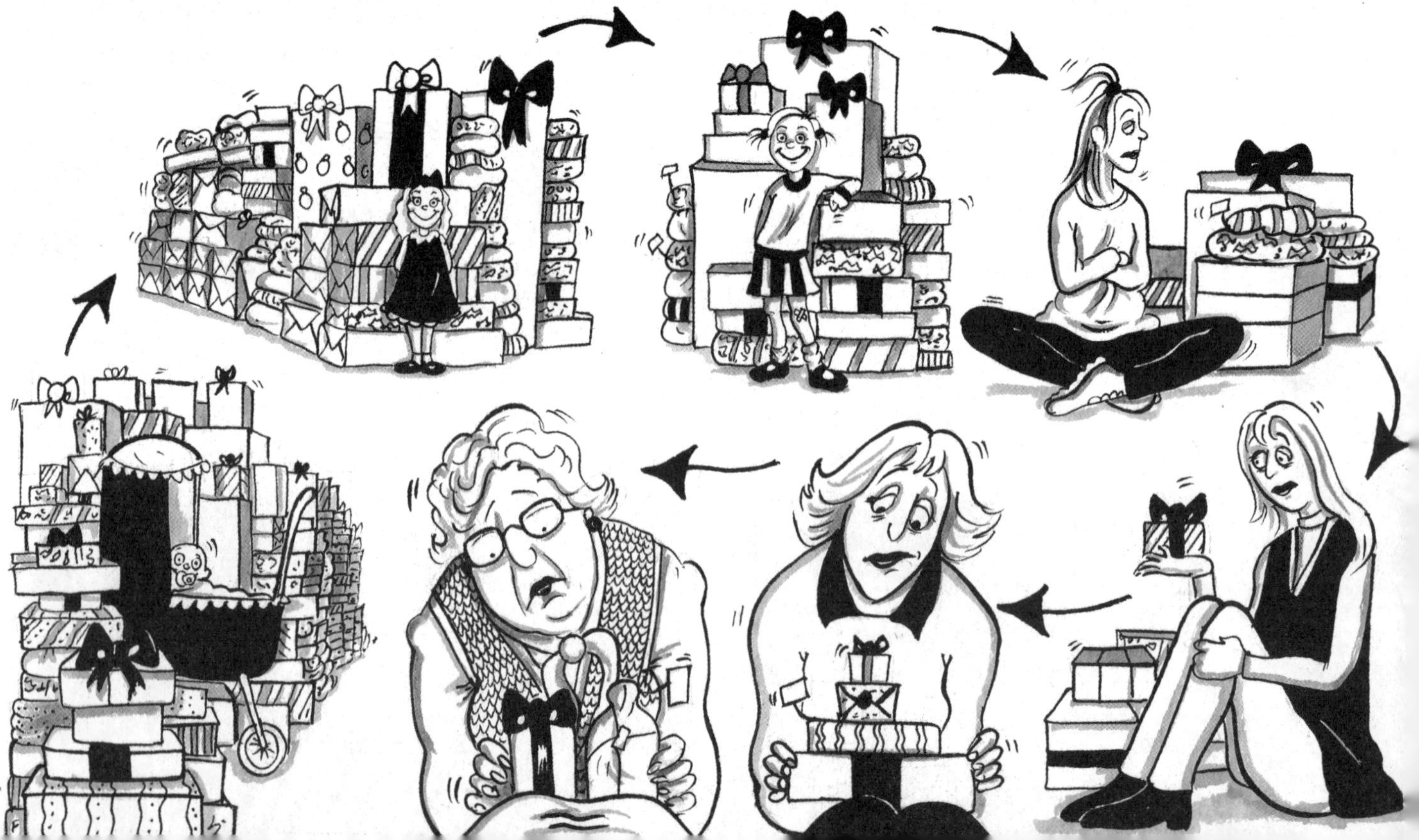

… They're always JUST what you wanted …

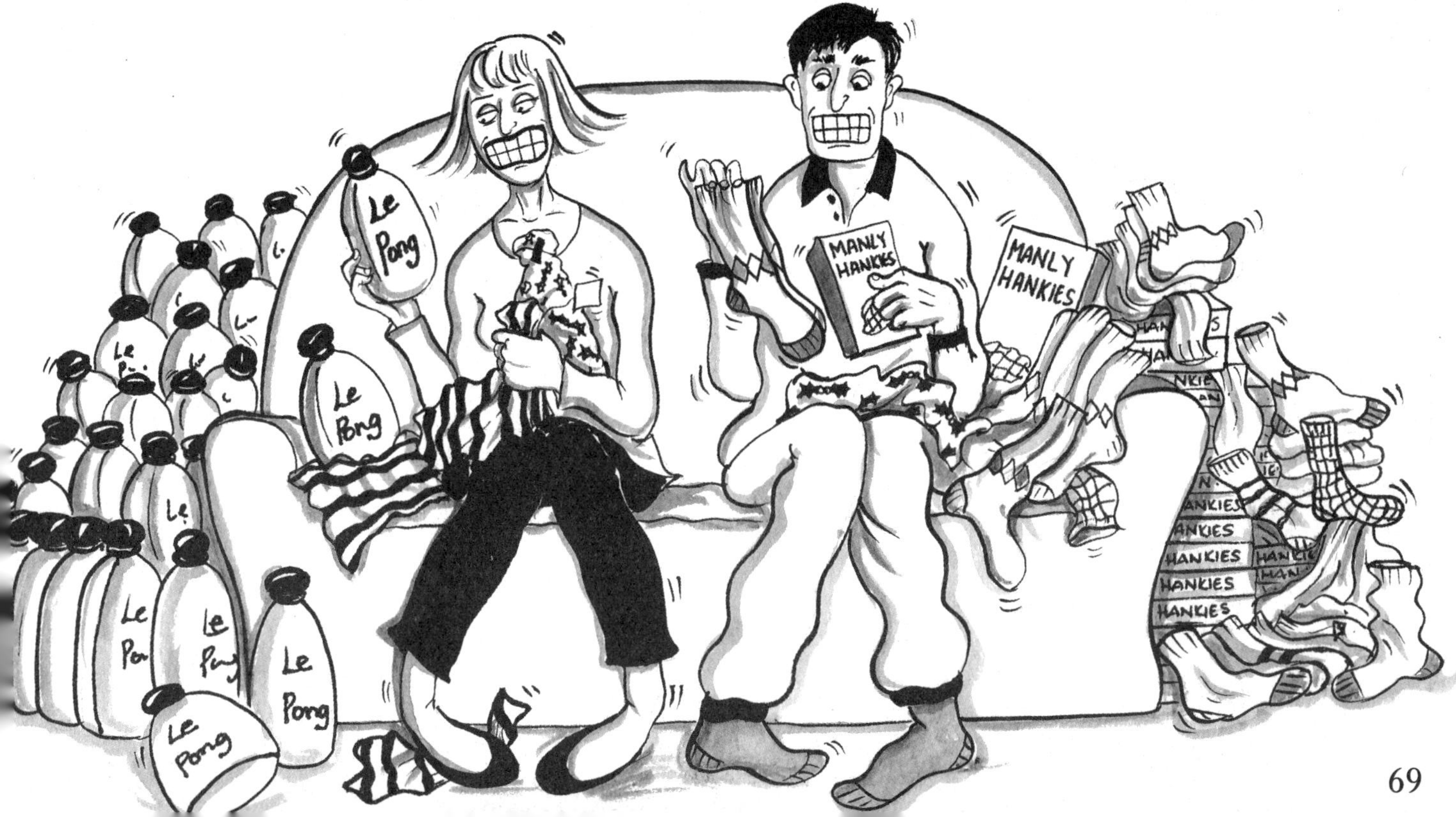

Le Pong
Le Pong
Le Pong
Le Pong
Le Pong
MANLY HANKIES
MANLY HANKIES
HANKIES
HANKIES
HANKIES
HANKIES
HANKIES

… CHRISTMAS PRESENTS FROM HELL …

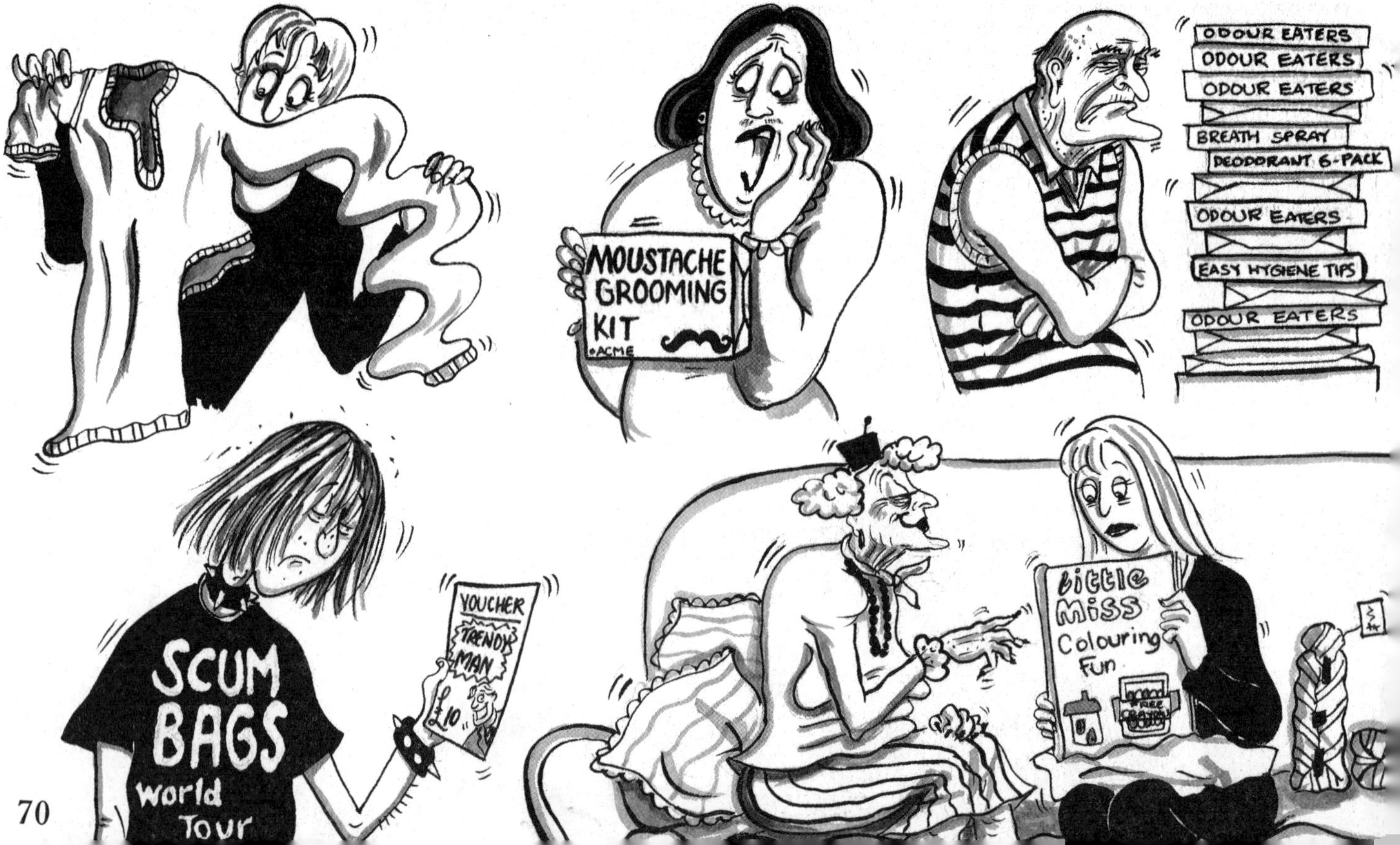

MOUSTACHE GROOMING KIT
©ACME
ODOUR EATERS
ODOUR EATERS
ODOUR EATERS
BREATH SPRAY
DEODORANT 6-PACK
ODOUR EATERS
EASY HYGIENE TIPS
ODOUR EATERS
SCUM BAGS
World Tour
VOUCHER
TRENDY MAN
£10
Little Miss
Colouring Fun

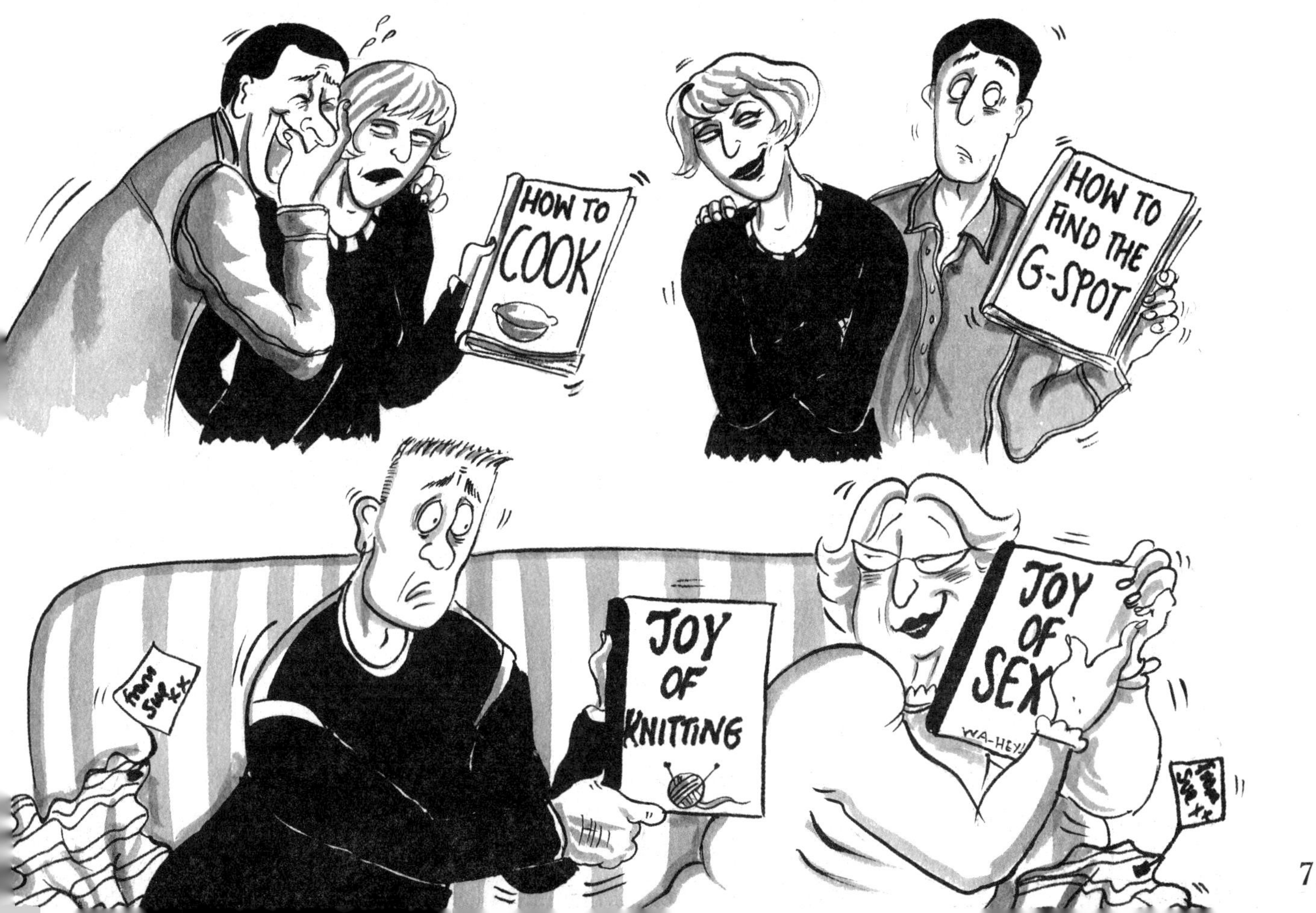
HOW TO COOK
HOW TO FIND THE G-SPOT
from Sue xx
JOY OF KNITTING
JOY OF SEX
WA-HEY!

CHRISTMAS TRAUMAS:

You know you're no longer YOUNG when …

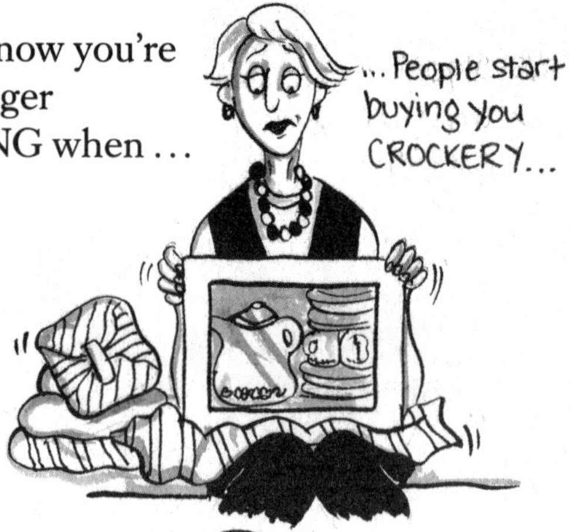
… People start buying you CROCKERY …

… You know you're a STUDENT when ..

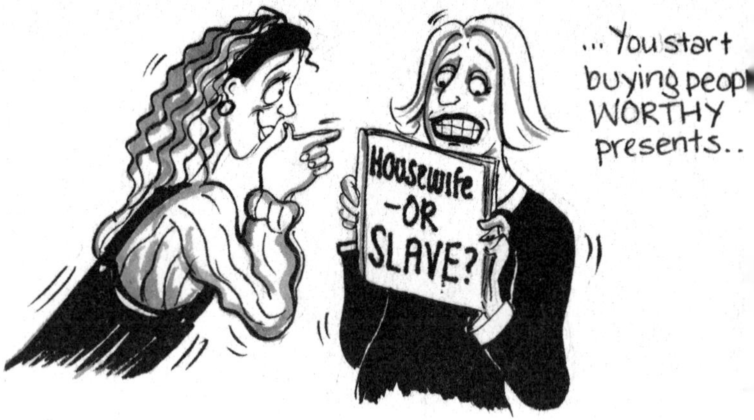
Housewife -OR SLAVE?
… You start buying peopl WORTHY presents..

… You know you're MIDDLE-AGED when …

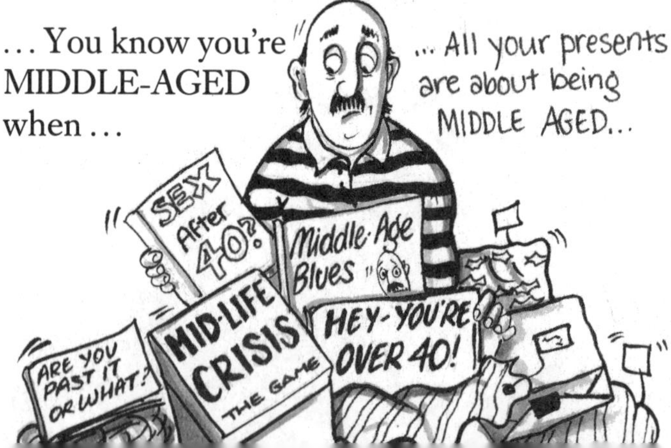
… All your presents are about being MIDDLE AGED …
SEX After 40?
Middle-Age Blues
MID-LIFE CRISIS THE GAME
HEY-YOU'RE OVER 40!
ARE YOU PAST IT OR WHAT?

… You finally know you're OLD when …

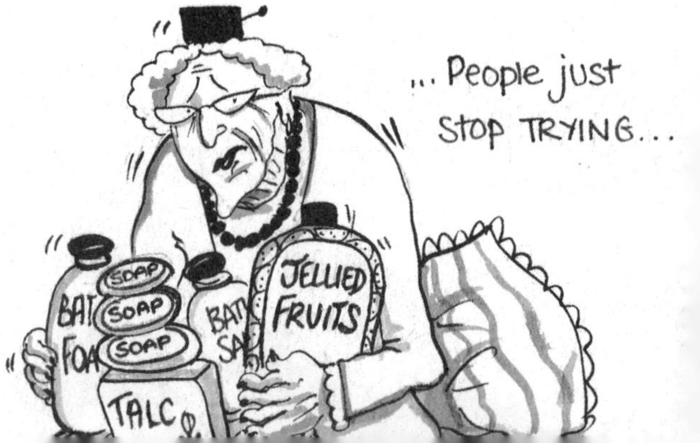
… People just stop TRYING …
SOAP
SOAP
SOAP
BAT FOA
BAT SA
JELLIED FRUITS
TALC

SEXY PRESENTS:

Lingerie
Surprise Holidays
Diamonds
Clothes
Anything Silk
Flowers
Luxury Chocolates
Love Nests
Cars
Jewellery
Perfume
Champagne

UNSEXY PRESENTS:

Nose-Hair Trimmers
Ear Waxers
Socks
Slim. Fast
Anything Crimplene
Toupees
Ties
Biscuit Selections
Ironing Boards
De-Icers
Lawn Mowers
Soaps That Look Like Chocolates
Chocolates That Taste Like Soap

CHRISTMAS COOKING

It all looks so easy in the kitchen of the TV cooks. All it takes is a few flicks of the wrist, a smattering of flour and eggs and ... presto! A meal fit for Royalty ...

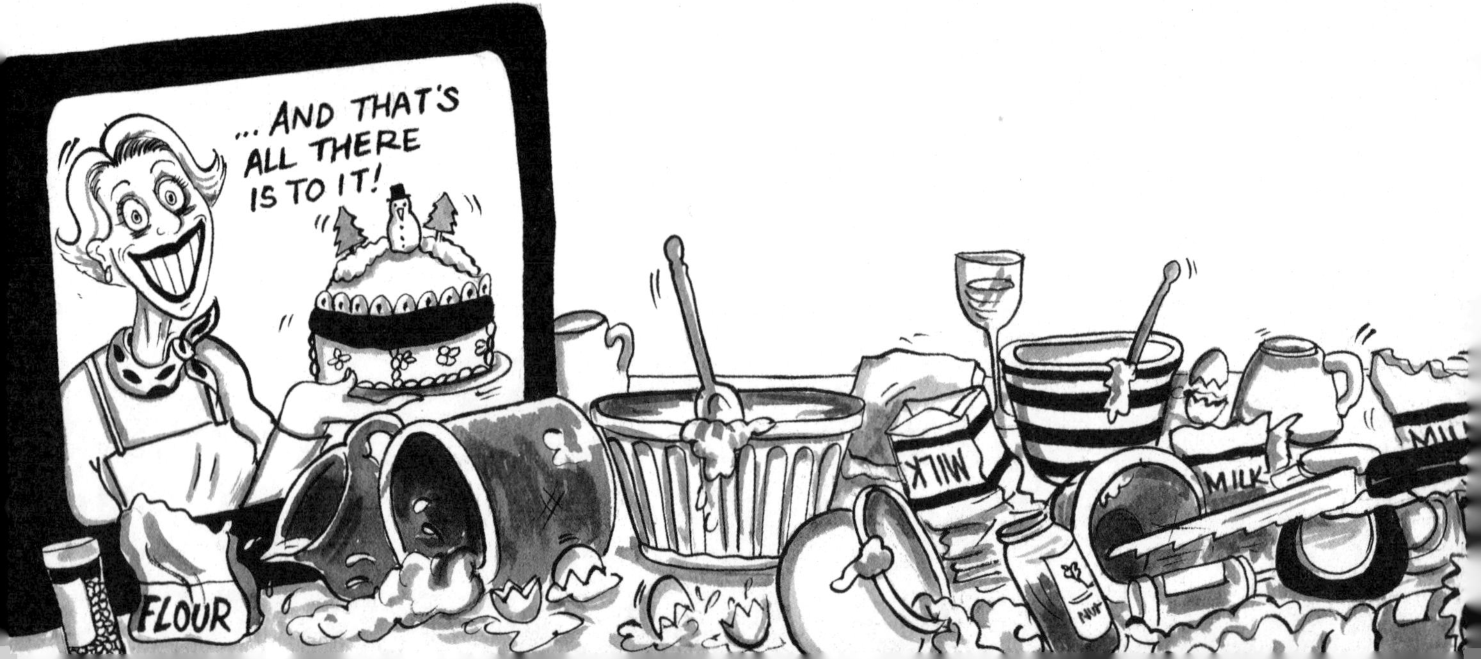
... AND THAT'S ALL THERE IS TO IT!
FLOUR
MILK
MILK
NUT

… But in *your* kitchen, your teenage niece has just announced she's a vegetarian, the kids have been watching a cartoon called "Timmy The Turkey's Last Day Out" and have started to cry, your blood pressure is at danger level, you're ready to run amok with the meat cleaver …
… and you haven't even put the brussels on yet!

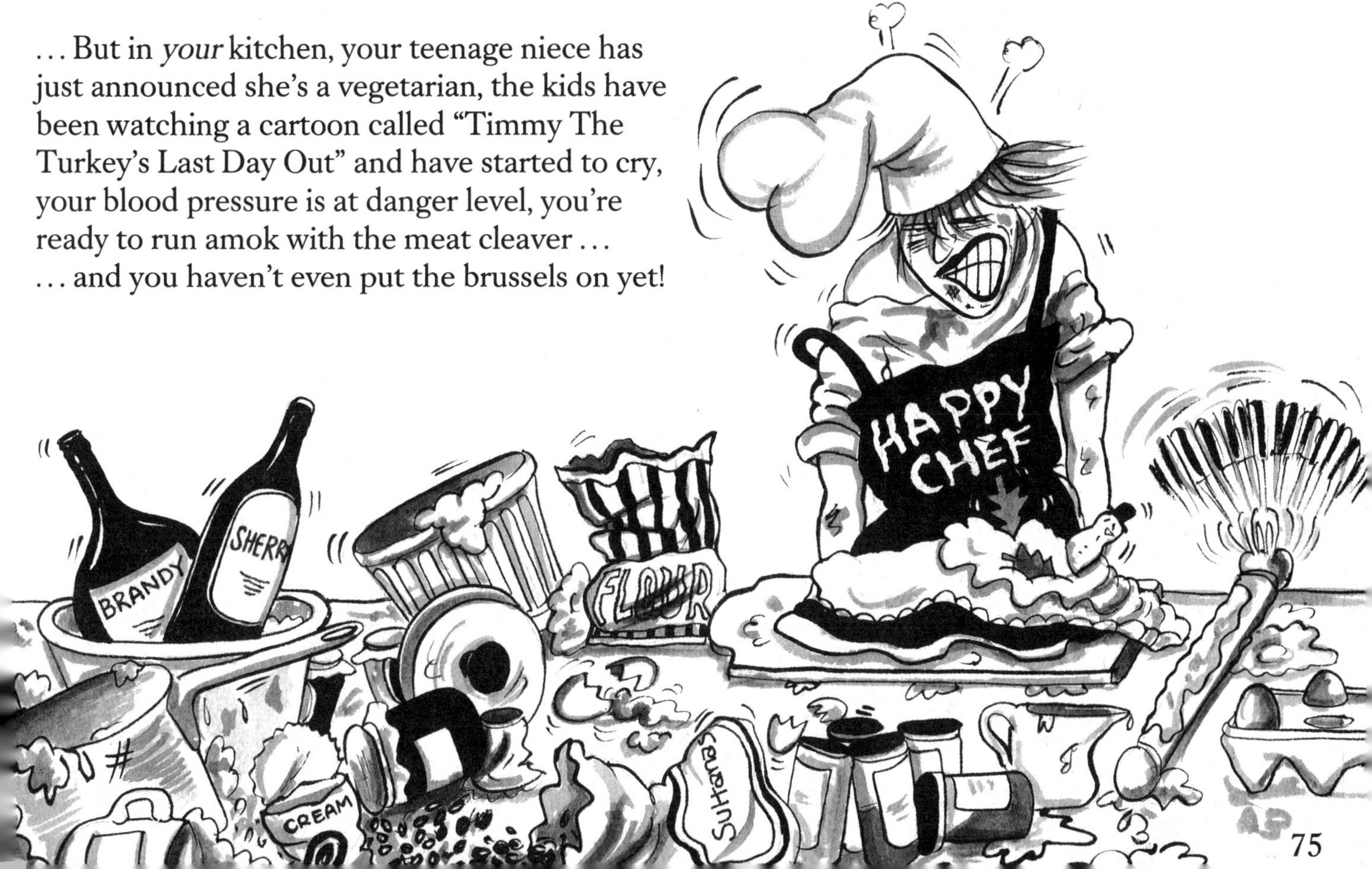
HAPPY CHEF
BRANDY
SHERR
FLOUR
CREAM
Sultanas

THINGS YOU HATE ABOUT CHRISTMAS

(7) Annoying Relatives …

Those who say …

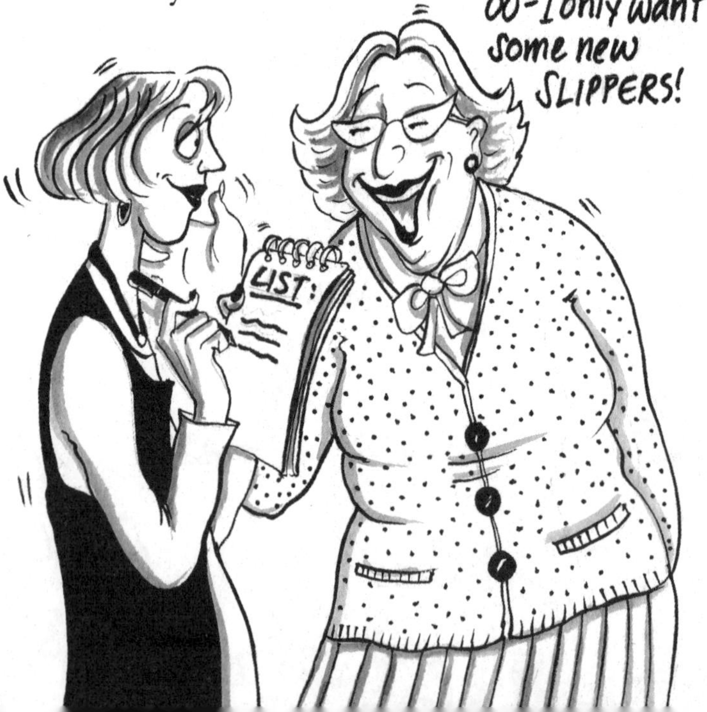
OO-I only want
some new
SLIPPERS!
LIST

… and when that's what they get …

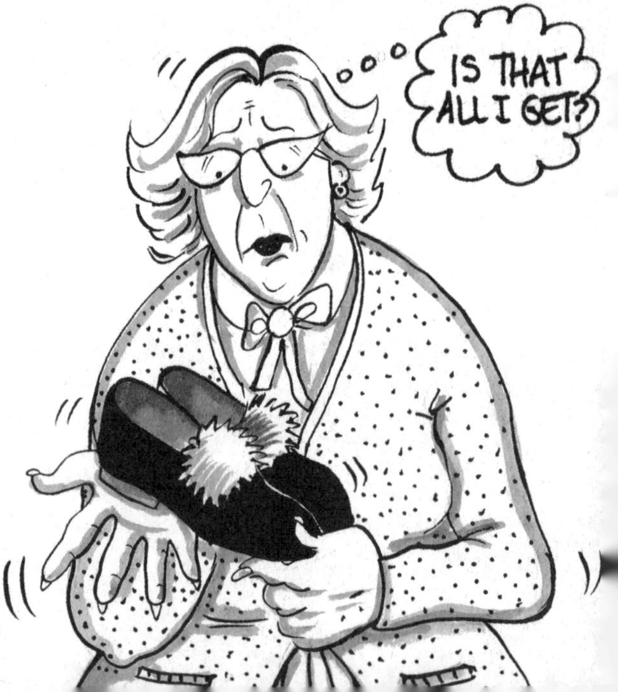
IS THAT
ALL I GET?

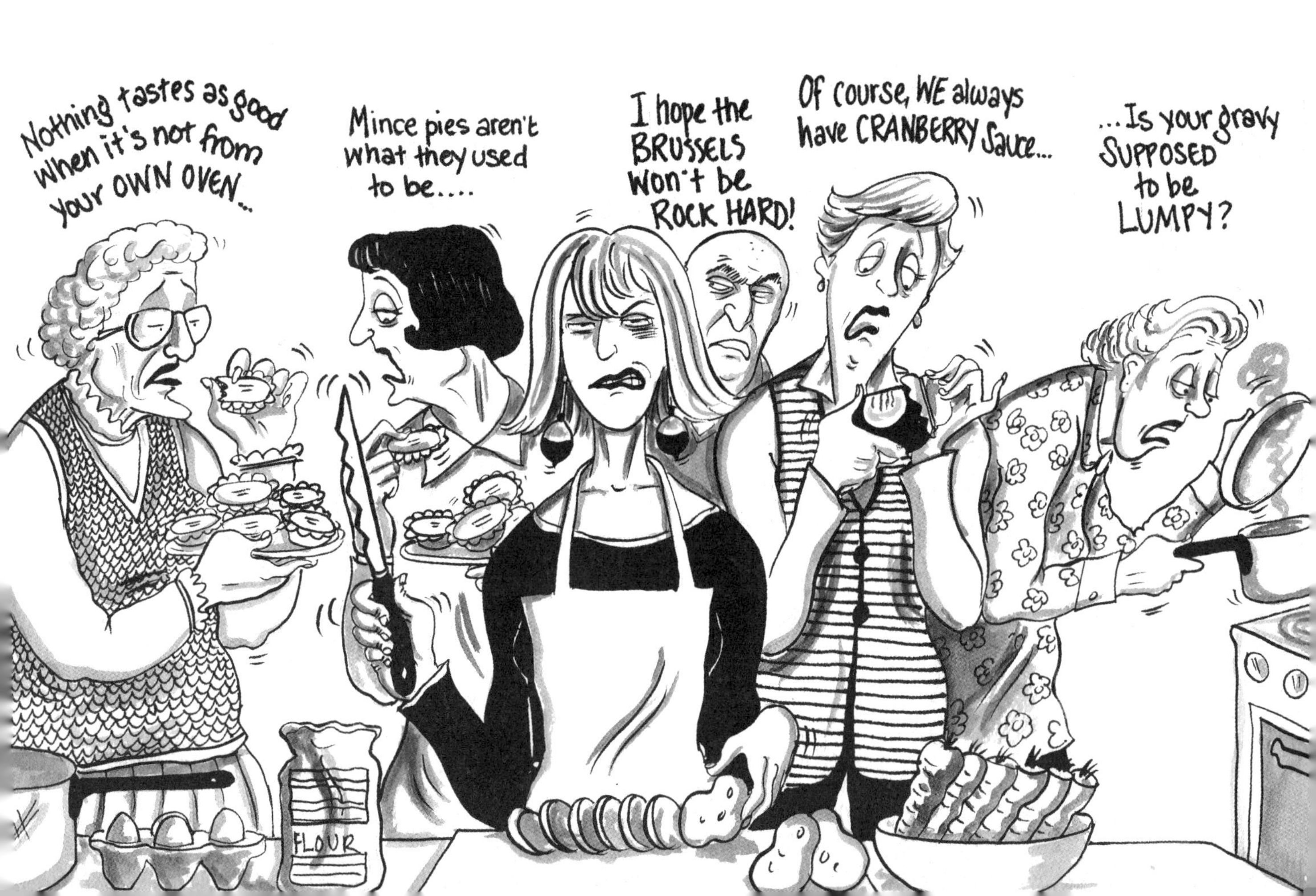
Nothing tastes as good when it's not from your OWN OVEN...
Mince pies aren't what they used to be....
I hope the BRUSSELS won't be ROCK HARD!
Of course, WE always have CRANBERRY Sauce...
...Is your gravy SUPPOSED to be LUMPY?
FLOUR

CHRISTMAS STUFFING ...

YOU SAY ...

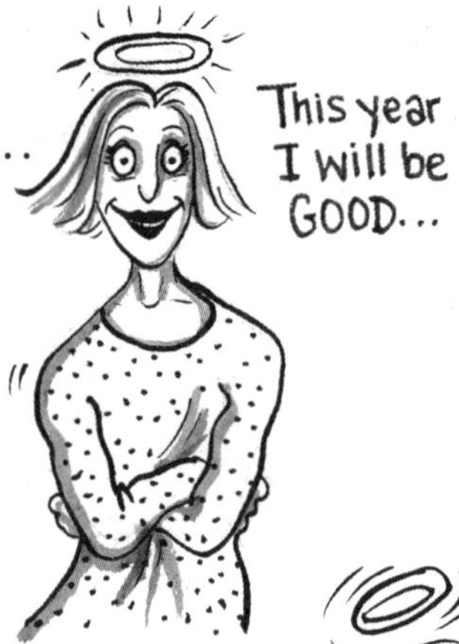
This year I will be GOOD...

You eat your Christmas Dinner ...

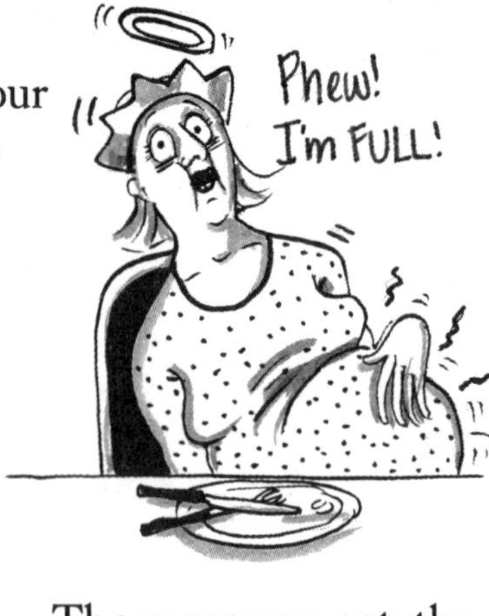
Phew! I'm FULL!

YOU SAY ...

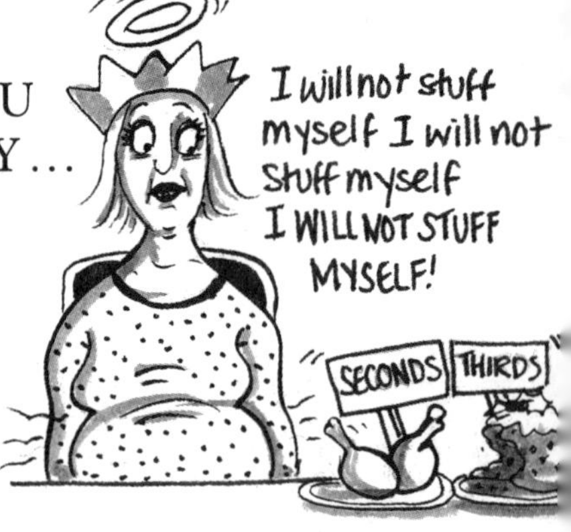
I will not stuff myself I will not Stuff myself I WILL NOT STUFF MYSELF!
SECONDS
THIRDS

... But your stomach has swollen to the size of a house and is crying out for ...

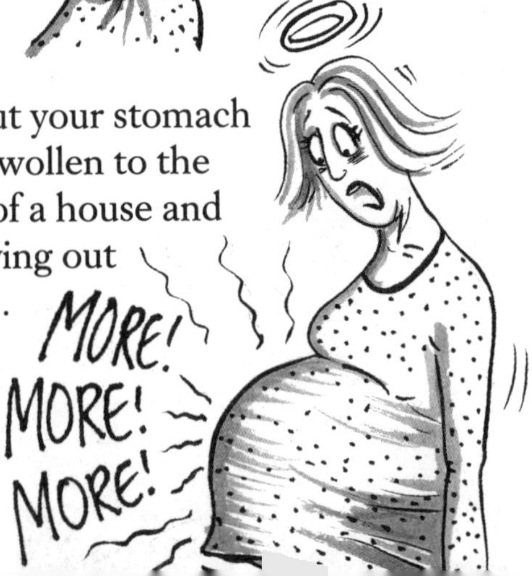
MORE!
MORE!
MORE!

The more you eat, the more you stretch, the more you want ... and the food may be in another room, but it won't leave you in peace ...

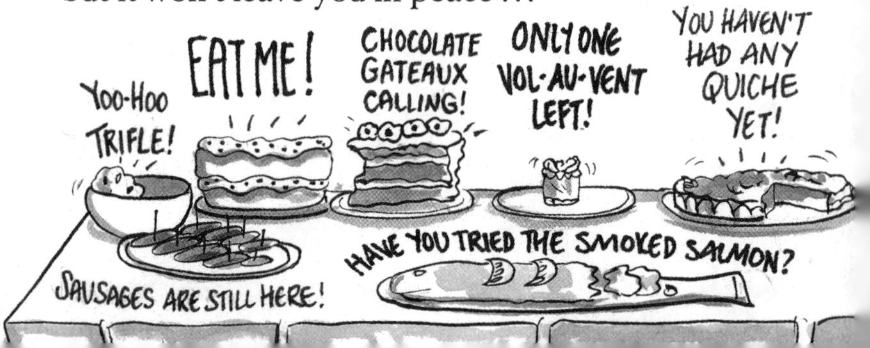
YOO-HOO TRIFLE!
EAT ME!
CHOCOLATE GATEAUX CALLING!
ONLY ONE VOL-AU-VENT LEFT!
YOU HAVEN'T HAD ANY QUICHE YET!
HAVE YOU TRIED THE SMOKED SALMON?
SAUSAGES ARE STILL HERE!

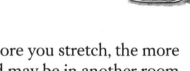

YOU
SAY …

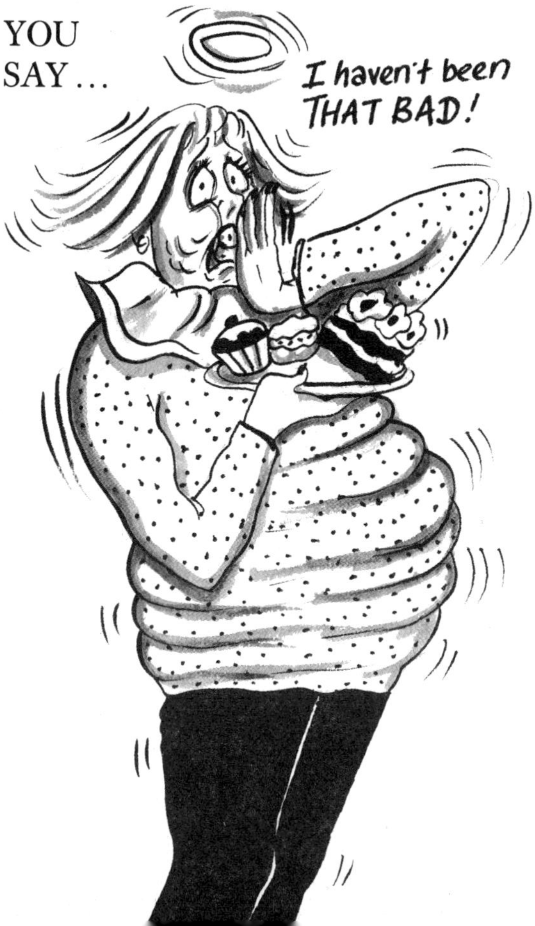
I haven't been THAT BAD!

… BUT YOUR
MIRROR SAYS …

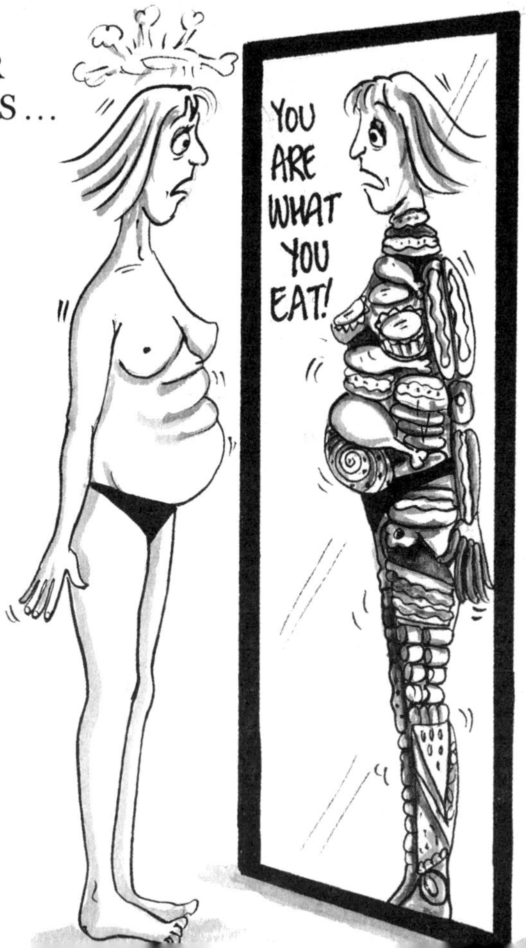
YOU ARE WHAT YOU EAT!

THINGS YOU HATE ABOUT CHRISTMAS

(8) That Turkey Feeling . . .

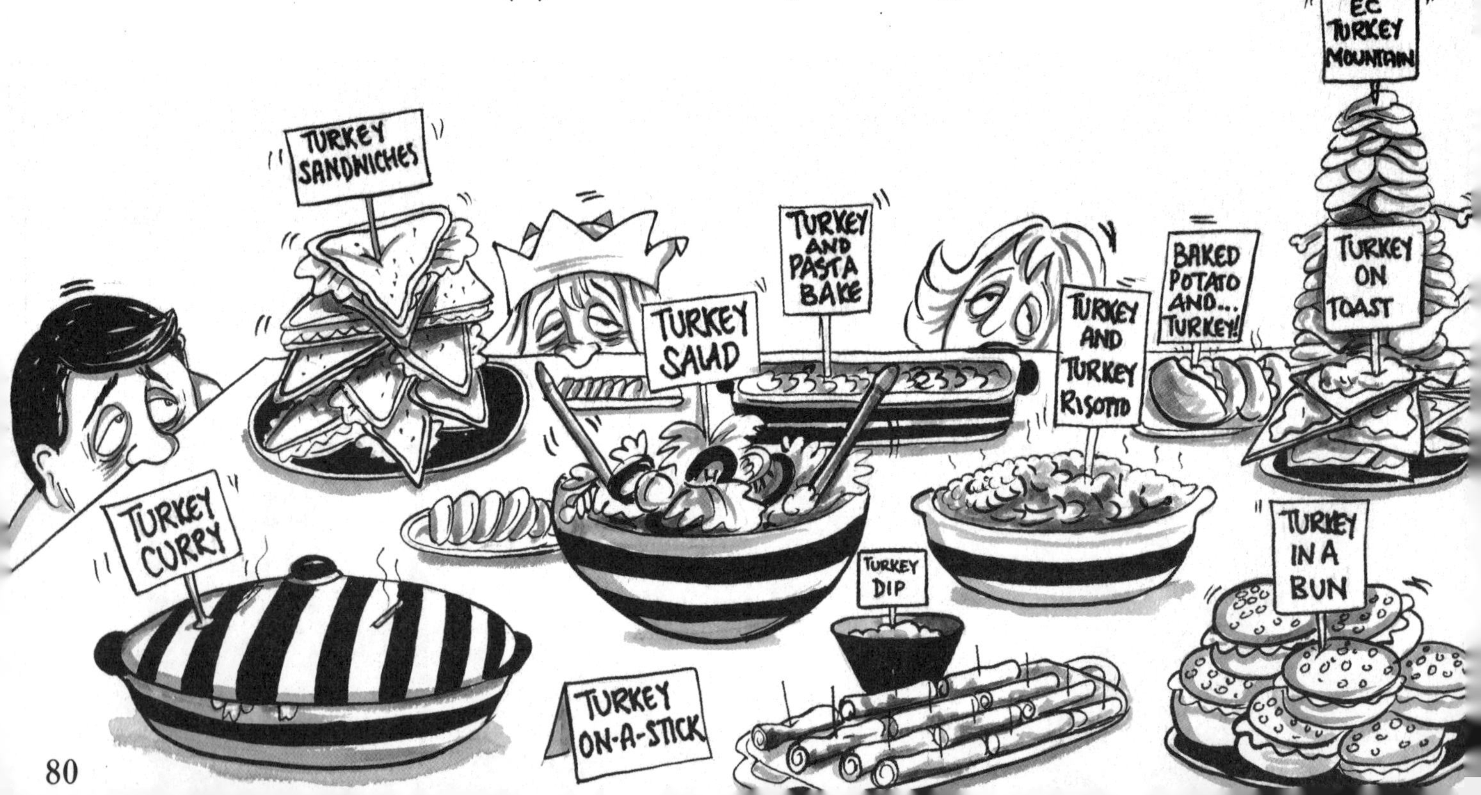
EC TURKEY MOUNTAIN
TURKEY SANDWICHES
TURKEY AND PASTA BAKE
TURKEY SALAD
BAKED POTATO AND... TURKEY!
TURKEY AND TURKEY RISOTTO
TURKEY ON TOAST
TURKEY CURRY
TURKEY DIP
TURKEY IN A BUN
TURKEY ON-A-STICK

... Turning Turkey ...

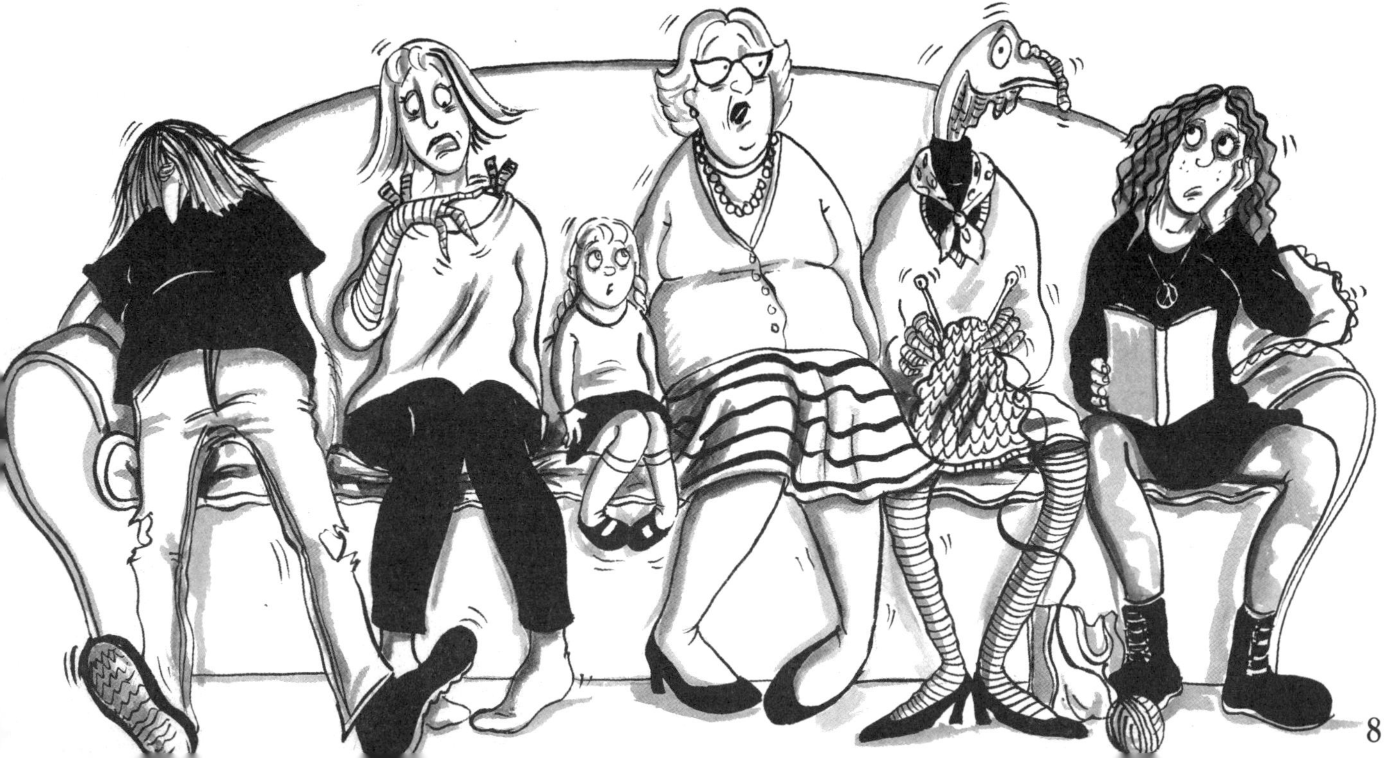

CHRISTMAS WISHES …

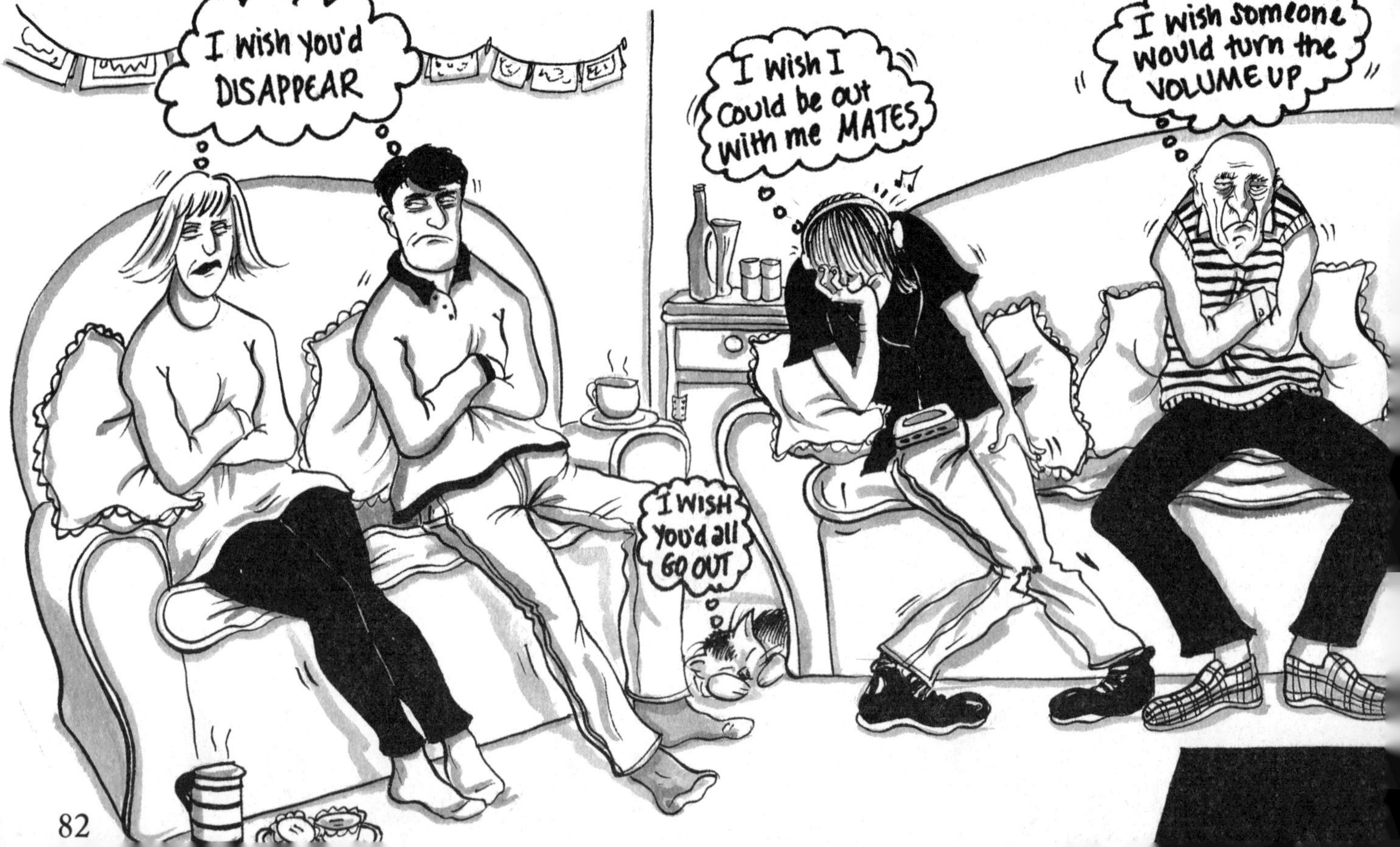

I wish you'd DISAPPEAR
I WISH You'd all GO OUT
I wish I could be out with me MATES
I wish someone would turn the VOLUME UP

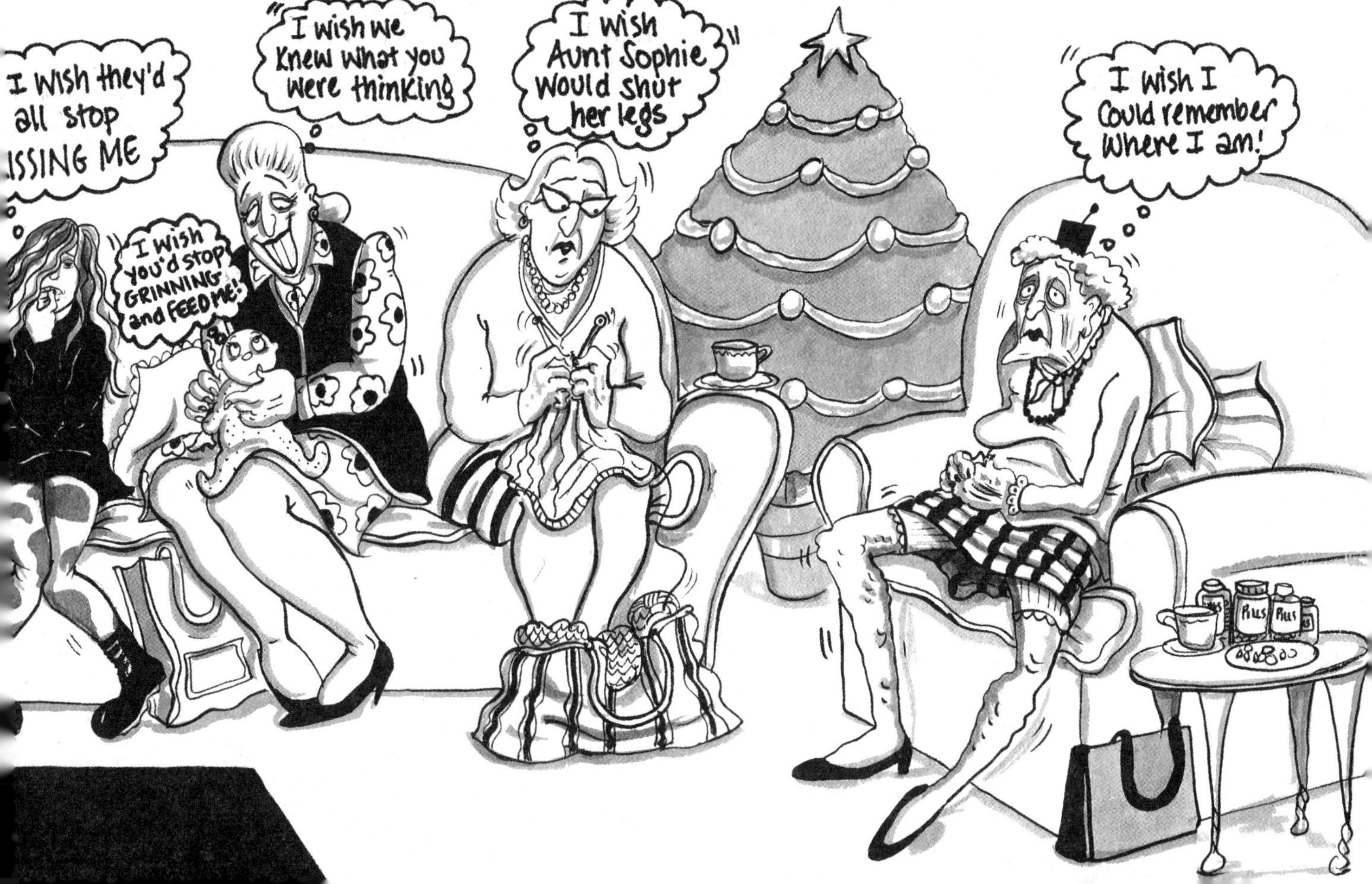
I wish they'd all stop ISSING ME
I wish you'd stop GRINNING and FEED ME!
"I wish we Knew what you were thinking
I wish Aunt Sophie would shut her legs"
I wish I could remember where I am!
PILLS
PILLS

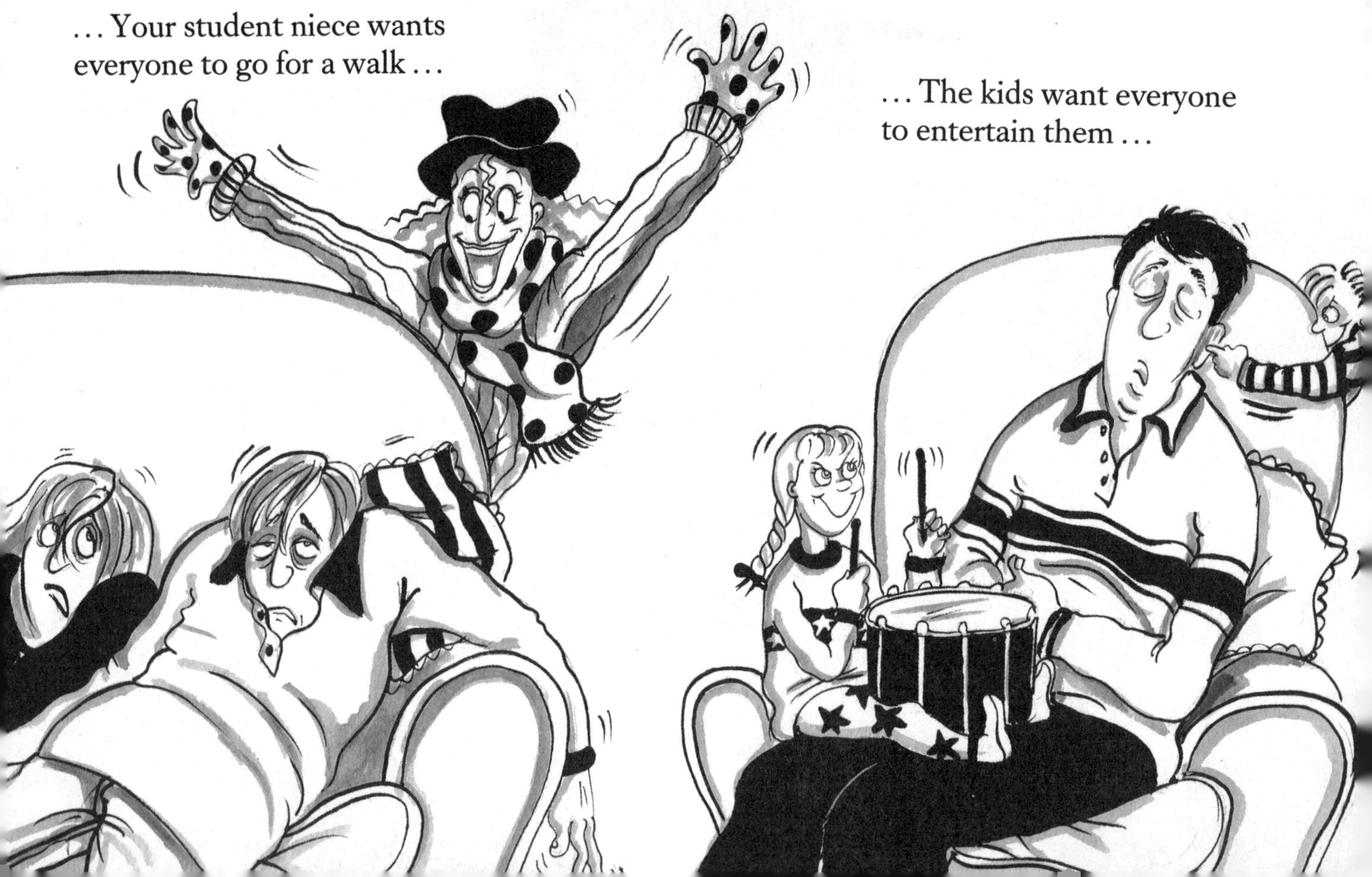
... Your student niece wants everyone to go for a walk ...
... The kids want everyone to entertain them ...

… Auntie wants
everyone to
play charades …

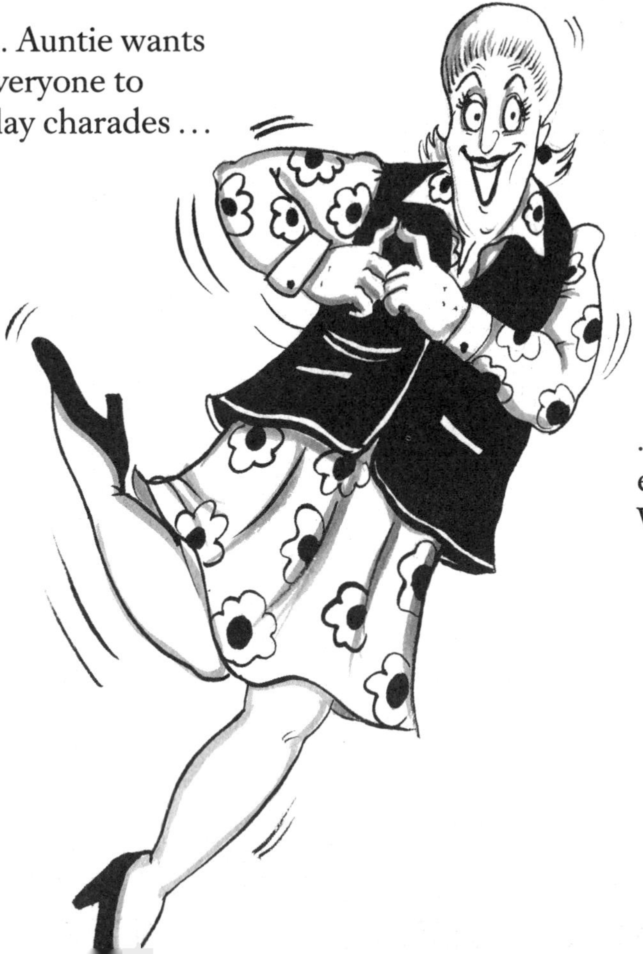

… Mum just wants
everyone else to
WASH UP!

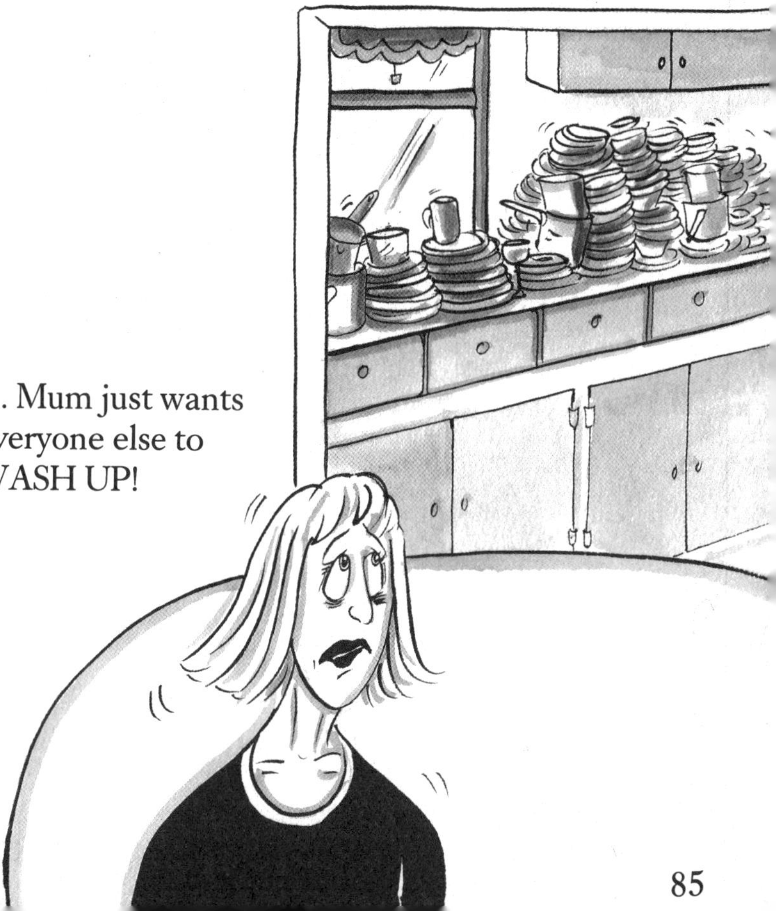

THINGS YOU HATE ABOUT CHRISTMAS

(9) Men At Christmas ... is it possible to have Goodwill Toward Them?

... Those who still think they can spend all day in the pub whilst you do all the work ... and then pretend to be asleep when it's time for the washing up ...

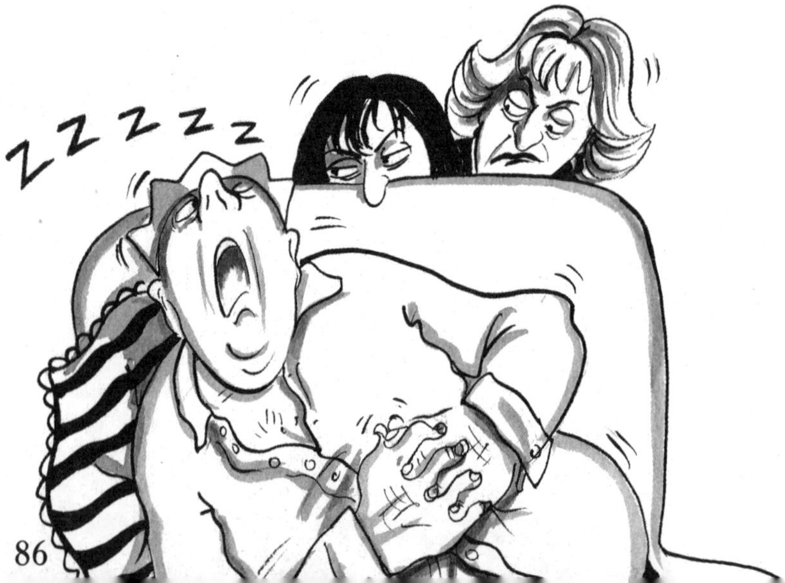
ZZZZZZ

... Those who expect to have a marvellous time but don't want to pay for it ...

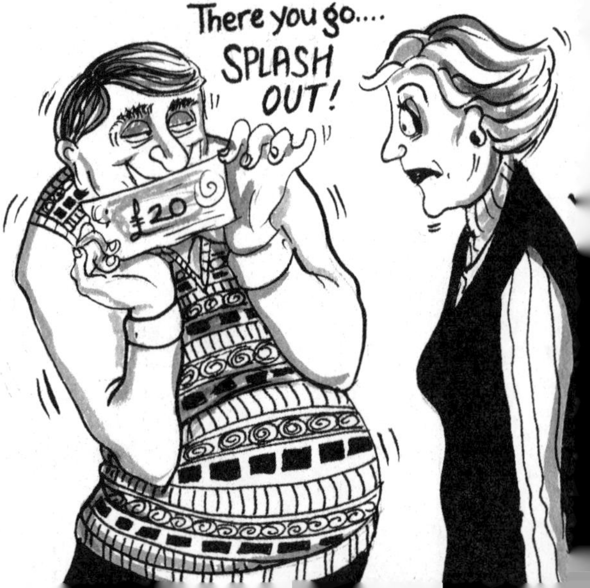
There you go.... SPLASH OUT!
£20

... Those who staple themselves to the sofa, superglue the remote control to their hand and move the TV to where only they have the best view ...

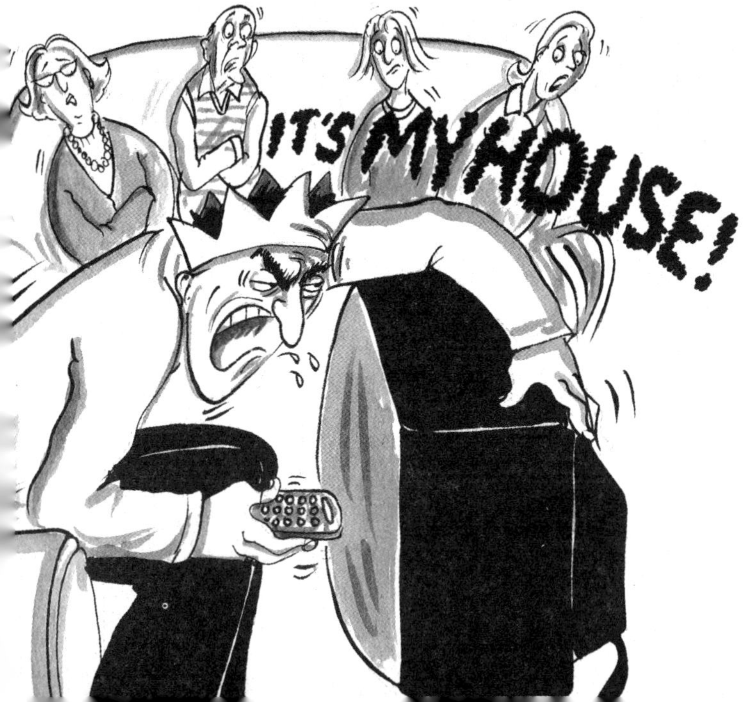
IT'S MY HOUSE!

... And those who peel the spuds once a year and want a STANDING OVATION!

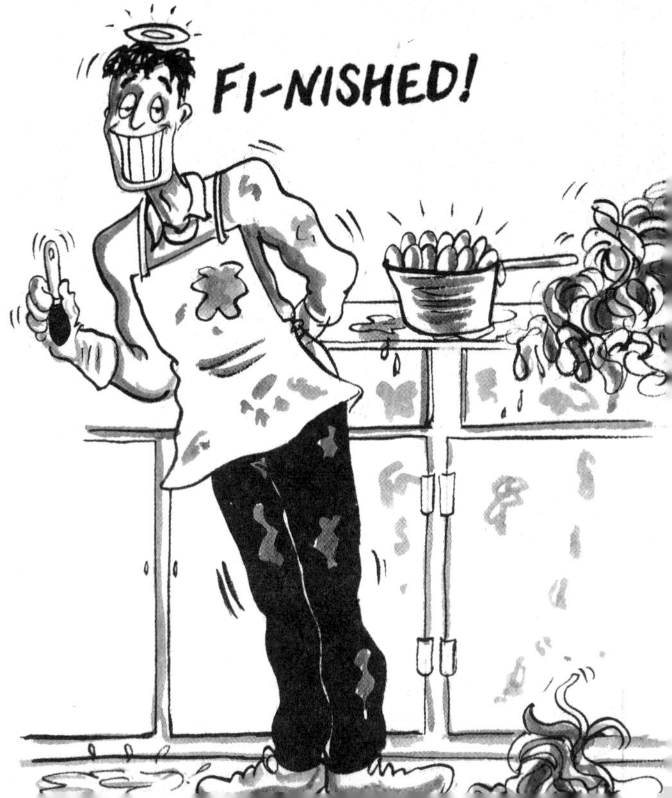
FI-NISHED!

CHRISTMAS REGRETS . . .

Buying Dad those cigars . . .

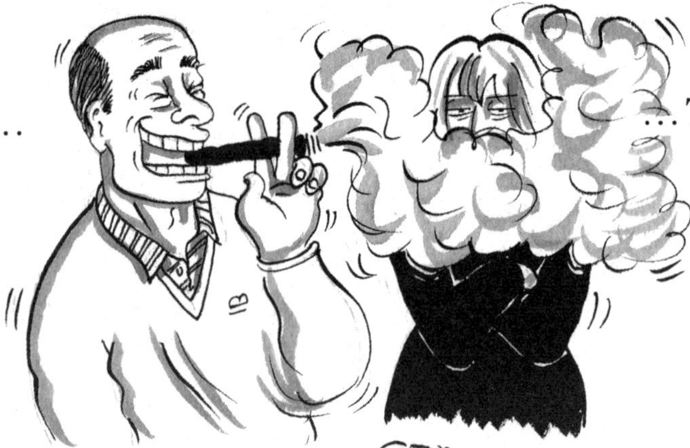

. . . The kids those noisy repetitive games . . .

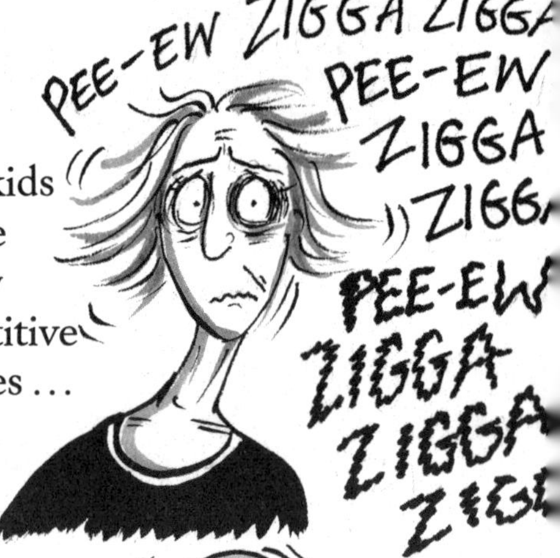
PEE-EW ZIGGA
PEE-EW
ZIGGA
PEE-EW
ZIGGA
ZIGGA

. . . Grandad something messy . . .

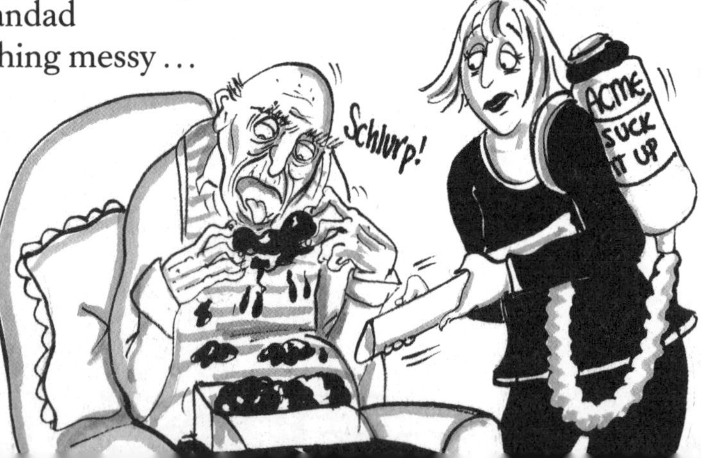
Schlurp!
ACME
SUCK
IT UP

. . . Uncle that Ginseng . . .

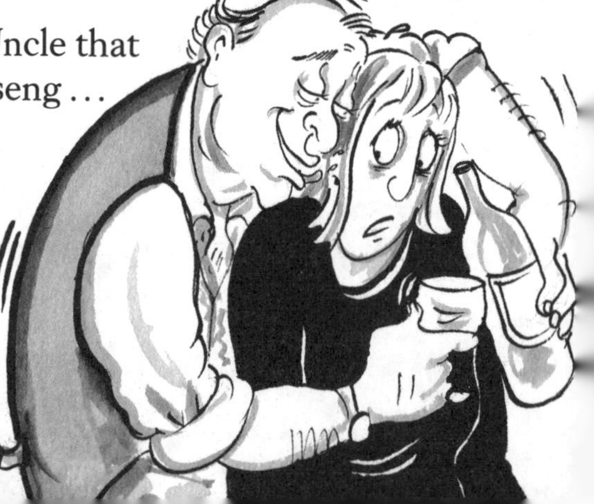

... But most of all, spending so much money!

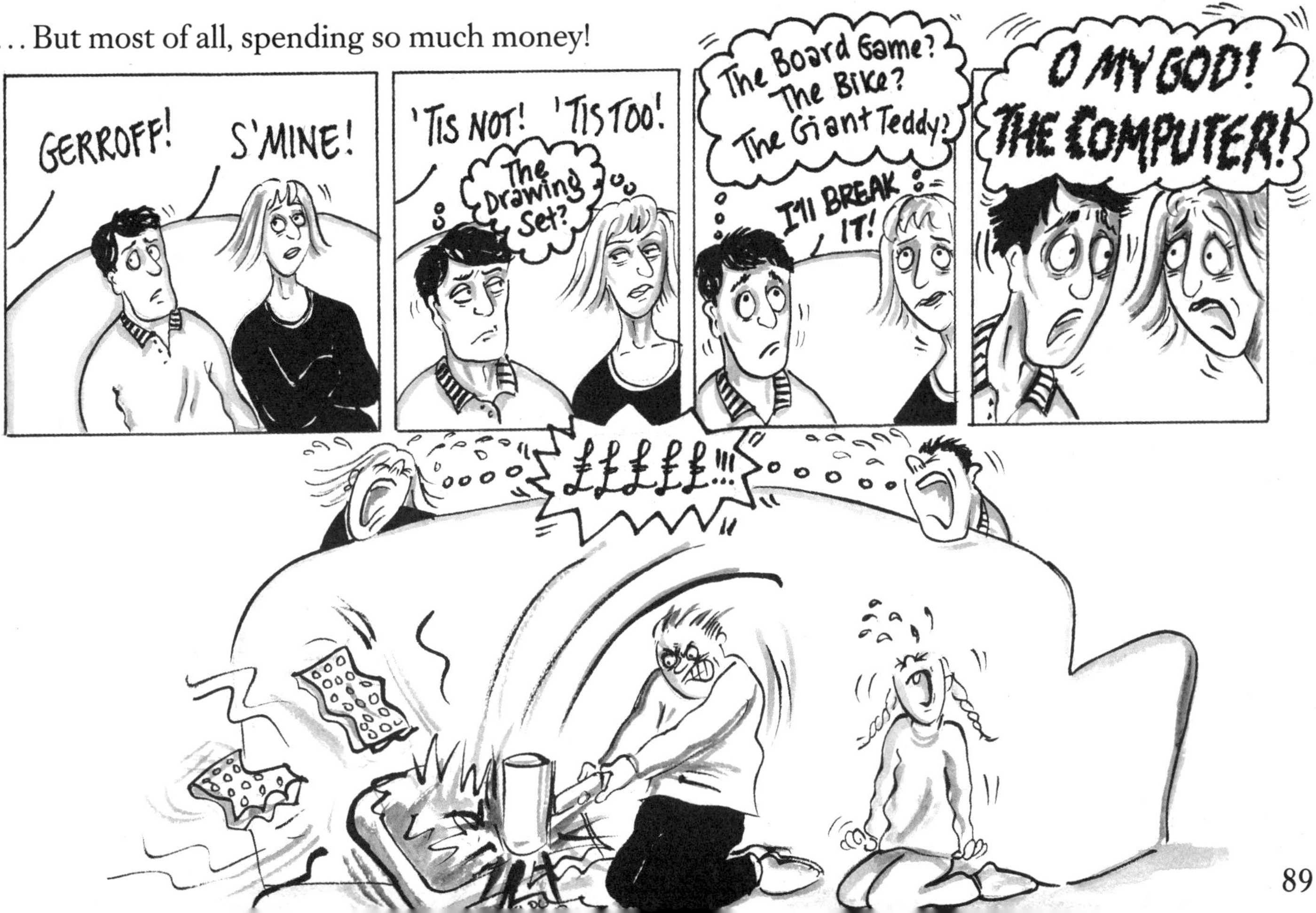
GERROFF!
S'MINE!
'TIS NOT!
'TIS TOO!
The Drawing Set?
The Board Game?
The Bike?
The Giant Teddy?
I'll BREAK IT!
O MY GOD!
THE COMPUTER!
££££££!!!

CHRISTMAS MYTHS …

It Snows …

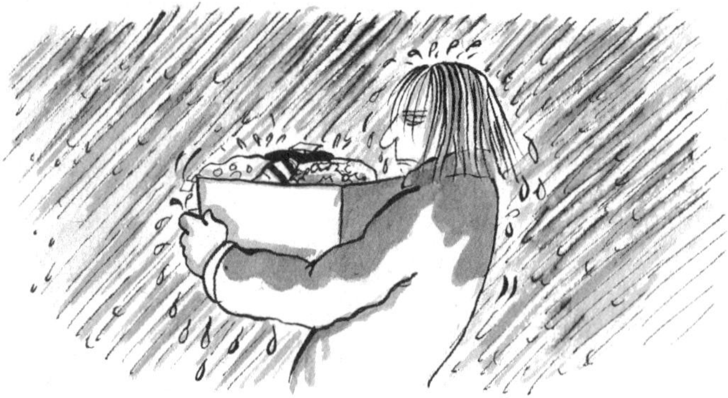

It's Romantic …

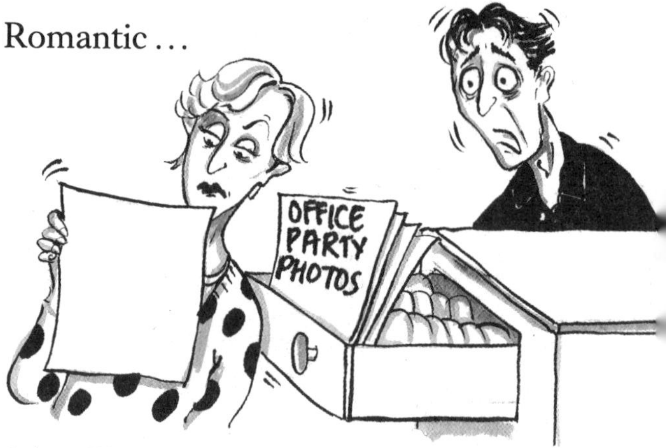

OFFICE PARTY PHOTOS

It Brings The Family Together …

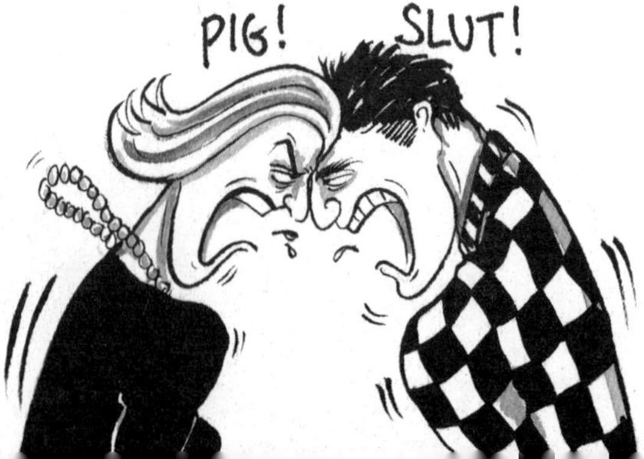

PIG!
SLUT!

It Makes You Remember *The Bible* …

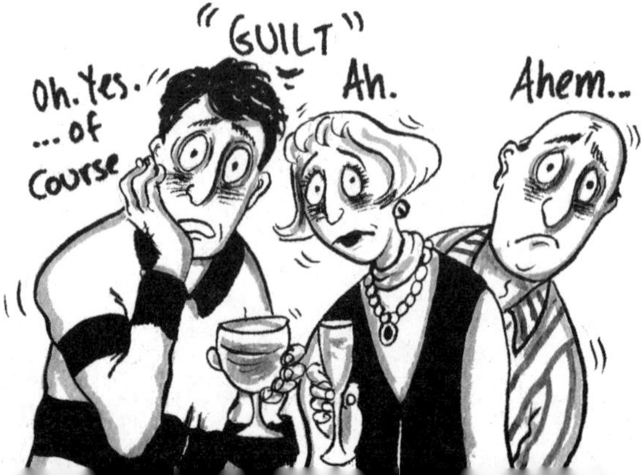

"GUILT"
Oh. Yes. ... of Course
Ah.
Ahem...

. . . It's Just For The Kids!

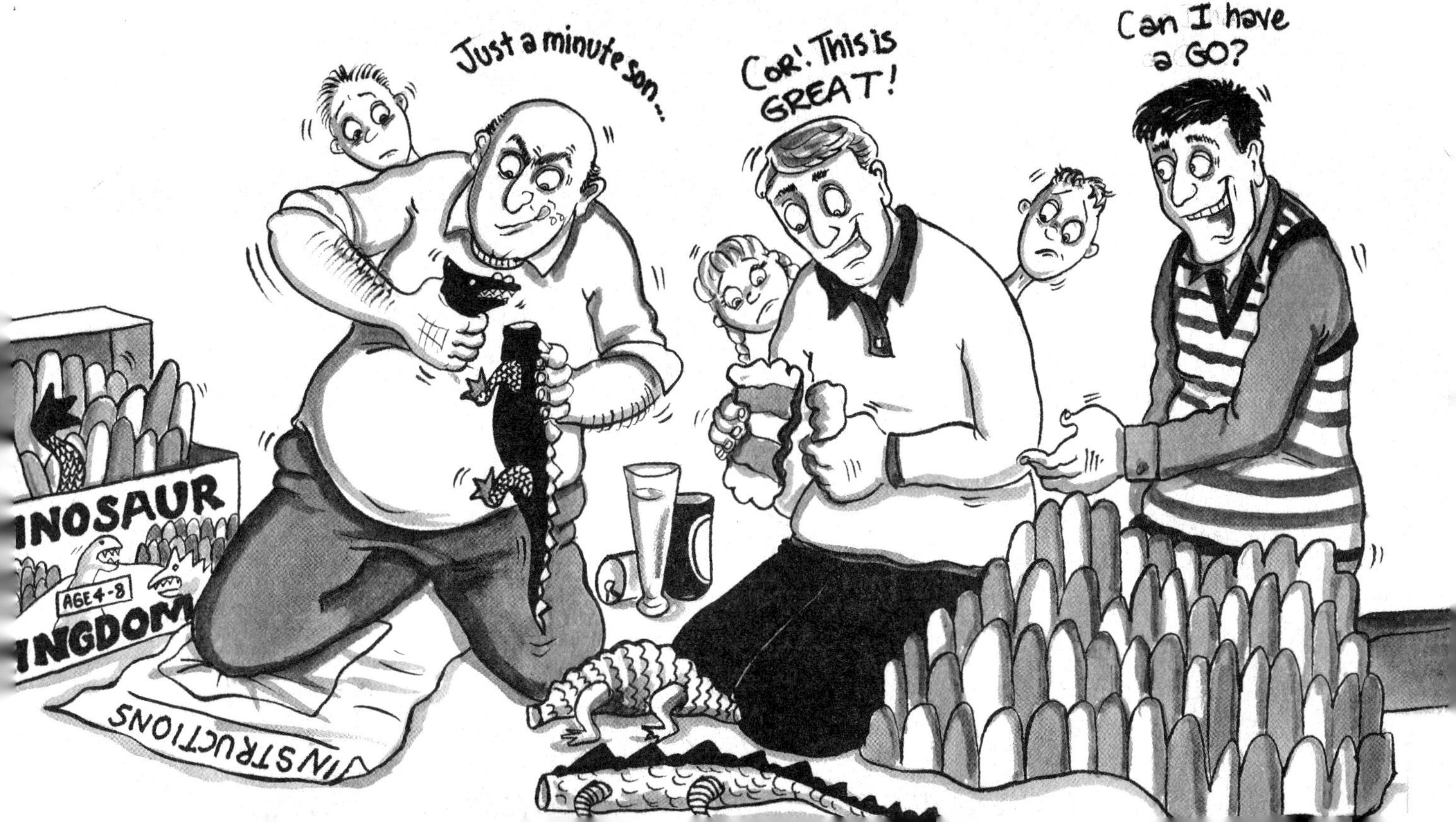

Just a minute son...
Cor! This is GREAT!
Can I have a GO?
INOSAUR
AGE 4-8
INGDOM
INSTRUCTIONS

CHRISTMAS TELEVISION

One of the things we row about most at Christmas has to be the television . . .

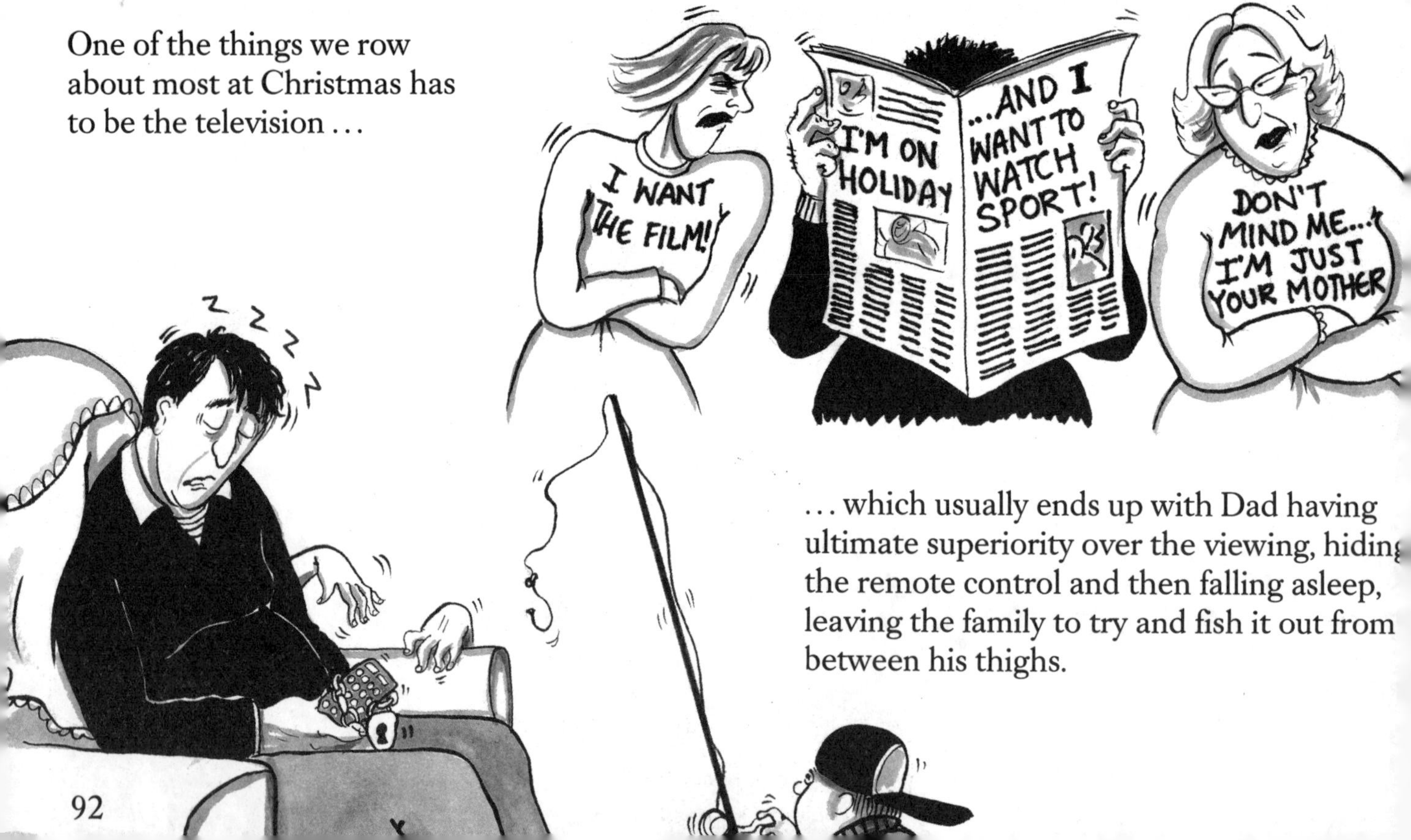
I WANT THE FILM!
I'M ON HOLIDAY
...AND I WANT TO WATCH SPORT!
DON'T MIND ME... I'M JUST YOUR MOTHER
Z Z Z Z

. . . which usually ends up with Dad having ultimate superiority over the viewing, hiding the remote control and then falling asleep, leaving the family to try and fish it out from between his thighs.

FILMS THAT REMIND YOU OF CHRISTMAS

(Because they're about Christmas …)

Scrooge
Miracle On 34th Street
White Christmas

FILMS THAT REMIND YOU OF CHRISTMAS

(Because they're on every year …)

Mary Poppins
The Sound Of Music
Chitty Chitty Bang Bang
The Wizard Of Oz

FILMS THAT HAVE NOTHING TO DO WITH CHRISTMAS

(But are always shown anyway …)

Zulu
Bridge Over The River Kwai
Spartacus
El Cid
Easter Parade

FILMS THAT ARE ABOUT A HAPPY FAMILY CHRISTMAS

(And make you feel guilty)

Meet Me In St Louis
It's A Wonderful Life
Little Women
The Railway Children

TISSUES

THINGS YOU HATE ABOUT CHRISTMAS

(10) Playing Games . . .

If you're an unmarried or child-free relative round for Christmas and are thinking of having a nice, quiet time . . . forget it!

It's the one time of year that parents can shift the 24-hour pressure to play games onto someone else.

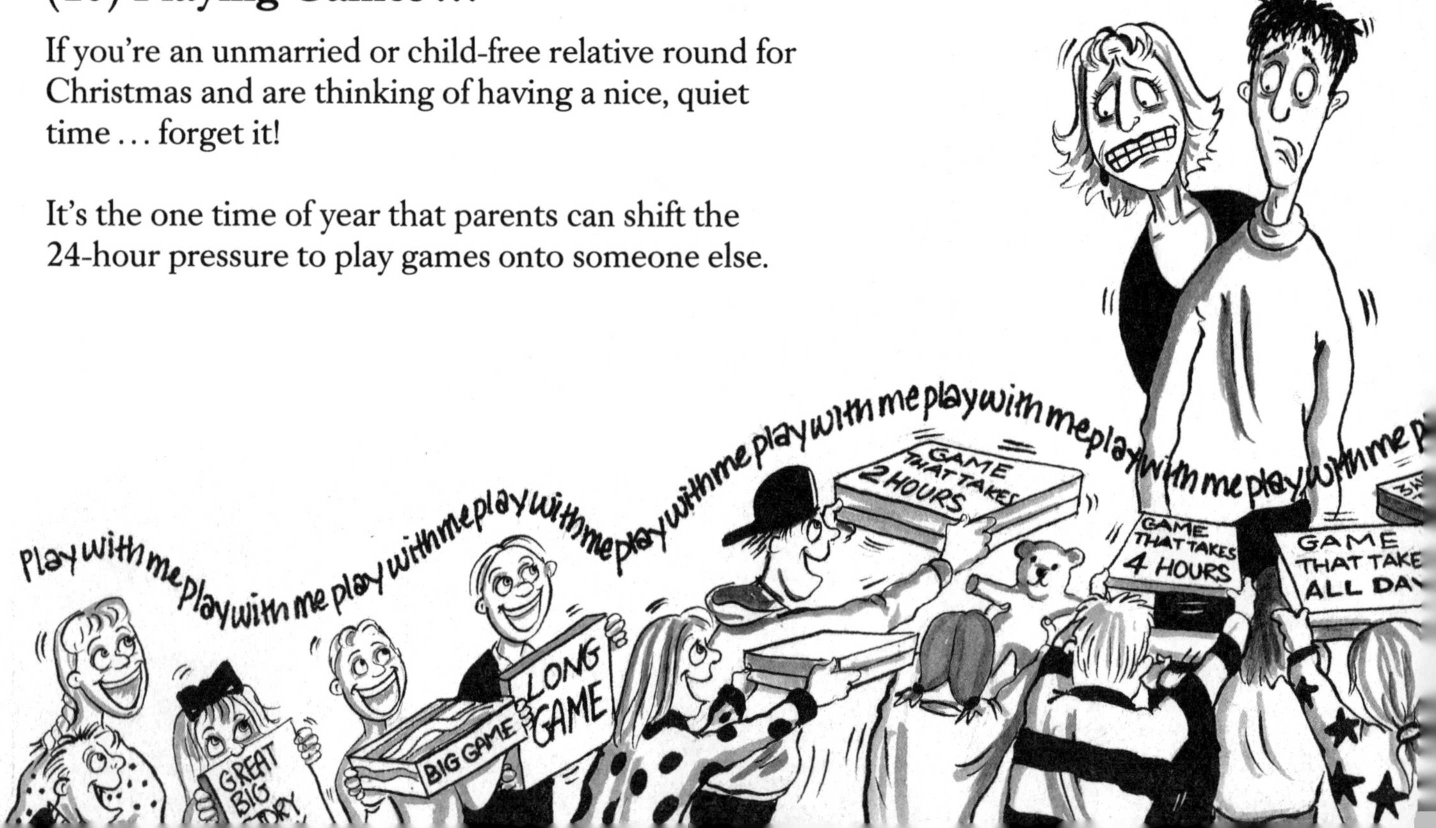

playwithmeplaywithmeplaywithmeplaywithmeplaywithmeplaywithmeplaywithmeplaywithmeplaywithmeplaywithme
GAME THAT TAKES 2 HOURS
GAME THAT TAKES 4 HOURS
GAME THAT TAKE ALL DA
LONG GAME
BIG GAME
GREAT BIG

You have to be adept at all levels of computer games, skilled at assembling all manner of pop-up books and complicated Lego worlds. You have to read stories using different voices and throwing yourself in it like a true Thespian. Sitting glued to the sofa will *not* be allowed.

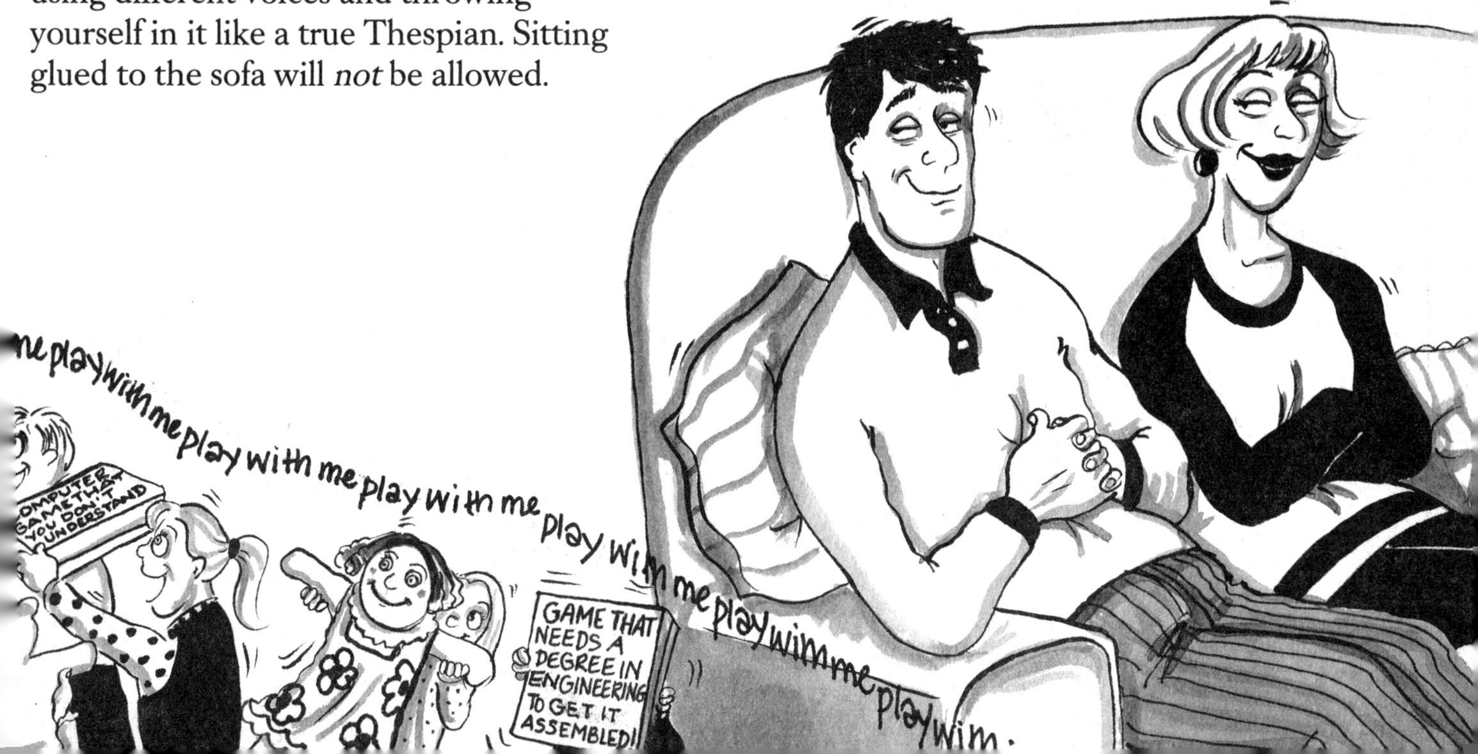
me play with me play with me play with me play with me play with me play wim me play wim.
COMPUTER GAME THAT YOU DON'T UNDERSTAND
GAME THAT NEEDS A DEGREE IN ENGINEERING TO GET IT ASSEMBLED!!

HOW TO SURVIVE CHRISTMAS

. . . Drop gentle hints to your relatives about the presents you want . . .

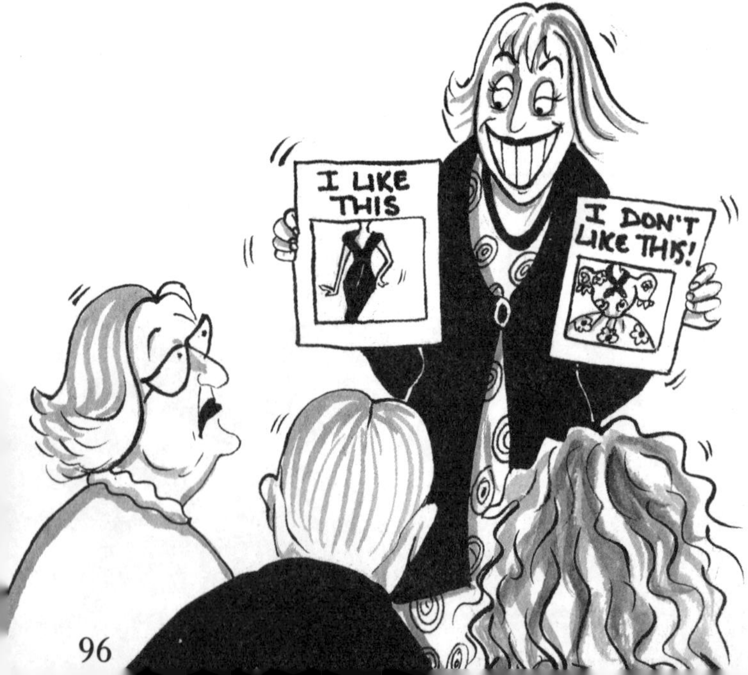
I LIKE THIS
I DON'T LIKE THIS!

. . . Encourage the family to do their share . . .

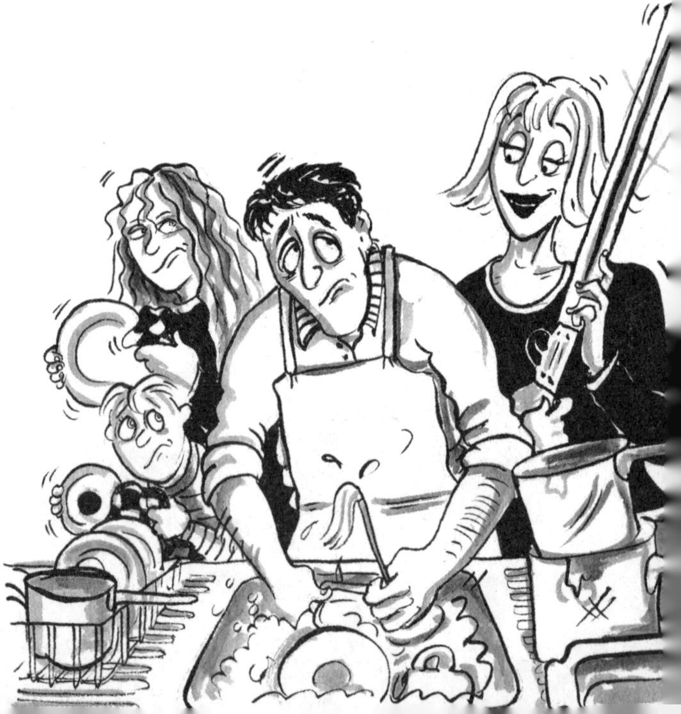

… Remember it's only once a year, hold on tight to that Smile-On-A-Stick …

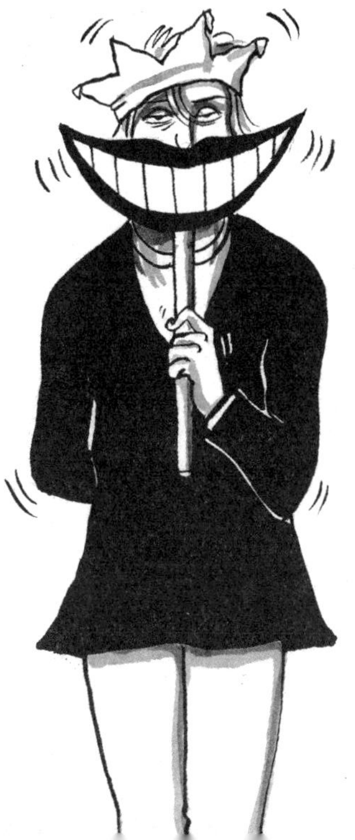

… and ALWAYS try to find a quiet place where you can escape!

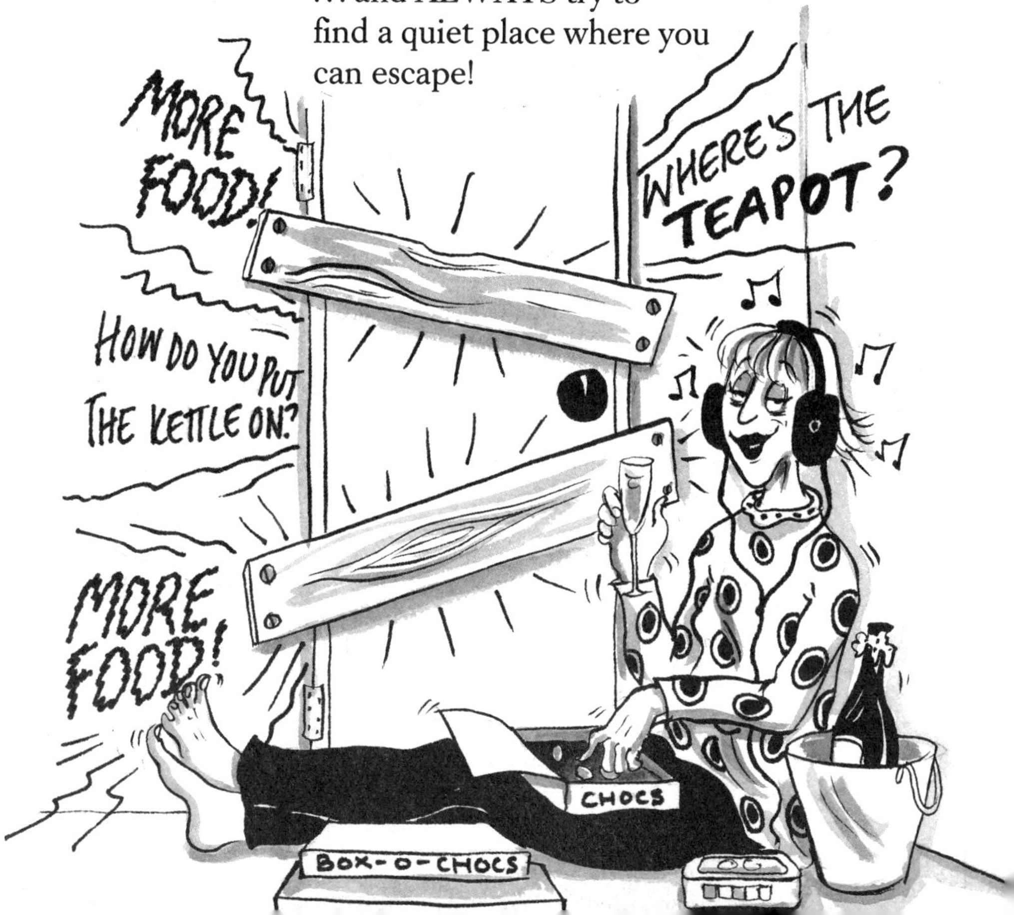
MORE FOOD!
HOW DO YOU PUT THE KETTLE ON?
MORE FOOD!
WHERE'S THE TEAPOT?
CHOCS
BOX-O-CHOCS

THINGS YOU HATE ABOUT CHRISTMAS

(11) Christmas On A Weekend …

You don't feel you've had any time off work …

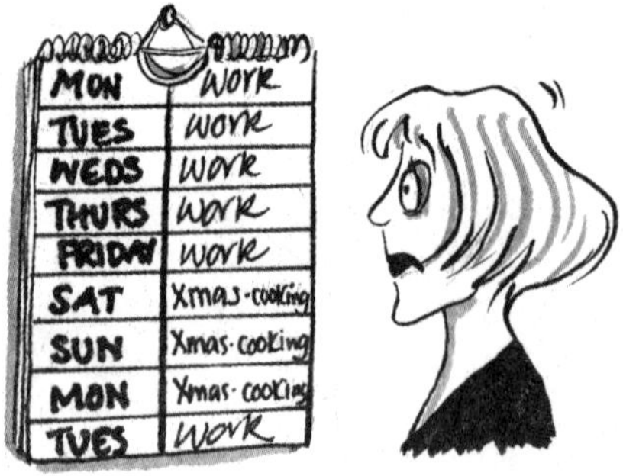

MON WORK
TUES WORK
WEDS WORK
THURS WORK
FRIDAY WORK
SAT Xmas-cooking
SUN Xmas-cooking
MON Xmas-cooking
TUES WORK

… You're stuck inside the house for longer because all the shops are shut …

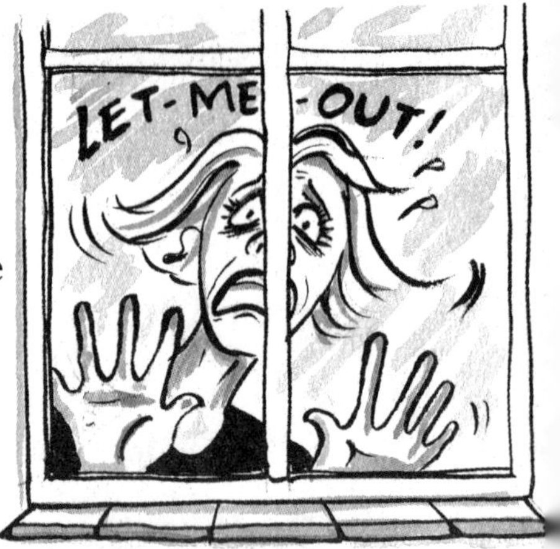

LET-ME-OUT!

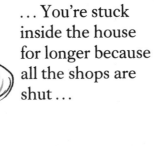

… There are a LOT more chances to open up old wounds, and niggle and wind everyone up for a really good row …

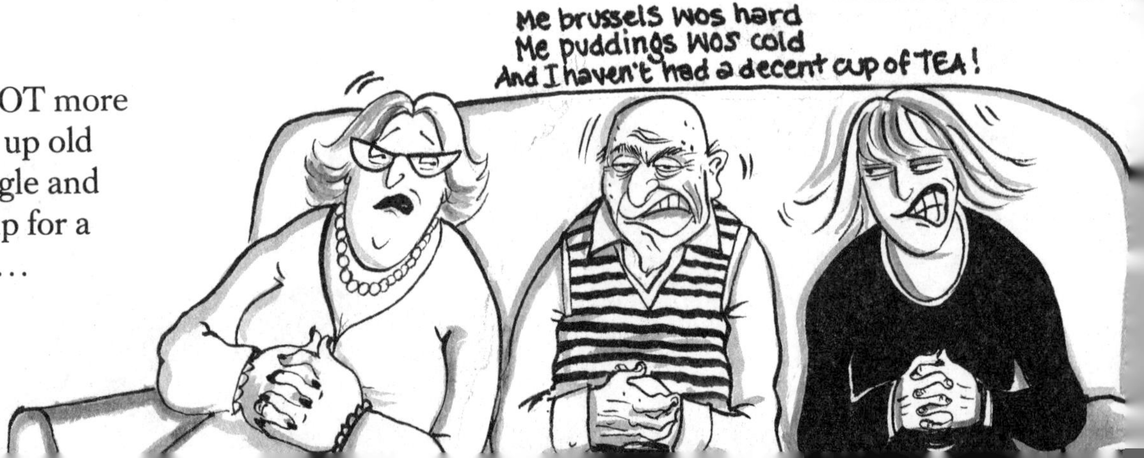

Me brussels wos hard
Me puddings wos cold
And I haven't had a decent cup of TEA!

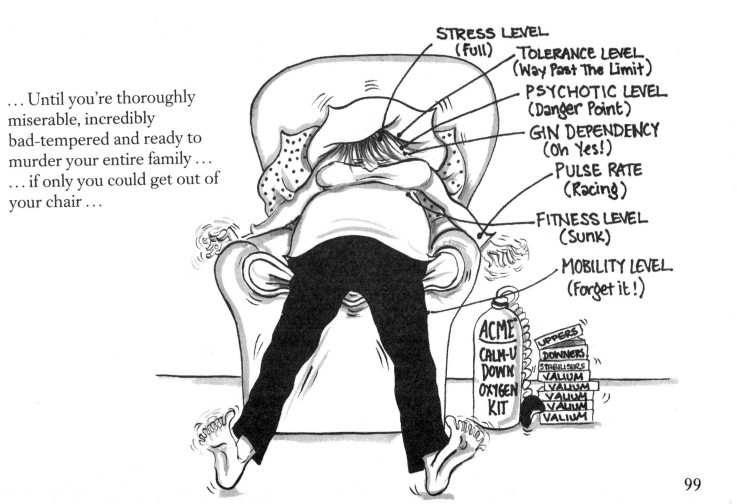

... Until you're thoroughly miserable, incredibly bad-tempered and ready to murder your entire family ...
... if only you could get out of your chair ...

STRESS LEVEL (Full)

TOLERANCE LEVEL (Way Past The Limit)

PSYCHOTIC LEVEL (Danger Point)

GIN DEPENDENCY (Oh Yes!)

PULSE RATE (Racing)

FITNESS LEVEL (Sunk)

MOBILITY LEVEL (Forget it!)

ACME CALM-U DOWN OXYGEN KIT

UPPERS
DOWNERS
STABILISERS
VALIUM
VALIUM
VALIUM
VALIUM
VALIUM

CHRISTMAS IS OVER!

(At last the shops are open . . .)

You haul yourself out of your chair, you squash into your coat that no longer fits, and you drag yourself out into the fresh air.

You have a change of scenery . . .

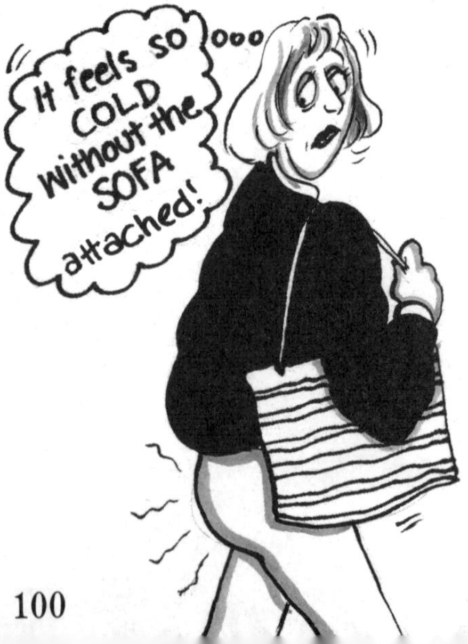
It feels so COLD without the SOFA attached!

. . . you get to look round the sales . . .

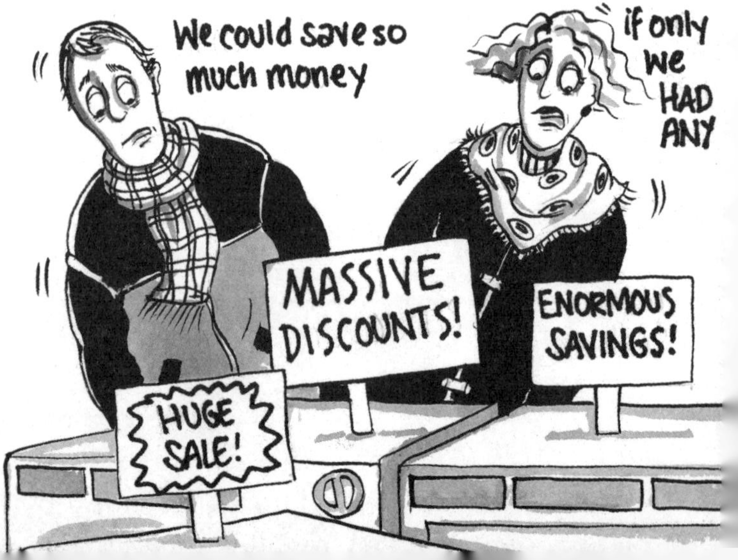
We could save so much money
if only we HAD ANY
MASSIVE DISCOUNTS!
ENORMOUS SAVINGS!
HUGE SALE!

… You can also start to get withdrawal symptoms from the TV …

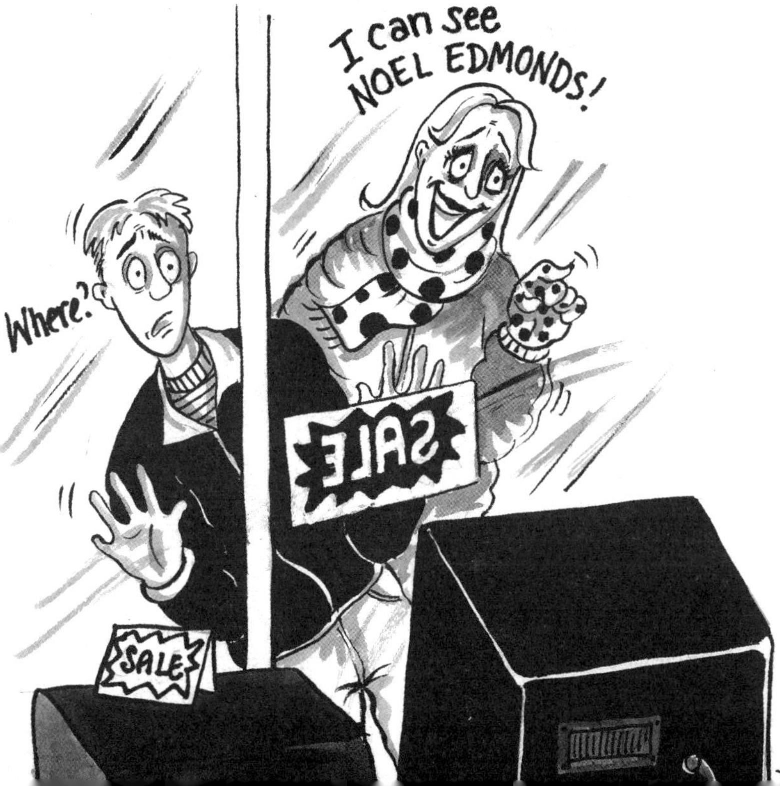
I can see NOEL EDMONDS!
Where?
SALE
SALE

… and the shock can sometimes be too much for you …

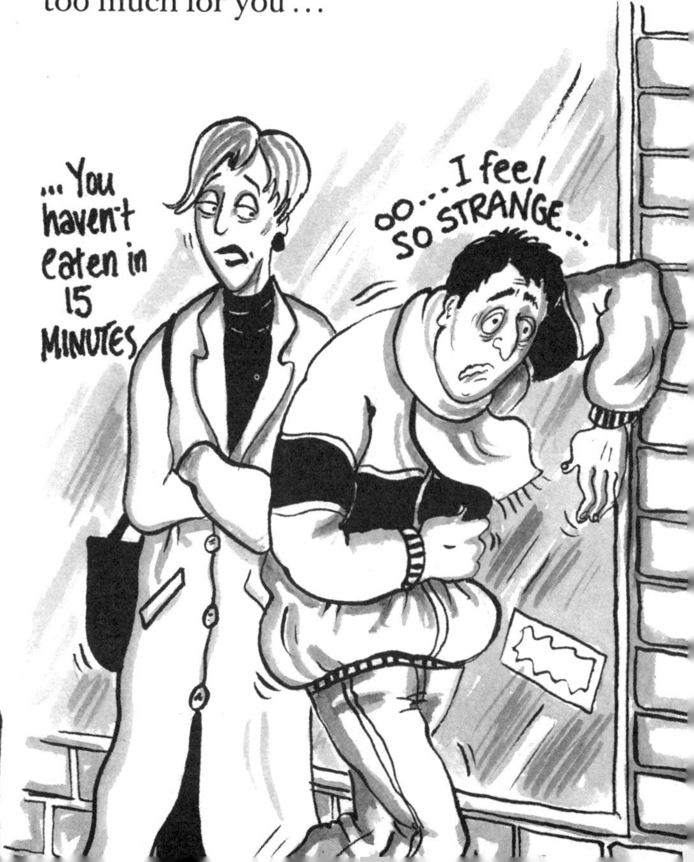
… You haven't eaten in 15 MINUTES
oo…. I feel SO STRANGE…

TAKING THE PRESENTS BACK ...

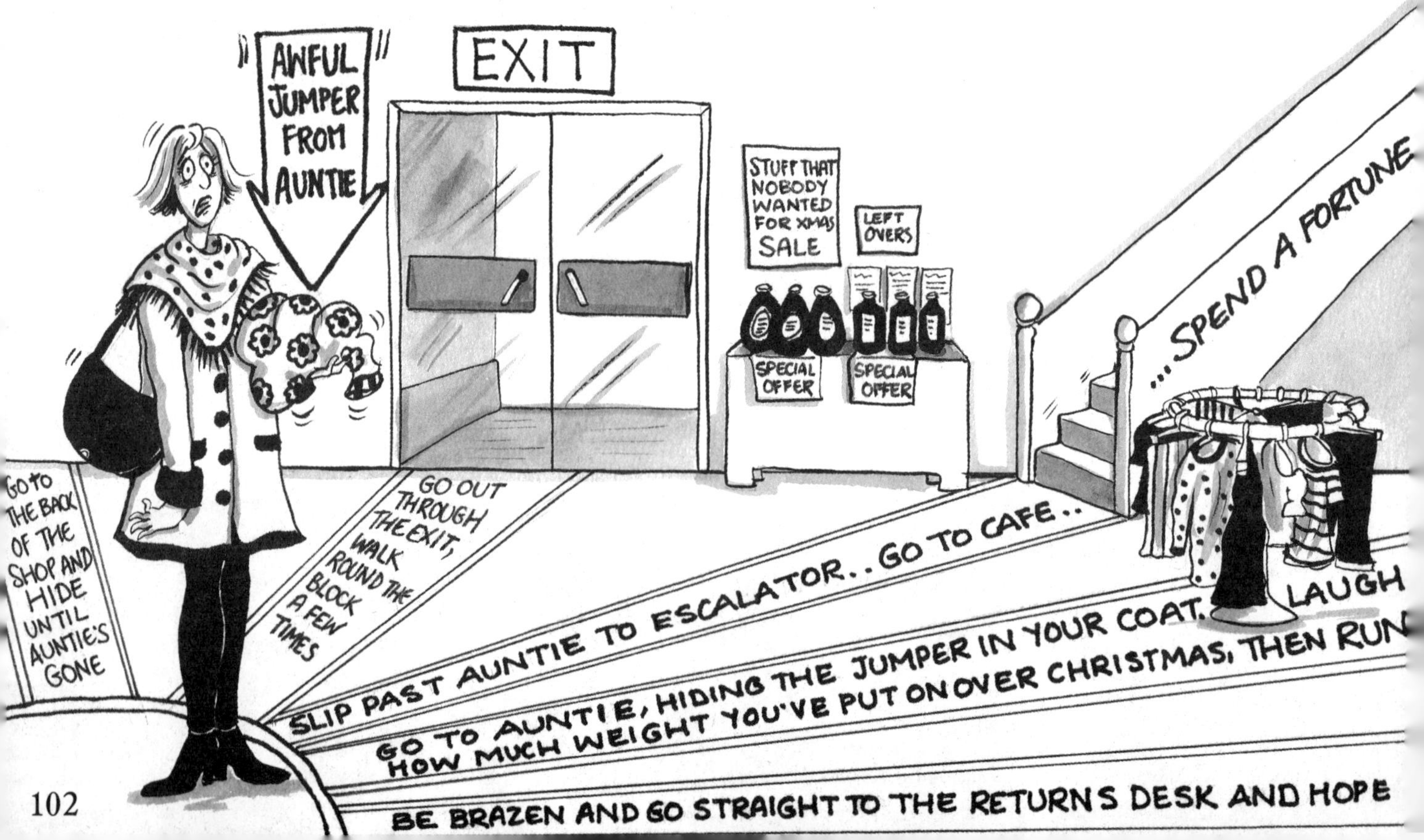
AWFUL JUMPER FROM AUNTIE
EXIT
STUFF THAT NOBODY WANTED FOR XMAS SALE
LEFT OVERS
SPECIAL OFFER
SPECIAL OFFER
GO TO THE BACK OF THE SHOP AND HIDE UNTIL AUNTIE'S GONE
GO OUT THROUGH THE EXIT, WALK ROUND THE BLOCK A FEW TIMES
SLIP PAST AUNTIE TO ESCALATOR.. GO TO CAFE.. ...SPEND A FORTUNE
GO TO AUNTIE, HIDING THE JUMPER IN YOUR COAT. LAUGH HOW MUCH WEIGHT YOU'VE PUT ON OVER CHRISTMAS, THEN RUN
BE BRAZEN AND GO STRAIGHT TO THE RETURNS DESK AND HOPE

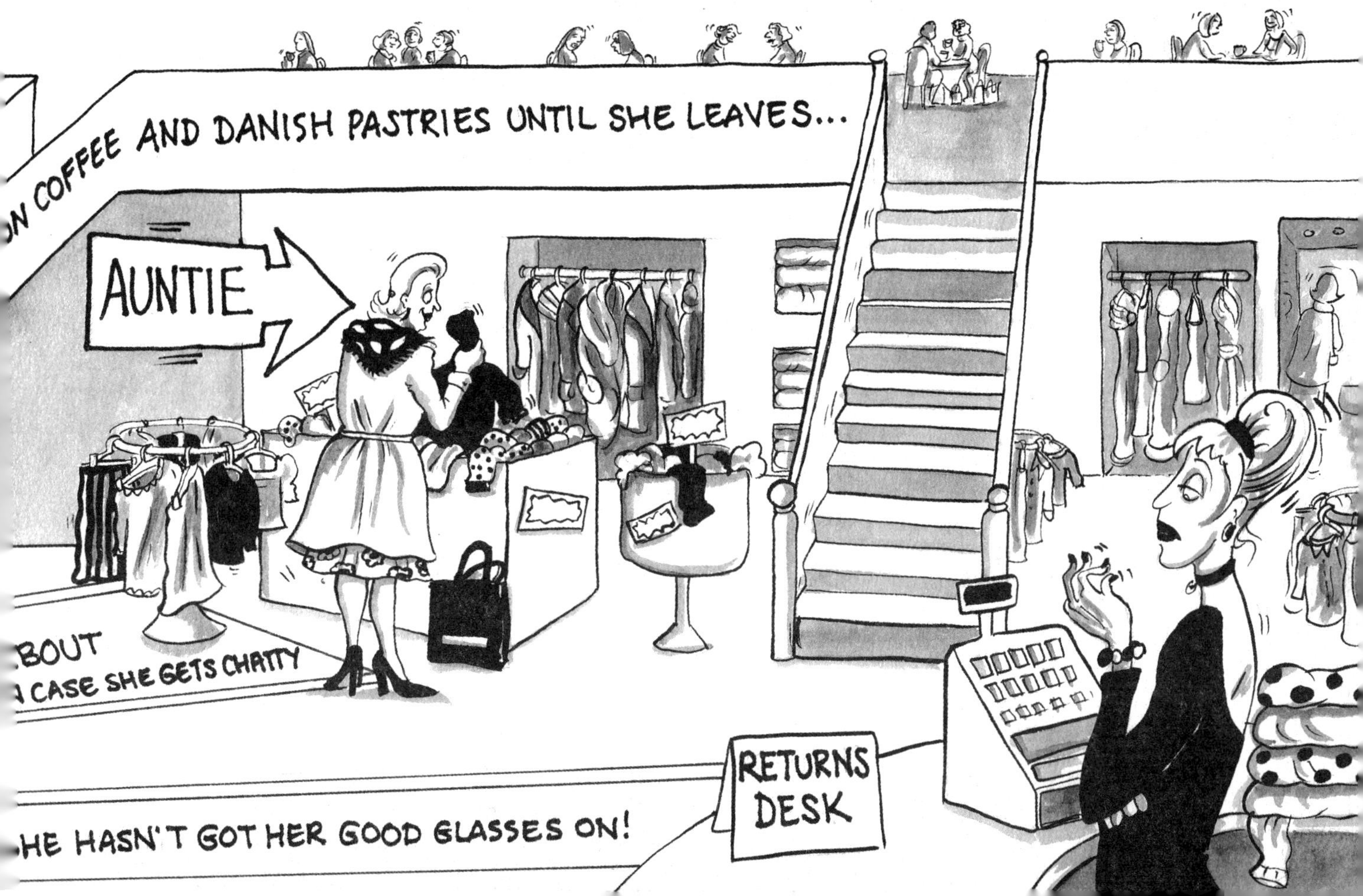

...ON COFFEE AND DANISH PASTRIES UNTIL SHE LEAVES...
AUNTIE
...BOUT
...N CASE SHE GETS CHATTY
...HE HASN'T GOT HER GOOD GLASSES ON!
RETURNS DESK

HUBBY'S SURPRISE PRESENT ...

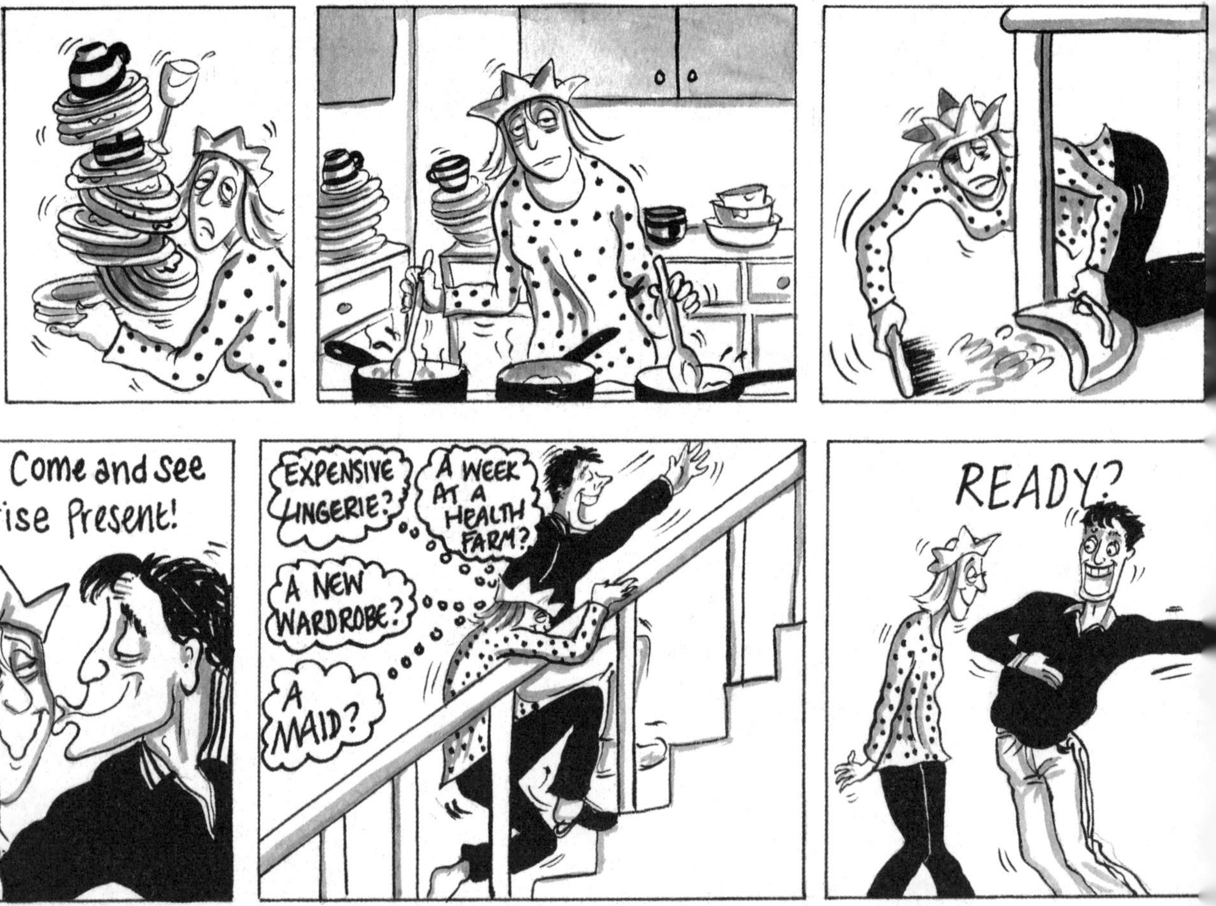
DARLING! Come and see your Surprise Present!
EXPENSIVE LINGERIE?
A WEEK AT A HEALTH FARM?
A NEW WARDROBE?
A MAID?
READY?

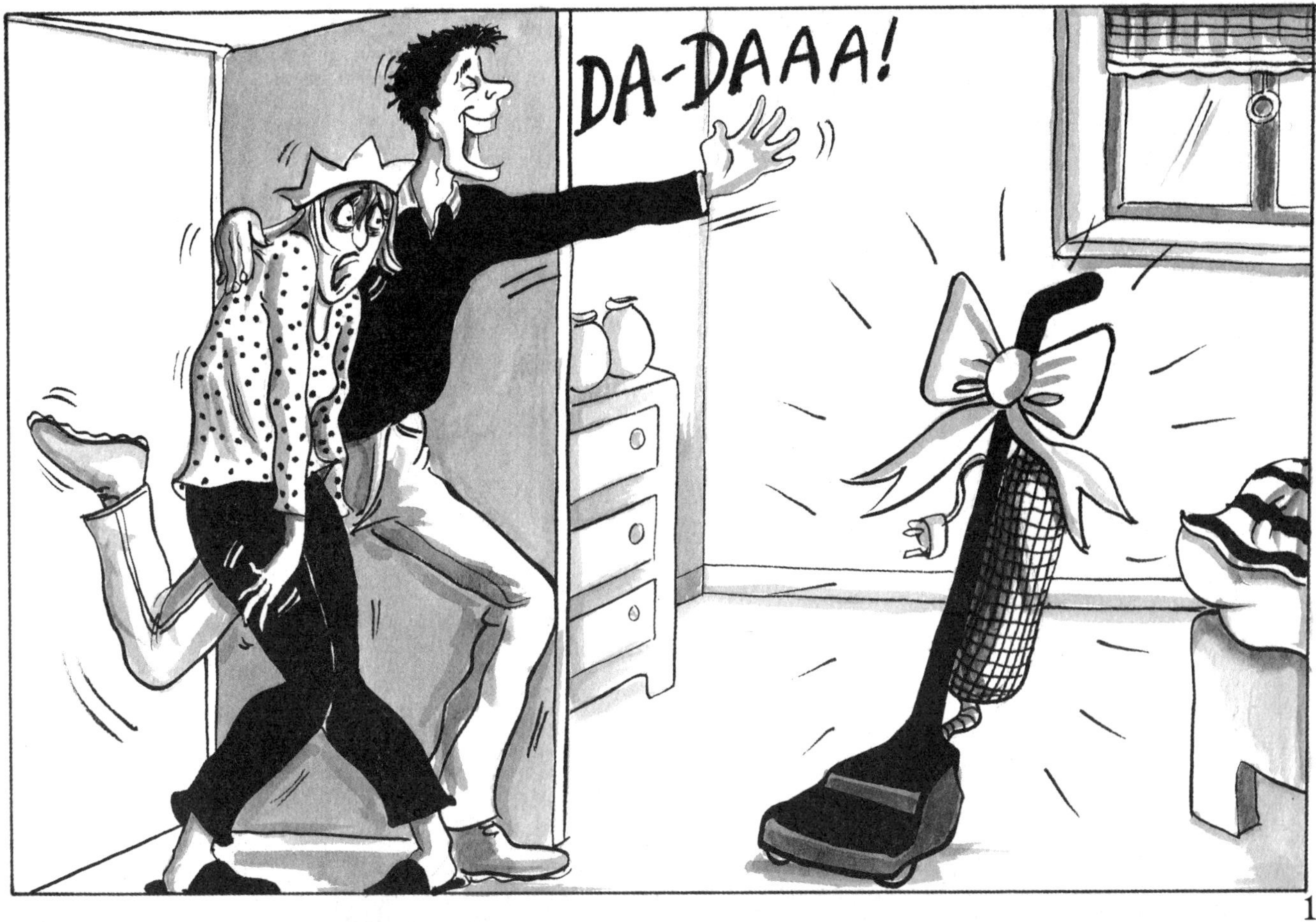
DA-DAAA!

THINGS YOU HATE ABOUT CHRISTMAS

(12) Hearing About Other People's Christmas ...

Their tinsel seemed brighter, their turkey looked bigger, their Christmas tree lights always seemed to work without any fear of burning the house down, they always seemed to be having a much better time than you ... and you can guarantee you'll meet them the minute you leave the house!

MR AND MRS PERFECT:

(They still *like* each other!)

We had a LOVELY TIME, didn't we darling?

Yes we DID, didn't we darling?

MR AND MRS OVER-ACTIVE:

(Make you feel instantly blobby)

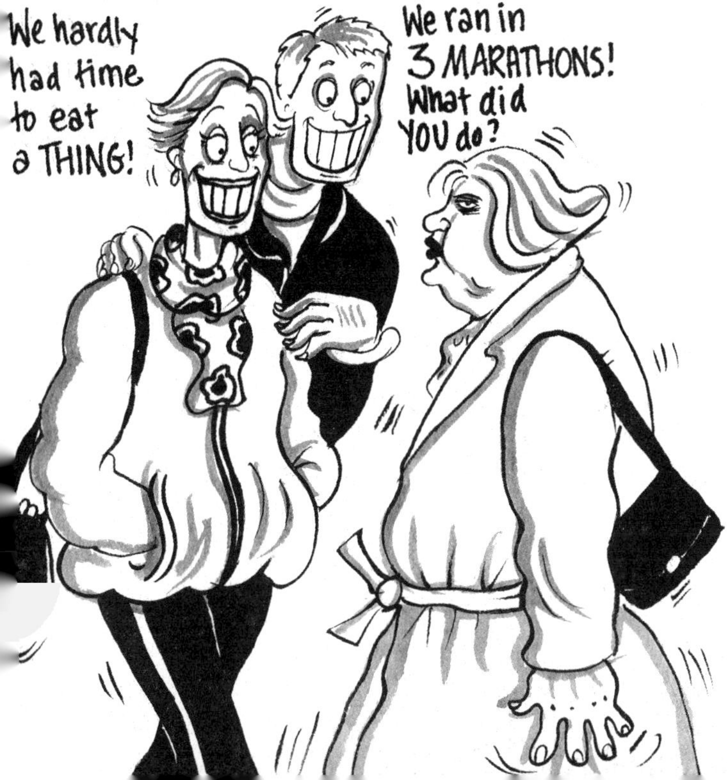
We hardly had time to eat a THING!
We ran in 3 MARATHONS! What did YOU do?

... MR AND MRS LOOK-WHAT-I-GOT:

(Just make you feel sick!)

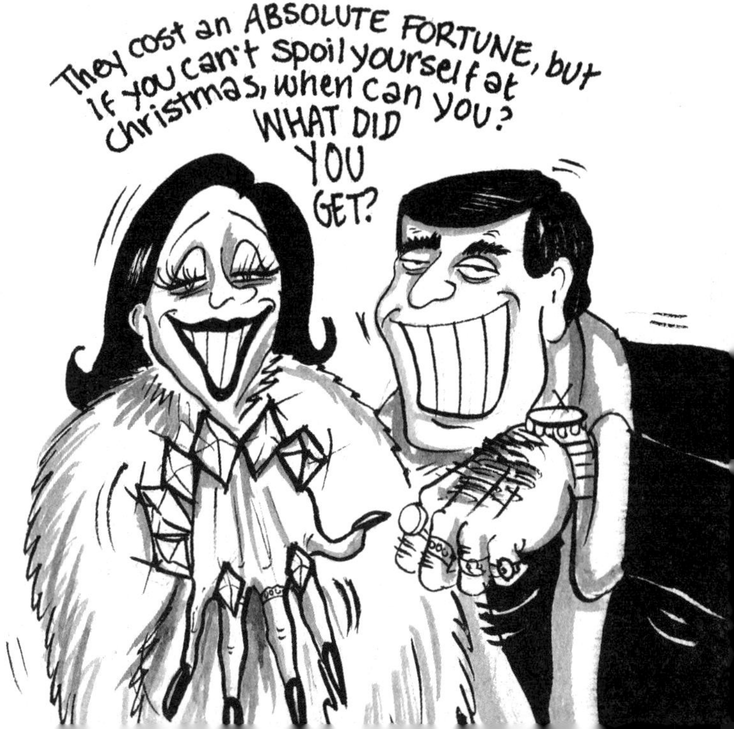
They cost an ABSOLUTE FORTUNE, but if you can't spoil yourself at christmas, when can you? WHAT DID YOU GET?

You finally manage to grab some Quality Time. You've sent the kids off to football, hubby to the pub, teenagers to the shops and you settle down in front of the box for the first time since the never-ending round of shopping, cooking, wrapping and washing-up began …

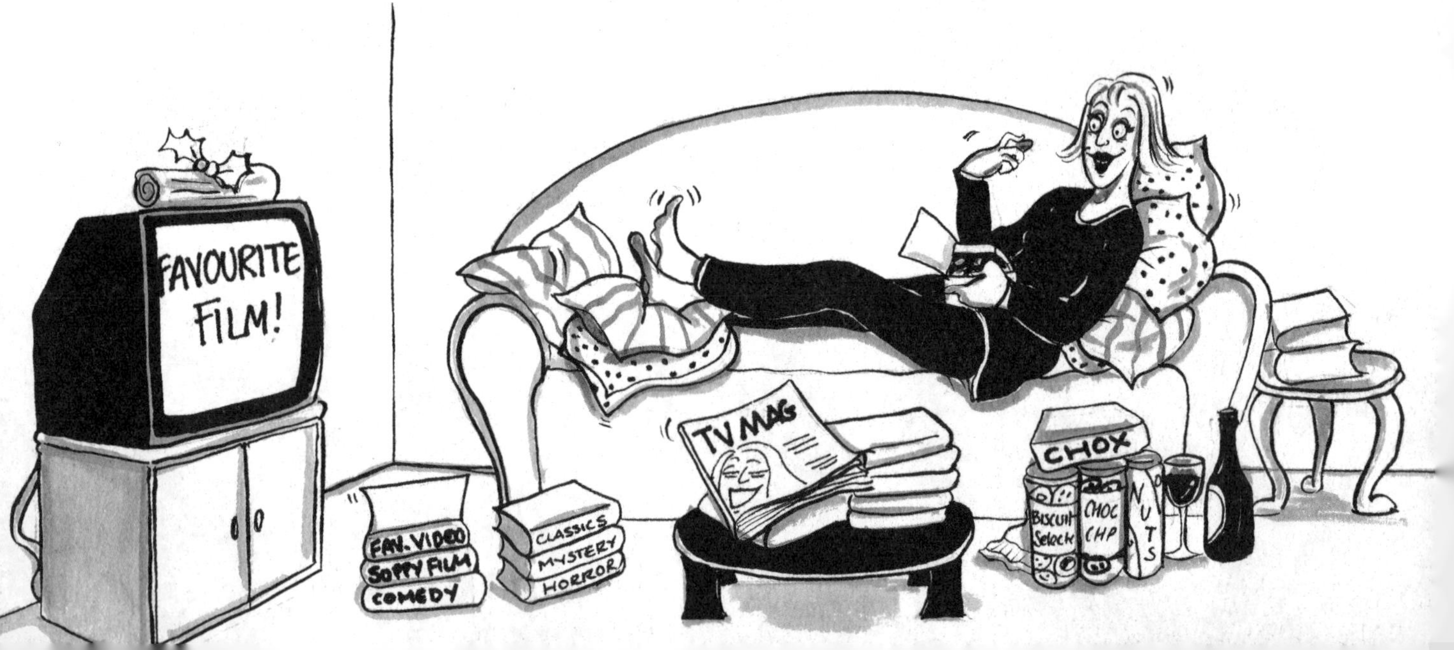
FAVOURITE FILM!
TV MAG
FAM. VIDEO
SOPPY FILM
COMEDY
CLASSICS
MYSTERY
HORROR
CHOX
BISCUIT Select
CHOC CHP
NUTS

… And you're just beginning to enjoy yourself when …

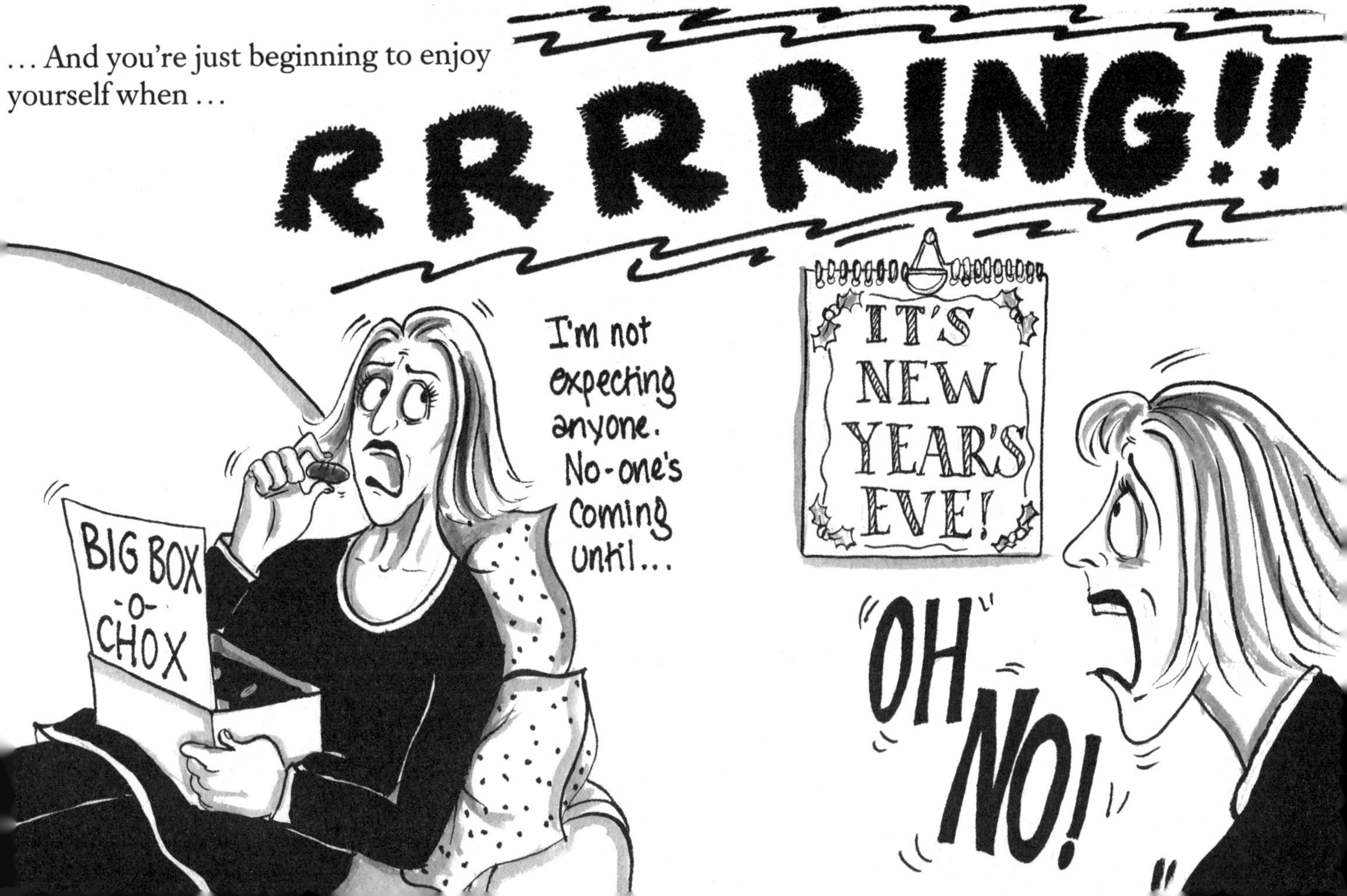
RRRRING!!
I'm not expecting anyone. No-one's coming until…
BIG BOX -O- CHOX
IT'S NEW YEAR'S EVE!
OH NO!

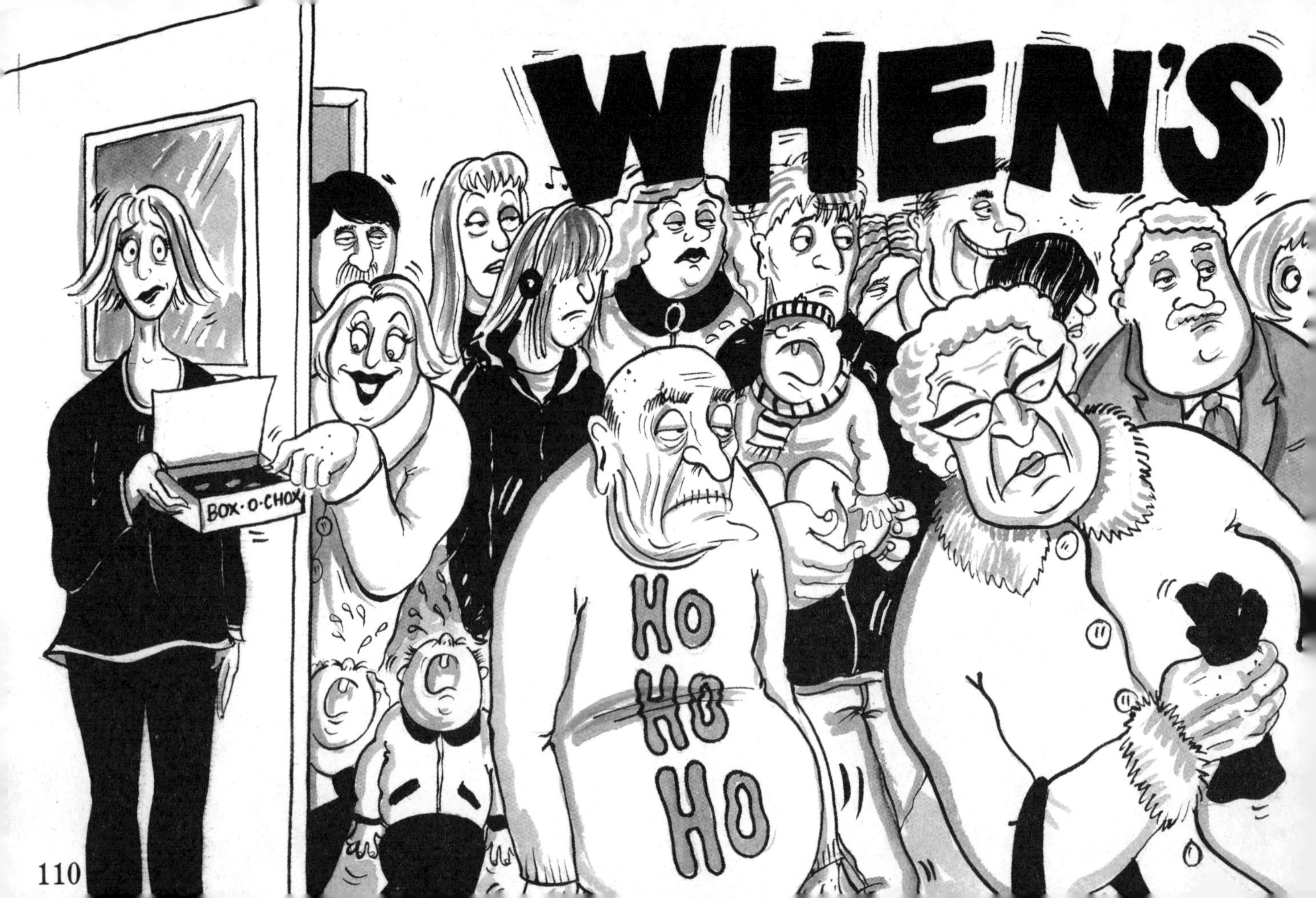
WHEN'S
BOX·O·CHOX
HO
HO
HO

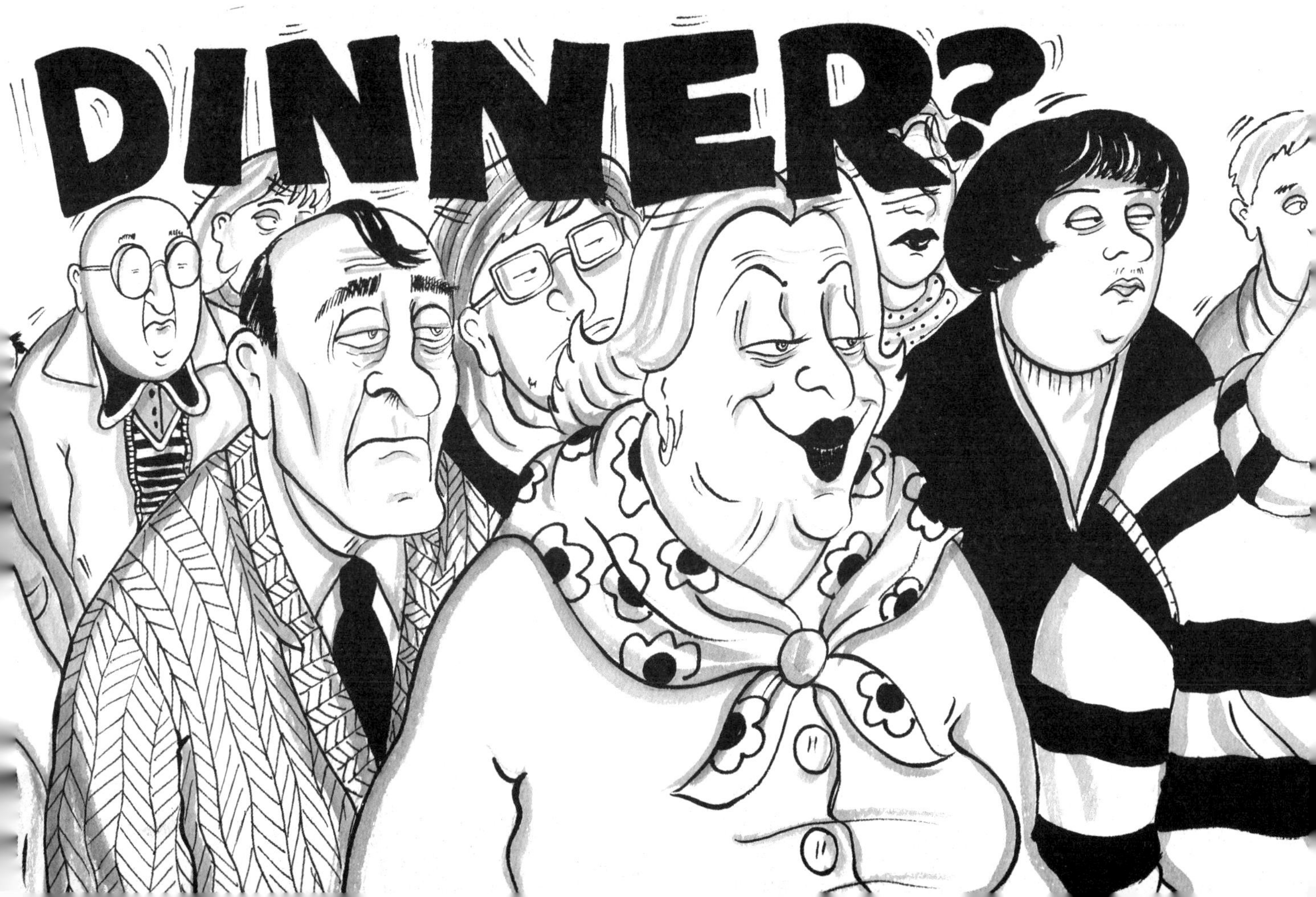
DINNER?

NEW YEAR'S RESOLUTIONS ...

We make them because over Christmas we've eaten far too much, have hardly left the sofa and have been horrible to our families.

By the time we get to New Year's Eve we're positively racked with GUILT!

FAVOURITE RESOLUTIONS:

Going on a diet.
Doing some form of exercise.
Being nicer to your family.

MOST IDEAL RESOLUTION:

Get your body frozen next November and miss the whole thing!

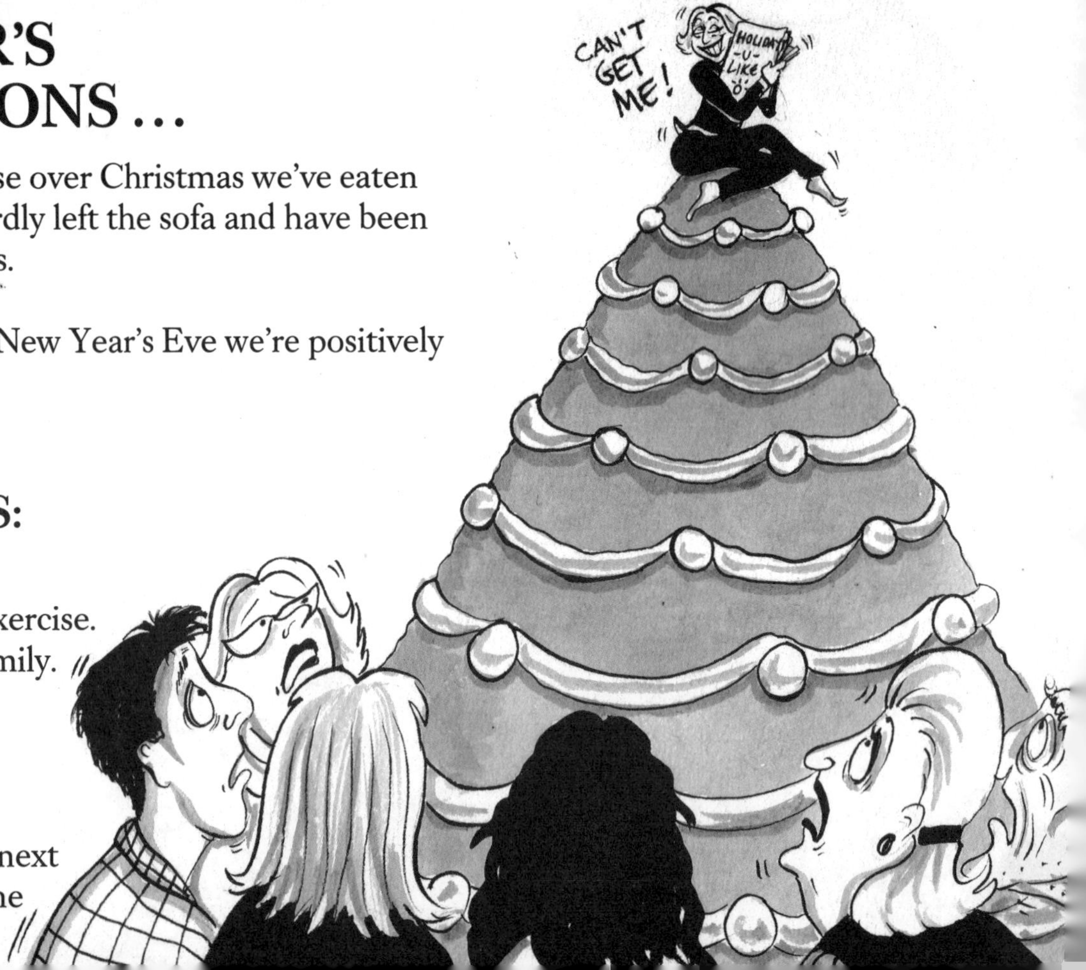
CAN'T GET ME!
HOLIDAY -U- LIKE